# MEDITATIONS
## on
# THE EPISTLES OF JOHN

Meditations of
## S. H. FROEHLICH
Delivered in Zuerich in the Years
1840-1842

*(Translated from the German)*

## 06693

VOLUME ONE

APOSTOLIC CHRISTIAN PUBLISHING COMPANY
1327 West Colvin Street
Syracuse, New York

1958

**N.B.**

The King James Authorized Version (Oxford University Press) of the Holy Bible was used for the Bible citations quoted herein.

The comparatively few undecipherable parts of the original manuscript are indicated as an omission in this work by a series of ellipsis periods.

It is to be borne in mind in the reading of this work that it is composed of extracts only of the sermons, as they were written in the diaries.

The term "state (established) church" as used herein refers to the State Protestant and Catholic Churches, in which baptism of infants was substituted for the baptism of faith. The deceit since that time is much more subtle where the State no longer subsidizes the Church.

It will be noted that following some of the Bible citations, the abbreviation "ff." appears, the same as in the manuscript (in German, "Fahre fort"—in English, "Fare ye forth"), where more than the verse cited applies, and its meaning is to continue with the citation (beyond the given verse) as far as may be applicable.

APOSTOLIC CHRISTIAN PUBLISHING COMPANY

1327 West Colvin Street

Syracuse, New York

# INDEX

# INTRODUCTION
### AND
## A CONDENSED OUTLINE OF THE
## LIFE OF S. H. FROEHLICH

This book is the first of four volumes of extracts of sermons by Samuel Heinrich Froehlich* (1803-1857) on the three Epistles of John, taken from his diary, word for word. The sermons were preached regularly over a period of two years and five months (May 12, 1840-October 11, 1842) to the church at Zuerich, Switzerland.

In the early 1840's when the sermons on the Epistles of John were preached, the young congregations were assailed by dissension from within, in addition to the persecutions which they had been suffering from without. One leader gathered to himself those who fell away from sound teaching and wished to associate with such that had not a clear grasp of the baptismal truth, who were not even convinced of the necessity for baptism, and so they reverted to a laxity in church discipline. Another faction held that the promises of the covenant in baptism were wholly one-sided, that God gave promises but that no vow of obedience was necessary on man's part.

These false teachings attacked the very root. It was therefore necessary that strong and incisive teaching out of the Word of God be brought to overcome such fatal opposition and these sermons used the sword of the Word in this struggle to a successful end so that the truth was maintained, and of the apostate many came back upon their painful disenchantment, while others remained excommunicated.

Brother Froehlich's activities fell in that time when freedom of faith and conscience dawned upon the nations of nominal Christendom (Revelations 3:8):

> "I know thy works: behold, I have set before thee an open door, and no man can shut it; for thou hast a little strength, and hast kept my word, and hast not denied my name."

which he believed was the "Then" in the Savior's parable, "Then shall the kingdom of heaven be likened unto ten virgins which . . . went forth to meet the bridegroom (Matthew 25:1 ff.)." The candlestick was re-

---

*The title "Brother" is generally omitted for the sake of brevity.

i

established upon its place on the continent of Europe where the light had flickered out for the descendants of those who in previous centuries were true witnesses.

Froehlich knew whereof he spoke concerning the established state church for he had been an integral part of it in every sense of the word, and then by the grace of God saw the light of the truth. He appeared in the time of the beginning of freedom of religion and conscience, when so-called Christendom had fallen into degeneracy and the State Protestant and Catholic Churches dominated the governments of Europe, to teach anew the true Gospel of Jesus Christ as it was taught by the apostles. He had been planted, so to speak, in the very soil of the Protestant state church and although his conversion in it was not brought about by it, yet thereafter he was still in, though not of, it and thus it became the field of his missionary effort. In this encounter, the mission of bringing the Gospel into the field of the great false churches of false Christianity, which had already been elevated to the position of the state religion in the beginning of the fourth century, he was a pioneer of his time.

## Early Life and Conversion

Samuel Heinrich Froehlich, the son of a sexton, descended from a Hugenot (French Protestants of the 16th and 17th centuries) family, by the name of DeJoyeau, a French word meaning "the joyful," who lived in France. When Louis XIV revoked the Edict of Nantes under which the Hugenots were allowed to live in France, and after St. Bartholomews Night (August 24, 1572) when many thousands of Protestants were massacred, the remaining families fled in all directions. The DeJoyeau family sought refuge in Switzerland where the name was later translated into "Froehlich" ("joyful").

In a letter to the English Continental Society of London, England, written in November 1831 (after his expulsion from the state church), making application for an assignment as an itinerant preacher in the Rhine Country, S. H. Froehlich gave a detailed account of his awakening and conversion (below). It is felt that since what Froehlich received from the Lord was by revelation, this account, besides being helpful to souls seeking God among us who heavily feel the burden of their sins and their separation from God, may enable souls outside the activities of our congregations, who are entirely unfamiliar with their teachings and to whom this would be a new message, to understand to the full extent what conversion by reconciliation and regeneration means (for whom the publication of these writings is as well intended). Further, it is hoped that this account may set aright those who confess having gone through conversion, as to any benefit to be expected from a so-called theological education, to better prepare them to work for the Lord. Also that it may clearly show that one must be accepted by Christ as well as to accept Him himself, and that there is no such acceptance without conversion and baptism. In the letter above-mentioned, he wrote, in part:

"As to my outward circumstances, I was born July 4, 1803, in Brugg, a small municipal city of the Swiss Canton of Aargau. From my youth, the idea of devoting myself to the ministry was made so much a matter of course by my parents that I never considered anything else, although I did not in the slightest degree feel the great importance and responsibility of the vocation and still less did I realize what was required to fulfill the duties of the office which preaches reconciliation. Much rather was I to learn it in the way of a trade instead of a profession.

**1820**
**1823**
Accordingly I was instructed in the necessary rudiments for this purpose in the school in my native city, up to my 17th year and was advanced to the extent that upon my removal at Zuerich on New Years Day 1820, I was not only at once taken into the Collegium Humanitatis, but also, contrary to custom, after a year's course, promoted to the Gymnasium Carolinum.

According to the practice there, in the following years I progressed class by class and pursued my studies mechanically, without spirit or life, indeed without any real interest, however not without absorbing the principles of theology and rationalism from the teachings of Dr. Schulthess and others, although quite unnoticed and unconscious thereof. When I came home on vacation with my head full of fancies, I caused my god-fearing mother, who is now dead, many tears and even paraded with bare-faced fluency the glories of the new teaching, "That there was no devil, no hell," etc.

In the four years of my stay at Zuerich I advanced thus far that I should enter the actual class of theology, but I preferred to go to Basel to study theology in the newly organized university under the still famous name of Dewette, and others. That was in the latter part of the year 1823.

In the meantime the might of SIN and the power of DEATH had grown up hand in hand with UNBELIF, since it cannot fail that where the head of the old serpent rises, its members also rise and, of necessity, stir. I became enwrapped and entangled in such a horror of sin that I shudder now when I think of it, and the saddest of all was that in accordance with my very principles I could pass over it so lightly and so easily quiet and deceive myself, that I could even formally say to myself, "That which I am doing is not sin."

O woe unto me, if God had been a man or had dealt with me as a man! He would have shattered me as a potter's vessel. Nevertheless, at one time during this period, I preached on Psalm 51:10, "Create in me a clean heart, O God . . . ," from which I now comprehend what all the so-called beautiful sermons of the Rationalists amount to! Fortunately, this was my first and last sermon in this state of ignorance.

Soon after I went to Basel. However the hour of my enlightenment and release from the dominion of darkness had not yet come. Even deeper was I destined to fall into the depths of Satan. For fully another year and a half I lived without God and without the knowledge of His Son Jesus Christ and of myself. What Schulthess begun in Zuerich was completed by DeWette in Basel. I became utterly carried away by the idealism with which he treated the scriptures. I thought that this was the true way and was sorry only that I did not have the wings to follow him in his flight. I honored him almost as a god. I felt no need of the Living God and had no thought of conversion from my sins.

During my stay in Zuerich I also entirely neglected prayer, even the mechanical prayer learned from childhood seemed ridiculous. In Basel, "Witschels Morning and Evening Sacrifice" appealed to my taste, not so much for the sake of prayer, but because it appealed to my idealism and—with all my sins—I wished to be pious. For that purpose those were the right "sacrifices" that cost nothing. My benighted spirit had by way of Basel the opportunity to cultivate and develop itself more. There were among the students some who belonged to the Community of Brethren. These were distasteful to me from their very name, without knowing any other cause. It was a blind zeal like that of Saul. I became a scoffer, a slanderer and a blasphemer.

On my transfer to Basel I was commended by the State Rector of my native city to the courtesy of one of his friends in Basel, Pastor P. He received me in a very friendly manner and introduced me into a society of long standing composed of young students who met every Thursday evening to read and discuss the Greek New Testament. Of these students the most were inclined toward the Community of Brethren. For this very reason I felt uncomfortable among them and in everything became an opponent. When they finally decided to begin

iv

and close the hour with song and prayer, I became angry and stayed away and also made others desert them, so that gradually the class almost disbanded, until after my conversion when it was again brought to renewed life and blessing.

Nevertheless, the true God and Father of our Lord Jesus Christ was not alone in His exceeding patience and longsuffering in bearing with me in this time of my blindness, for this beloved Pastor P. was tireless in his endurance with me. As often as I visited with him (which was not very frequently) he greeted me with the question, "Well, how are things going in the most important matter of all?" What he meant by this and what the most important matter of all was, I could not imagine. Each time I became embarrassed and still did not wish to let him notice it.

**April 6 1824** Once however when he asked me again as to the most important matter of all, I could not help but ask him the counter-question, what he meant by this. The dear pastor almost laughed at this question, but he composed himself, grasped the opportunity and began to preach to me of repentance to God, knowledge of one's self, faith in Christ, etc. But he preached to deaf ears. I understood not a word of all he said. His sermon seemed in part foolish to me, in part vexatious.

Yet I was honest enough to write down at home in my diary the main thought which had stayed with me and as it still stands there under date of April 6, 1824, namely: "Through the knowledge of God, man comes to the knowledge of self; that is the truth which Christ taught us and to which we arrive only through repentance." But that was all and besides I do not know whether I wrote it correctly or not, for the sinner does not attain to self-knowledge through knowledge of God, but much more the reverse: "Through the knowledge of self, one comes to the knowledge of God (John 16:8)."

> "And when he is come, he will reprove the world of sin, and of righteousness, and of judgment:"

From that day on however, a whole year passed before I felt the slightest trace of this knowledge of self, and from the above it is clear that if the grace of God wished to make something of me to His glory, it certainly had in me the greatest of all sinners, a fit object in whom to manifest, even in me, the greatest riches of the patience and pity of our Lord Jesus Christ, that I in turn should have pity towards my brethren in the flesh who still wander in error along the course of this world and after the prince of darkness. Finally, it pleased God well to awaken me from the sleep of death. He passed by me and saw me lying in my blood. He said to me as I thus lay in my blood, "Thou shalt live (Ezekiel 16:6)!"

**April 1825** It was in the month of April 1825 when I was spending my Easter vacation in Brugg. All the circumstances are as fresh in my mind today as if it had happened yesterday. I cannot however recall that there were many previous preparations or any special circumstances to work towards it. A very soft voice, which was neither terrifying nor depressing but nevertheless very convincing and penetrating, spoke in the depth of my soul, "It cannot remain thus with thee. Thou must change!" And at the same time it drew me irresistibly onward. I knelt for the first time before the hidden God and with uplifted hands solemnly gave the vow of fidelity, that from now on it must be different with me.

True, I did not as yet grasp and understand correctly what I said. Indeed I also did not as yet know the Lord Jesus Christ and the necessity for His atonement and redemption, for it was not yet the burden of my load of sin which had driven me to the Savior of Sinners, but merely the conviction, "Thou must change; otherwise thou canst not become a minister."

From now on, with all earnestness and might I wished to shun sin, which I now recognized as sin, and knew not that it did not lie within my power to overcome a mastery which had for so long bound me with chains of darkness. But it was as if the Lord, to Whom I had made my vow, had taken me at my word, although it was really He Who had taken me by my hand and with all His goodness drawn me to Him.

Beginning with this day the whole scene changed. He never left me. I found rest and peace nowhere. My whole body, indeed the whole world, became too narrow for me. I sought for something which should fill the endless emptiness which had now arisen in my soul and I did not find it. I went out into mountain and forest, knelt and prayed and cried out in lonesome places. My whole being was longing, sorrowfulness and anxiety. I sought the Lord Jesus Christ with ardent fervor and many tears. That was the *first period* of my awakening.

The first piece of literature that fell into my hands was Fenelon's Religious Works, translated by Claudius. In it I found for the first time a name for my spiritual condition, for up to this time I had been an inexplicable riddle to myself and I did not know what was to become of me. Therefore it was, in a measure, a consolation to see that others had experienced similar things. Especially did I believe to recognize myself in the 14th chapter of the first part, which bears the superscription, "Concerning the inner workings of God, to bring man back to the true end for which He created us." As yet I was far from seeking to be represented therein; it was Another Who did lead me and He led me into an extraordinarily difficult and dark path.

Now for the first time my suffering began. What I had to go through from now on, in a literal sense, is inexpressible. Everything that fire and water, hammer or sword may bring about, is as nothing compared with the unfathomable sea of trouble and misery wherein I thought I must sink. I wept night and day and writhed like a worm in the dust when it is trodden upon. Had I had authority over myself, I would often have taken my life through anguish and despair. But the Lord held me in His hand in such a way that I could not move. The price that I paid was a higher one than this earthly life. Like Job I lay in the dust. In no human being, in no friend could I confide, nor could I reveal myself to anyone. All theological or rationalistic lectures became an abomination to me for I was now in another school.

All my letters of that time bear the stamp of my inner condition. My sisters feared that I was losing my mind because the tone of my letters was radically different from what it had previously been. They consisted for the most part of scriptural passages. For a long time I remained in this fiery furnace until at length faith in Jesus Christ the Crucified brought me rest, peace and light, and made place within me for a new creation.

From then on Jesus Christ was the center of my whole life and sphere of activity. However I was kept constantly under the discipline of the Holy Spirit, for not until now did the struggle against my old nature and against the law of sin, which dwelt in my very members, become serious. But even with all my new transgressions, the faithfulness of the Lord did not forsake me. Both of these things, my sins and His grace, humbled me greatly.

**October 1825**     That was my last half year in Basel and the *second period* of my conversion from darkness to light and from the power of Satan to God. And so after a stay of two years in Basel, I was obliged to return to my home principally for economic reasons, in October 1825. Here in my father's house a new school or period of my life began, in which I was to be further trained, developed, strengthened, invigorated and grounded so that I should not enter as a novice into the important office which preaches atonement.

**1826** Here I applied for the examination as a candidate for the Ministry, which was postponed to the following Spring 1826. At the request of my parents I preached for the first time in my native Brugg, the Sunday before Christmas, and met with such general approval that I should have become anxious and afraid if the honor of the Lord had not counted for more with me than all personal vainglory among men. I did not again preach here until Good Friday 1826, and that proved to be a veritable Good Friday for me. Instead of expressions of praise, I reaped only ridicule and reproach. It produced an entirely different effect from the praises I had received; it was necessary and wholesome for me.

Now for two entire years there came over me fiery tribulations that are beyond description. Only He Who knows the heart, knows what I suffered through it. I preached Christ here, there and everywhere in the country. But in every minister who allowed me to preach I gained a new opponent. With such preparation and forebodings I approached my examination.

The principles which I brought to light in the compositions made such an unfavorable impression upon the members of the church council that I failed in the examination and was put back a year. The Lord had resolved upon this also for my further testing and purification.

In the course of this year, oppression and misery often rose to the extreme, both from within and from without. After a sermon which I was compelled to preach in September 1826, in a church of a member of the church council, among other things he wrote to my parents, who were already troubled and dissatisfied because of my set-back: "It is bad and dangerous (and this impressed the whole church council at the trial sermon) that your son is not on the right road with regard to his doctrine and teaching, and in all sincerity he should be advised to enter upon a better course, if he wishes to be accepted into the Ministry and is to make the proper success of his future calling. On this point I gave him my opinion in a friendly and earnest way. Now it depends upon whether he will give ear to good counsel. In any case he will do well if he will soon present new sermons composed in a different spirit." That was the occasion that also in my case the saying should be fulfilled: "A man's enemies will be the members of his own household."

From this quarter, too, they now began to vehemently urge upon me that I should preach in a different manner and indeed like others so that I be not excluded from the Ministry entirely. I however could not say a word in answer to this. In the midst of these blows and storms,

I had to keep still like a lamb that is led to slaughter, like a sheep which is dumb before its shearer. The Lord however, amidst all these attacks of the foe, still gave me patience and courage to endure everything. Yes, even death rather than abandon the recognized and experienced truth.

With all this my body was not spared. In that very month of September 1826, I had a sudden attack of sharp pain in the chest, so violent that I could hardly draw a breath and for many days seemed near death. That was followed, for an entire year, by cramps in the chest and most difficult respiration. But never did I experience more vividly in my heart the unspeakable friendliness of the Lord Jesus than just at this time, toward the end of the year 1826. Without doubt it was to strengthen and prepare me for the ensuing darkness and the storms of opposition." (End of quotations from Froehlich's letter aforementioned, November 1831.)

## Chronology (Beginning in 1827)

The first period in the conversion of S. H. Froehlich was one of an awakening (in April 1825), the second, one of being brought from darkness to light and from the power of Satan to God (in October of the same year). There was an interim of seven years from the time of his conversion to his baptism in 1832.

On May 27, 1827, Froehlich was confirmed for the Ministry in the Protestant state church after repeated examinations. Of this acceptance he wrote that it was brought about through no fault of his. After waiting for some time he became parish administrator of the congregation Leutwil (Aargau). There was still no thought of a position and his suffering continued for another year, inwardly and outwardly, until Easter 1828, when he received an assignment as tutor in a private family near Schaffhausen.

It was not until his transfer to the vicariate of the Probstei Wagenhausen (Thurgau) in August 1828, that an essential change in him took place. There his spirit became a thing of life and he felt in his element.

In December 1828, he accepted a call as vicar to the congregation at Leutwil. The hand of the Lord was with him and gave his word such power that the testimony of the Crucified Savior pierced the hearts of the hearers like a two-edged sword and called forth a great awakening in the congregation of 1,800 souls and the once poorly attended church was now crowded. The evil one could no longer look on passively. He was accused of attracting members from neighboring parishes, but he remained for two years without taking fright at the threatenings. The adversaries of the Gospel however sought after reasons to put away this new preacher who was in their path.

At Easter 1830, the church council introduced, in place of the old Heidelberg Catechism, a new rationalistic one for the instruction of children. After examination of the book, Froehlich could not persuade himself to use it because, instead of a positive faith in Christ, it laid a foundation for nature- or reason-religion. Because of this and other trumped up charges of arbitrariness he was haled before the church council on September 27, 1830. He defended himself and held his ground on the basis of his conviction and was, for the time being, being dismissed without a decision from the hearing.

## Removal from Ministry of Protestant State Church

As two Basel divines, who had been sent privately to investigate and persuade him, could achieve nothing, the church council recognized the futility of its efforts. With reference to his removal, Froehlich wrote (to his beloved congregation in Leutwil): "My deposal was revealed to me by the church council without further ado on October 22, 1830. and, in fact, so quickly that I had no opportunity to preach a real farewell sermon. Accompanied by many thousand tears and good wishes I went my way on October 25th." A teaching which demanded regeneration through repentance, faith and baptism, was bound to call forth opposition from the consistory, which suffered from dead formalism.

On June 4, 1831, Froehlich was called before the district magistrate of Brugg, who gave him the following decisions of the Aargau government:

(a) He is removed from the list of the Aargau clergy;
(b) All churchly functions, i.e., teaching, baptism, holy communion, are strictly forbidden him;
(c) All officers of the Canton, Protestant and Catholic, have received strict orders, if he enters their jurisdiction, to have him arrested and reprimanded and sent back to his home (state-church) congregation.

The breach with the state church was thus made final. What shall he do now? Submit or assert himself against the whole power of darkness? His inner conviction no longer permitted him to practise infant baptism, at which, according to the old liturgy, the baptismal candidate is addressed by name and asked five questions. These questions the sponsors answered in the name and in the stead of the child. First question: Do you renounce the devil and all his works and all his ways. Answer: Yes, I renounce. Second question: Do you believe in God the Father, etc.? Answer: Yes, I believe. Third question: Do you believe in Jesus Christ? Answer: Yes, I believe. Fourth question: Do you believe in the Holy Ghost? Answer: Yes, I believe. Fifth question: Will you be baptized in this Christian faith? Answer: Yes, I will.

Froehlich wrote: "This play with holy things I could no longer carry on in my conviction." For this reason it was no longer possible for him to be a clergyman in the state church. He strives after clarity and unceasingly brings his need and desire to God in prayer.

## New Beginning

Froehlich returned to his paternal home in Brugg, where he, for a year, quietly prepared himself for the work God had appointed for him. It seemed to him that he was being sifted like wheat and, like Joseph in prison, was waiting for the Lord's deliverance. But he could not remain inactive for one cannot stop a living spring.

An invitation to Wilhelmsdorf in Wuerttemberg, Germany, seemed a sign from heaven for him and he preached there for a congregation that had separated from the state church (1831). However this church was not receptive to his doctrine for it clung to infant baptism and had gone out from the state church only on account of the liturgical baptismal formula.

In this new beginning, Froehlich served several families at various places as private tutor. In addition, he associated with the old Baptists (Mennonites) and preached in their circles in 1831, and kept in contact with his former congregation at Leutwil.

## Continental Society in London

Through a preacher in Frankfort on Main, Froehlich learned to know the Continental Society of London which supported ministers and teachers. One of these who had been expelled from the state church, Pastor Bost, was active in Geneva. Through his mediation Froehlich offered himself for a diaspora-preaching place in the Rhineland in 1831.

In February 1832, Froehlich was baptized at the hands of Bost in Geneva and thereupon, at private meetings, proclaimed the true Gospel here and there. He pointed men to Christ for repentance, faith and baptism according to the words of Christ, as the first Christians had done.

On January 9, 1836, Froehlich wrote: "It never entered my mind that I should found a sect here on earth, rather it was and is my purpose to gather children to God. If I could not place my confidence in the Lord my God, that He has called me to His Gospel, I would indeed repent to have begun something on which the Lord could not place His blessing or with which He could not be pleased. Now, however, I placed myself wholly into His hands that He might lead me according to His good pleasure."

## Evangelization

### FIRST MISSIONARY JOURNEY IN AARGAU

Froehlich began his missionary work in Leutwil, his former congregation. Hardly had the news spread that he was there when from 200 to 300 persons gathered every evening that he might preach the Word of Christ to them. Some also came to spy on him; the majority however from desire. Within a week many hearers, whom he had instructed before and in whom God had prepared the way, requested baptism. Froehlich examined them carefully to be convinced of the uprightness of their faith and of their knowledge, and admonished them to count the cost of following Christ. Then he baptized them according to the instruction of the Lord and on Palm Sunday he could celebrate the Lord's Supper with 38 members for the first time.

Meanwhile the foe was not idle. When many were gathered together, a gendarme appeared and ordered that all who had sheltered Froehlich must appear before the district magistrate. As Froehlich did not permit himself to be intimidated and continued to preach the good tidings, a summons followed and he was told to leave the village at once and to return to his native Brugg. In vain did he refer to the highest Aargau court and traveled to Aargau to the magistrate. He was dismissed with a warning.

Later on, a gendarme dragged Froehlich out of a meeting and brought him to the magistrate at Lenzburg. In answer to the question, "Who had commanded you to preach?" his reply was, calmly: "Christ." The angry official raised his hand to strike him but withdrew it under a stream of profanity. Finally he tore his clothes and emptied his pockets in order to find his books; then he ordered the gendarme to put him in prison. When Froehlich appealed to the fact that the magistrate at Aargau had not arrested him, he was finally allowed to go free, and began his wearisome journey to Brugg.

## SECOND MISSIONARY JOURNEY IN THE CANTON BERNE

As it seemed impossible to be active further in Aargau, Froehlich once more turned to Pastor Bost at Geneva: "I have been declared scot-free. In Aargau I was arrested and banned. Where shall I go?" In the mission field he felt himself a beginner and a novice. He would like to go with Paul to learn of him "how with simplicity and shrewdness the Gospel might best be spread."

The new constitution gave religious freedom and freedom of conscience. When Froehlich appealed to it before the officials, he was told that he may believe what he chooses but that he cannot convey it to others.

In July 1832, Froehlich journeyed to Berne to meet with Bost. But he had departed because those who would prevent the interview had informed him that Froehlich was behind bars in Aargau. That the wearisome and costly journey might not have been undertaken in vain, Froehlich resolved to go on a missionary journey *from* Berne.

## THIRD MISSIONARY JOURNEY IN EMMENTAL

On August 11, 1832, Froehlich made contact by letter with Christian Gerber, Langnau in Emmental, elder of the Baptist Church there, whom he had never seen, but of whom he had been told. The agreement of their views on baptism attracted him thither.

Ten days later he himself traveled to Langnau and visited Christian Gerber, who then was nearly seventy years old. At a meeting of all the deacons, Froehlich laid before them by way of introduction, a copy of the letter to the English Continental Society in which he, on May 14th of that year, had answered six questions. (For questions and answers see "Individual Letters and Meditations," S. H. Froehlich. Copy obtainable upon request to Apostolic Christian Publishing Company, 1327 West Colvin Street, Syracuse, New York.) The gathering seemed to be agreed with these explanations.

Froehlich held daily meetings in the area, mostly accompanied by the elder of the church. The attendance grew larger and larger and on Sunday, September 2nd, the number of hearers at Langnau was between four and five hundred. According to the custom of the time he preached for three hours. The word is not without fruit but the foe senses the danger. On the following morning the state church pastor raised his voice in warning in a meeting of the citizens. Despite the fact that a deacon who was present, defended the accused fearlessly, Froehlich was haled before the magistrate, who decided after a brief hearing that Froehlich was to leave the territory within 24 hours.

Back at Brugg, Froehlich could not, in spite of the prohibition, keep from visiting the persecuted churches in Aargau. In Leutwil where there were 45 baptized souls, a penalty had been placed upon anyone who would permit the meeting in their homes. "We have a great cloud of witnesses before us, who, for the sake of freedom in Christ, were ready to sacrifice goods and blood, whose imitators we should be in patience and faith," he wrote on September 24, 1832.

### Fourth Missionary Journey to Zuerich and East Switzerland

In October 1832, Froehlich began his activity in Zuerich, where two of his sisters lived. They were, as yet, undecided to go his way, but they were no longer offended by him. He found no hearing however with his former acquaintances.

Great was the joy of seeing one another again when he, in Canton Thurgau, visited the congregation Wagenhausen at Stein on the Rhine where he had served as vicar four years before. Although the teaching of the baptism of believers met with opposition, he parted from them in the good hope that they would finally find the way.

In St. Gall also he met with opposition on account of baptism, while he found many receptive hearts in Herisau. On November 21, 1832, he reached Wattwil, where a year before a simple laborer, Adolf, of Zuerich, who was active for the kingdom of God, had worked, and after his expulsion by the authorities, had left many awakened ones behind. Here Froehlich remained several weeks, in which he held meetings and strengthened the knowledge of the baptism of faith, and deepened it. In Hauptwil (Thurgau), where he had never been, he learned to know the Brunschwiler family, who sought after divine truth and who was deeply touched by his word and teaching about the baptism of faith. A daughter of this family, Susette, he chose, in 1836, as his life's partner.

# London

In Hauptwil, Froehlich received an invitation from the Continental Society of London for a visit of three months. First he concluded his visits and then returned to his home. At the end of January 1833, Froehlich went to London where he stayed almost five months. The journey led him, instead of as he had at first anticipated, down the Rhine over Antwerp, via Paris. In the archives of the "Strict Baptist Church," which upheld the baptism of faith, there are records of his stay. Froehlich felt himself very lonely in the world metropolis London, like Elias on Mt. Horeb, and wrote: "Behold, what doest thou here in England? I do not rightly know why I have come here, and yet I was called thither, and by the will and guidance of the Lord. I have been zealous for the Lord, and I am here now, and wait as to what I am to do."

As much as Froehlich treasured it to have support ($100.00 per year), he saw that this was bound up with difficulties. The Continental Society was now suffering from financial cares, so that it was not in position to support him nor to pay Bost's salary in Geneva. On its advice he returned to the continent to work, "where the Gospel is not known or preached and where one may find tolerance and entry." The recommendation that the zealous missionary might work in Strassburg, as only in France was the freedom of preaching the Gospel allowed, cannot be followed as settling there (likely for political reasons) was not possible. Froehlich returned to Brugg.

## Return

Boldly Froehlich once more took up his work in his native city after his London visit, in midyear 1833. During his absence two brethren from Wuerttemberg, Germany, had directed the congregations in Aargau. One of these had been arrested at a meeting, the other during a visitation of the sick, and had been held for weeks in the Lenzburg prison. In September 1833, both were brought to the border; their personal property was sold at public auction to defray the costs.

A Berne brother was banned from the Canton Aargau and moved to Toggenburg, from where he sent an urgent call to Froehlich as several souls longed for baptism. "Bitter experiences have taught me not to be too hasty in this matter," he wrote in September 1833 in his diary, "for some whom we have baptized, have apostatized when Satan started to rage. Everyone who permits himself to be baptized must be ready, not alone to receive the blessings of the Cross of Christ, but also to take up the Cross of Christ."

## Storms

In the beginning of October of the same year, 1833, a message came from the English Continental Society that for lack of funds it had to be dissolved. Froehlich did not allow himself to become discouraged on this account. Bravely he started out on a journey through Aargau, to Suhr, Rupperswil, Hunzenschwil, Schafisheim, Aesch and Teufental. He held meetings everywhere, despite the persecutions that followed him at every step. "As long as I kept silent I was left alone, as soon as I began to testify of Christ persecution came." For the first time three elders were ordained to serve the churches in Aargau.

In Hauptwil (Thurgau) also, where Froehlich continued the work which had been begun, the Word found response. The meetings were attended by 200 persons and by the beginning of the year 1834, the number of baptisms had risen to 60. This development was bound to bring the opponents to the fore. There were public warnings from the pulpits, also threats, and the newspapers descried the enthusiasts and sectarians. The participants at the meetings were manhandled to the shedding of blood with stones and sticks. Twelve state church pastors demanded the removal of Froehlich out of Hauptwil. At the end of February, a mob of several hundred people destroyed a house, the inhabitants of which barely saved their lives.

Now the storm broke loose generally. All newspapers brought reports so that Froehlich became known and was reviled throughout Switzerland. He had to flee from Thurgau and on his passport it was noted that he had been expelled as a sectarian. Now the police watched him wherever he went.

The persecutions which Brother Froehlich encountered and endured continually were intensive and appalling, and are only briefly touched upon in this Introduction. They are given quite extensively in his diaries.

## Extension

The persecutions brought Froehlich in October 1832 to Zuerich to his sisters where he could remain a week. In Zuerich the truth began to find a way. The movement spread farther and farther through Froehlich's tireless activity and reached over into other areas. Even the newspapers could not stop this, though they agitated: "The sect of the Re-baptizers is growing in the Cantons of St. Gall, Appenzell, Thurgau, and Zuerich," and publicly called upon the government of the Canton Aargau to prevent the "dangerous sectarian" S. H. Froehlich from moving about. In Appenzell believers were beaten till blood flowed and fined up to 100 gold pieces, a large amount at that time.

In his addresses and talks, Froehlich used an earnest, clear and positive speech, which awakened the lukewarm and chastened the opponents of the truth. This led to a decision of the spirits; the one to repentance, the other to enmity.

## Expulsions and Departure

Early in 1837, Froehlich was forced to the realization that he could not remain long in his native city as his marriage took place without state-church copulation, being blessed however by the united prayer of the congregation at Hauptwil. As this was not according to state-church order, its validity was not recognized by the civil authorities. The home (state-church) congregation at Brugg denied the young woman the right to be received into citizenship, although the publication of the banns had taken place, and the marriage sanction, the marriage certificate and the immigration sanction had been granted. All petitions to the authorities of Cantons Aargau and Thurgau, as well as an interview with the federal president at Berne, to obtain recognition of the marriage were without result.

On March 20, 1843, Froehlich was expelled from the city of Zuerich as a sectarian, five months after the completion of the series of sermons on the Epistles of John. He appealed, but this was denied on April 10th, after an interim of five days. He traveled to Wil, Hauptwil and later to St. Gall, where his family visited him by day. It was impossible for him to stay in Hauptwil as a reward had been offered for his capture. On June 27th he was also expelled from St. Gall. He fled by night to Rapperswil and sought refuge at Hirzel, a small village on Zuerich See.

In June 1844, Froehlich made one more attempt in Brugg to bring his marriage papers in order. He was told that the marriage could be recognized only if he would allow the baptism and confirmation of his children. As his conscience forbade this, there was nothing else to do than leave his fatherland altogether and settle in Strassburg, where, at last, he had in prospect to find a homestead. For the time being he could not take his family along; that was not possible until June 1846, when he finally succeeded in obtaining legal recognition of his civil marriage and then after seven years of enforced separation he was united with his family in a home in Strassburg. Although Froehlich could achieve nothing for himself in Switzerland for legal recognition of his marriage, yet he was a pioneer with respect to it for others in a matter which weighed down so heavily upon the believers.

# Determination

The brotherhood met in the Rohr July 10, 1843, to make petition for the recognition of their society. They resolved that the congregations should hold fast to their principles according to the Word of God, and to carry them out whatever the cost might be. Opposition was asserting itself everywhere. Yet it was not possible to repel the light that had appeared. The good seed had been sown and had brought forth its fruits.

As he had been expelled from the Canton Zuerich in September 1843, he could not abide in one place very long in order not to expose himself to arrest and punishment. In his distress, Froehlich remembered the advice given him ten years before in London to settle in Strassburg where there was freedom of speech. This course he now took.

Froehlich's departure was a severe temptation for the congregations in Switzerland. In the storms of those years his experience was invaluable. An active correspondence shortened the distance that separated them, whereby the messenger service of traveling or visiting brethren was utilized. Of one of these trips, it is reported that he carried a package of 70 letters. By means of mutual visits the bond was kept close and especially were the various extended journeys which Froehlich made from his new home into Switzerland a blessing and joy to the churches.

Typical of the depth of his letters, we give here excerpts from letters written in September 1856, a few months before his death:

Zuerich, September 3-6, 1856

*To the Church in Berne*

I have received an invitation to a conference of Baptist preachers from Germany, France and Switzerland which will be held here from the 4th to the 8th of this month. It concerns the union of all the various and separated parties among the Baptists. However, as this union could be only an outward one, without the inner one of the Spirit of Christ and the truth, I cannot take part in the conference and have therefore written them a detailed reply outlining my reasons for declining.

Such a formal union would have the result that we would have to allow all such who differ with us in doctrine to teach in our meetings for thus they expressly write: "That the various bodies, *regardless of the differences of their views,* ought to work together for the one great purpose of the kingdom of God." Thus the matter has a good appearance and a fine title, but in itself a destructive character and poison.

Is it according to the apostolic rule and evangelical truth that men of the most varied opinions and views should unite themselves for one purpose in the kingdom of God? Is not that Satan in the form of an angel of light? I believe that here applies our Savior's warning that in the last days the seduction would be so subtle that if it were possible even the elect would be drawn into error.

---

We can insist upon nothing so much as that all brethren in the Lord be of one mind, endowed with one doctrine, and here it is declared that this difference has nothing to do with the working together in the kingdom of God.

I am therefore writing you this, that if anyone should trouble you about it, you may know the true state of affairs. For, for example, the Brothers L . . . . . received the invitation before I did and were willing to accept it and to attend the conference, until I came here.

To me, my life in itself is not precious. However, I rejoice if the Lord, through me, does things for the comfort and well-being of the brethren, for the church is everything to me and for her I will present what I am able to do and I also would be presented as a sacrifice if it is the will of our Father in Heaven.

All is grace and Christ does everything for His Father's sake, to the glory of His name, when He bestows gifts and powers to His servants and messengers. For it concerns the destruction of Satan's kingdom and rule on this earth and the restoration of God's kingdom and glory. To this end the Son came and paved the way to victory by His victory. It may be gradual, slow, as long as the Gospel is preached, and much is done in a false guise that should have prestige as if it were for God's kingdom and the hurt of Adam were healed (in the easiest way), as if nothing else were necessary than to just believe, but if the whole world remains in enmity against God in the disposition of the flesh, that amounts to nothing.

---

Zuerich (Thursday), September 4, 1856

*To the honorable Baptist Preachers' Conference,*
*esteemed Friends:*

You have honored me with a written invitation to your conference. But as I am not in position to accept this invitation, I at least feel myself obligated to reply to your letter, giving a few reasons. First and in general, I have a poor opinion of the benefit and results of such conferences, especially as they concern the truth and the kingdom of God. They remind me too much of the erstwhile church synods and councils where men desired to replace the missing truth by means of human inventions and wisdom, to great harm of the truth and the church of God. For just as there is only *one* truth, so also is the true church in itself just *one,* and this oneness (unity) has not to first be discovered or established by means of conferences.

Here the words of the prayer of the Lord (John 17:21) do not at all apply, for Jesus did not pray the Father that *many* existing organizations, each resting on its own foundation, might be merged into *one,* for under none of these organizations could another foundation be laid than that on which it already rests. Rather this was the prayer of the Son, that *all* who are converted to Him and, through the word of the apostles, become believers on Him, be completely *one,* even as He and the Father are truly *one.* This unity is accordingly given and exists in the true faith (by virtue of this intercession of Jesus) and should not first be achieved later on, between various separately-established organizations by means of conferences and all sorts of human endeavor.

On the basis of the divine truth therefore, such an intended union is impossible because the divine truth is not the foundation of these individual organizations, otherwise one would not primarily have to bring it into existence artificially. If a church rests on the foundation of the truth it will not afterwards confer with other organizations, otherwise it would mix the truth with strange additions and errors, and what is worse, no organization resting on a foundation of error is inclined to relinquish its false principles.

How is it possible then to have a union based on the truth? Where the foundation is *one* there the hearts are already *one,* and where the foundation is false, the individual hearts must make a new beginning. Now many have already passed judgment on me, that my foundation upon which I build the church, namely, my doctrine and my baptism are wrong, in that I ascribe too much to baptism and do not permit baptism to be an *opus operatum* or a formal confession of the believer and that as a result I, for 25 years, teach that he who *by baptism is born again* is no longer a sinner, but has become a child of God in order to walk in a new life as a righteous and holy person, otherwise God would be a father of sinners like the devil.

I maintain therefore, that every organization which teaches and believes that the man in Christ is a sinner also, like the man in Adam (I John 3), stands on a false foundation. And if they, under the circumstances, constitute a church ordained according to the Word and will of the Lord, then I must deny this. No apostle of the Lord would acknowledge them as such, inasmuch as they say that the various organizations, regardless of the difference of their views, should work together for the kingdom of God.

In a true church of God one permits no difference of views to arise or to obtain. Unity and agreement must exist even on points of minor importance, for just in this free choice of views Satan has his sport and his playground and thereby the door is opened to error (Phil. 3: 15-18; I Cor. 14:35-38; I John 2:22-27; II John 10 and Titus 3:10).* Division is better than the union of unlike elements. In our last times the kingdom of heaven is like unto ten virgins who cannot be united (made one) because of their inner differences, even though there is apparently a formal unity in their endeavors. Each must look out for herself; the end will reveal who was right and who was wrong.

By a formal union, all those who teach otherwise would have the right to teach in our church, without the inner unity of the doctrine of Christ, and that shall not be.

I do not love strife and commit every strange servant unto the Lord. I however have been judged of all and therefore say with Isaac (Genesis 26:27), "Wherefore come ye to me, seeing ye hate me and have sent me away from you?"

---

Finally, we would have to unite with such organizations that have accepted those who departed from us or who were expelled, whereby they prove sufficiently that we do not belong to *one* church, for the one church of Jesus Christ has not many entrances but only one.

In general, different churches cannot become one in Christ, although the many local churches in the time of the apostles were really only one church of Christ. This is my answer and I now leave it to you as to what you may think of it. It is a matter of indifference to me whether I am judged by you or in a human way. It is the Lord however who judges me aright. To Him I commit the matter until He comes; then each will receive the praise of God that is due him. This I know, that the true brotherly love rests only on the truth as it is in Christ Jesus and I would not deceive myself with such brotherly love. Where the truth is and conquers, there the community of saints is of itself and without conferences.

---

*All these passages should be carefully read.

Samuel Heinrich Froehlich died January 15, 1857, aged 53½ years. His last words:

"I shall die, Lord my God. Mayest Thou keep Thy holy ones from temptation that is in the world, that they may not perish but abide in Thee, and give them eternal life. For the prince of this world is prepared with his whole power of darkness, and preachers of unrighteousness who seek to destroy Thy work, to mislead Thy elect. Thou knowest that I have not sought glory before men but only to further Thy glory and have declared Thy name before all, and have not been ashamed of Thee and have fought until this hour."

Then after speaking with Brother Weiler, who had watched at his bedside, about experiences of faith and his fears, and about the congregations and his family, he committed himself to the Lord, saying, " . . . I do not regret our going out; we would and should let nothing frighten us, and if all unite to honor God, then there is no enmity and no foreign spirit can work among us. My soul is saved and I am comforted in the Lord."

The special endowment which God gave to this faithful servant is still today our good! An idea of Brother Froehlich's diligence is formed when one considers that in one year he held up to 450 meetings, generally consecutively, chapter for chapter, verse for verse, of various books of the Bible. Besides this he held many children's instruction meetings, undertook visitations and tiring journeys, and annually wrote from 200 to 300 letters (in duplicate) annually, and his diary. His diaries from 1827 to 1856 are extant with the exception of that for 1839, and were put at our disposal by his family, for which we are very grateful.

The mortal remains of Samuel Heinrich Froehlich were buried in Strassburg, where he had taken refuge during the period of persecution. A simple grave-stone in the St. Helena Cemetery, which stands to this day, marks the end of his earthly pilgrimage.

# Meditations on the Epistles of John

## Chapter I

## The Work of Enlightenment

May 12, 1840 (Tuesday)

In the evening meeting I began preaching from the First Epistle of John.

> "That which was from the beginning, which we have heard, which we have seen with our eyes, which we have looked upon, and our hands have handled, of the Word of life;
>
> "(For the life was manifested, and we have seen it, and bear witness, and shew unto you that eternal life, which was with the Father, and was manifested unto us;)
>
> "That which we have seen and heard declare we unto you, that ye also may have fellowship with us: and truly our fellowship is with the Father, and with his Son Jesus Christ."

This epistle (without apostolic greeting) was not written to beginners but to previously enlightened and anointed believers, to establish them in the truth and to further them in the knowledge of the Son of God, and it shall serve the same purpose for us.

The work of enlightenment is progressive and is wrought by the inner as well as by the outer witnessing of the Holy Ghost, in order that we may learn to know the entire will and counsel of God unto our salvation, until the full light of day, for the more we learn to know Christ, the more comfortable we shall be to Him and the more greatly we shall be made willing and capable of obedience unto the will of God.

But the less we know Christ, the more the darkness of sin and death controls us, for the knowledge of Christ dispels the former darkness because He is the Light and Life of men, just as the darkness of the devil is the death of men; and although the darkness is so powerful that it has covered everything, the Light is still more powerful yet and overcomes the darkness in all those who become converted unto the light and let themselves be enlightened and made alive by Christ.

1

But the conversion of men must precede as a condition of the new life, and whoever does not care to be converted by the call of God because he prefers darkness to the light, remains in death eternally. Therefore the Lord sent John in the wilderness before Him as a messenger of light calling men to repentance, that he witness of the Light Which was to come. But, instead of believing in the Light and being converted from darkness through him, men wished only to rejoice for a time over the appearance of a new prophet, although John was no prophet but the angel of the Lord Himself, who, with his baptism of water unto repentance, should prepare the way in order that they might be, later by Christ, baptized with the Holy Spirit unto the renewing of the divine nature (John 1).

On the whole, in the beginning of his first epistle, "That which was from the beginning, . . . declare we unto you," John plainly refers to the beginning of his gospel. The old is ever again also the new (I John 2:7 ff.).

> "Brethren, I write no new commandment unto you, but an old commandment which ye had from the beginning. The old commandment is the word which ye have heard from the beginning.
> "Again, a new commandment I write unto you, which thing is true in him and in you: because the darkness is past, and the true light now shineth."

Where the knowledge of Christ and His will is concerned, we can never finish learning, according to which we shall walk like children of God. But in the beginning was the Word, the Son of God, and the Same appeared in the flesh to take away our sin and to relinquish the control of the devil over us, if we receive Him in faith as the Word of Life and also become sealed by the Spirit of Truth, Which He sends in His stead, to establish, in peace and joy, the righteous or the children of God, unto fellowship with the living and true God.

May 14, 1840 (Thursday); Evening Meeting; I John 1:1 ff.
(with light and power)

If John understands the Son of God by "That which was from the beginning," we must, by this "Beginning," think not of any definite time—for instance of Genesis 1:1—but of eternity, because our thoughts and ideas are still terminable and restricted (defined by space and time); so we cannot yet comprehend what is beyond (the unending and eternal) and the Word of God therefore condescends to our limited knowledge and speaks of a beginning, and we must meanwhile satisfy ourselves therewith in this respect, for as long as we walk by faith the searching into the divine essence and perfection is not our concern or problem. We shall not speculate about the nature of God but shall believe His Word and become simple-minded and humble like children, or we shall eternally not attain unto the true knowledge nor enter into the kingdom of God (Matthew 11:25 ff.; 18:3 ff.; I Corinthians 1 and 2).

"At that time Jesus answered and said, I thank thee, O Father, Lord of heaven and earth, because thou hast hid these things from the wise and prudent, and hast revealed them unto babes.

"Even so, Father: for so it seemed good in thy sight.

"All things are delivered unto me of my Father: and no man knoweth the Son, but the Father; neither knoweth any man the Father, save the Son, and he to whomsoever the Son will reveal him."

---

"And said, Verily I say unto you, Except ye be converted, and become as little children, ye shall not enter into the kingdom of heaven.

"Whosoever therefore shall humble himself as this little child, the same is greatest in the kingdom of heaven."

# Chapter II

## The Perfect Revelation

Our present knowledge of God, in comparison to the future one, is like the age of a child in comparison to the age of an adult (I Corinthians 13); all is still incomplete and piecework, even in the case of the most perfected ones. The perfect revelation for the believing and humble children of God is held in safe-keeping for eternity, but they must now become prepared for it and be advanced to such a degree in the knowledge of God and in the fellowship with Him and in His spiritual way of viewing things, that they may later enter the opened portals of the city of God and kingdom of the glory of Christ.

The Son of God came to the world and appeared in the flesh so as to take sin away—destroy the works of the devil—and, in place thereof, raise up in us the righteousness of God, and by faith in this mystery (of the Gospel) we attain unto that knowledge wherein eternal life is found (John 17). But the unconverted, the unenlightened, the soulful man understands and grasps nothing of this systery; it is foolishness to him in his own blindness and darkness, which he considers wisdom and in which he despises God in His wisdom and crucifies the Son of God because He declared Himself to be what He is and the world with its false wisdom, what it is, namely, of the devil (James 3:15 ff.; John 8):

> "This wisdom descendeth not from above, but is earthly, sensual, devilish.
> "For where envying and strife is, there is confusion and every evil work.
> "But the wisdom that is from above is first pure, then peaceable, gentle, and easy to be intreated, full of mercy and good fruits, without partiality, and without hypocrisy."

for it is the nature of all human wisdom to be speculative only and it makes men's minds conceited, puffed up, haughty and lets their hearts remain in sin. It can rise no higher than the old heathenish question, "What shall we eat, drink, wear?" and those who obtain the most of these things are praised (or envied) by all and looked upon in astonishment as if they were filled with wisdom. Yes, even Seneca, a respectable heathen man, censures the schools because they turn out nothing but speculative minds and no righteous men. And although we preach the true, divine wisdom (Christ) to men, they will not have it and they do not understand it.

Countless Jews saw and heard the Word of Life Who appeared in the flesh, but they did not recognize Him or believe Him, and the highest point to which Jesus had brought His own disciples after several years—and no further—was when He could say: "They . . . have known surely that I came out from thee, and they have believed that thou didst send me (John 17:8)." Their further guidance was necessarily taken over by the Holy Ghost. But this is the true, divine wisdom, to which Christ is made unto us of God (I Corinthians 1:30), that makes our hearts pure, chaste, righteous, holy and our walk godly, humble and peaceable.

In comparison to such wisdom from above in the children of God, all the wise of this world are nothing but fools, for they fail the purpose

4

of being in the world and the aim of their life and must die in their sins because they do not believe that it is Christ, by Whose death and resurrection we must become new men of God, since only he who leads a holy life *in Christ* knows God and attains unto his designation.

May 17, 1840 (Sunday); Morning Meeting; I John 1:1 ff.
(with power and joy)

> "That which was from the beginning, which we have heard, which we have seen with our eyes, which we have looked upon, and our hands have handled, of the Word of life;
> "(For the life was manifested, and we have seen it, and bear witness, and shew unto you that eternal life, which was with the Father, and was manifested unto us;)
> "That which we have seen and heard declare we unto you, that ye also may have fellowship with us: and truly our fellowship is with the Father, and with his Son Jesus Christ."

If we wish to know what "Christ is the (divinely spiritual) life of men" means, we must know and consider what life in general is (as opposed to death), for, by nature already, man has a life but it is not Christ the divine life, but a physical (soulful) one which passes away, an activity or laboriousness for the earthly and transient; and his spirit (his new light) is so darkened that he no longer has knowledge of God nor fellowship with Him and he can neither seek nor find God of himself because he cannot *see* Him, and nothing has value for him except the visible, and his whole wisdom consists in what he would like to eat, drink and put on—for his body. Instead of turning to the Creator of all things, he turns his heart to the creature, makes it his god and becomes an idolater, for the devil uses the visible as a snare by which he draws men away from God and unto damnation.

Fallen man entrusts nothing to God, the Only and Veritable One, not even the temporal, to say nothing of the eternal. His whole life on earth is a continuous chain of trouble and sorrow, how he may procure a life free from care by earthly abundance, but only the fewest obtain this and they have more worry and care by reason of their mammon than they had before. Besides, nothing that perishes is really one's property; in the last shipwreck one must leave it all behind. But he who is rich in God has his riches as his real and eternal property which he takes yonder with him ("omnea mea mecum porto"), and even in a

5

profane epithet he who is proud of his riches is called a fool, as if he were better on that account. Christ however has given us the right directions for leading a life free from care (Matthew 6), namely, in faith to God and in striving after His kingdom, but who believes what He says is true?

And yet the temporal is the very least that God does for us. Thus those who choose mammon for their god cannot serve nor cling to nor trust the living and true God for they make Him a liar by their unbelief. On the other hand, in faith and in knowing the Father and the Son is life eternal, just as the air, which is also invisible and yet so powerful, is the element of the natural life of men—"Luft" (air) is derived from "Leben" (life) as "Gruft" (grave) comes from "graben" (to dig), etc. —and we must ever inhale it (breathe) so as to live and if God would not give us breath we would all fall down and die; and although men *daily* see how they live and die by the will of God, they nevertheless do not notice God, how closely He surrounds us everywhere, that we might feel and touch Him with our hands if we were not spiritually dead (Acts 17:27).

> "That they should seek the Lord, if haply they might feel after him, and find him, though he be not far from every one of us:"

Just in the same way, God shall become the very life of our spirit so that we breathe in Him and could no longer live without Him (John 3:8).

> "The wind bloweth where it listeth, and thou hearest the sound thereof, but canst not tell whence it cometh, and whither it goeth: so is every one that is born of the Spirit."

Thus the invisible air is the inhalation* of the invisible God, Who, as a Spirit, surrounds us everywhere and as soon as He, by Christ, has become our new spiritual life, we have fellowship with Him. But if Christ has become our life, that He thinks and wills, speaks and acts in us, it is then proved by our having become dead and having died to sin but alive for God and His righteousness, for Christ can do no evil, only the good, for the evil is from the devil and those who do it are his, not God's, children.

But because we, by nature, would nevermore know nor find God, He has come nigh unto us in His Son, appearing in human form, so that

---

*In the meaning of the word *inhalation,* of that which is inhaled.

He could be seen, heard and touched—yes, even the Father in Him (John 14)—and this Christ will now come unto us by His Word and Spirit and dwell in us as the Eternal Life. But whoever will not hear or receive Him so as to come from death to life by Him must blame himself for being lost (John 15), for the eye-and-ear witnesses have written and testified to us of the Word of Life for this purpose, that we shall believe them and become believers and be saved through their word.

May 17, 1840 (Sunday); Afternoon Meeting
(a continuation of the previous text)

There seems to be something irreconcilable about the Word of Life in what John says, not only in "which we have heard [speak]," but also in "which we have looked upon, and our hands have handled." This contradiction and riddle however is solved when he says: "The life was manifested [the invisible, hidden God has become visible and manifestly revealed in His Son]," and again: "And the Word was made flesh, and dwelt among us (John 1:1, 14)."

In Christ, the human and the divine have been wondrously united in one Person, that one may no longer excuse himself for lack of knowledge of God, for whoever would not believe it now, would have to touch with his hands like Thomas (Luke 24:39; John 20:27 ff.) (below), what Jews, Gentiles and Christians have testified of the Incarnate and Crucified Christ with one accord to the world.

> "Behold my hands and my feet, that it is I myself: handle me, and see; for a spirit hath not flesh and bones, as ye see me have."

---

> "Then saith he to Thomas, Reach hither thy finger, and behold my hands; and reach hither thy hand, and thrust it into my side: and be not faithless, but believing.
> "And Thomas answered and said unto him, My Lord and my God.
> "Jesus saith unto him, Thomas, because thou hast seen me, thou hast believed: blessed are they that have not seen, and yet have believed."

# Chapter III

## The Power of the Living God

This Christ and Son of God is the Medium (Expedient and Mediation) by Whom the living God would impart and reveal Himself to dead men (for death rules over all in Adam): for only the living God is the true God; and because He is the Living One, He vivifies and pervades all things, and even the life of natural man is an effluence of His power and proof of His omnipresence, which however is so shamefully sneered at and misused by sinners that, in their darkness, they do evil in His sight, as if He (Who has made the eyes) did not see! Men are such fools because there is no fear of God (which is the beginning of wisdom) before their eyes (Psalms 14 and 53; Romans 3). So mad and blind are they all that they think the living God is far away (in heaven) and the devil just as far away (in hell), so that they may sin without being disturbed. What gross darkness that is!

And yet, we all are surrounded by God just as we are by the air, "For in him we live, and move, and have our being;" whether we believe it or not. But as a dead body neither inhales air nor has any need of it, so also the spiritually dead neither feel nor find the living God all around them; yes, as a corpse exposed to the air soon begins to decompose and give off an offensive odor that men hasten to get it under the ground, so also have sinners (the spiritually dead) gone into corruption and putrefaction (stench as the Hebrew gives it in Psalm 14:3):

"They are all gone aside, they are all together become
filthy: there is none that doeth good, no, not one."

and thus God from heaven beholds all men in their natural state as a putrefying carrion because He has not withdrawn His presence (as a spirit) from them, although their heart is far from Him.

It is therefore not enough that we are in God so as to have the true and eternal life, but God must be in us also and live and walk in us; then we truly know Him, and as the right use of the law brings about the fear of God, which however does not yet save us, so also must the Gospel of Christ, from this beginning of wisdom, then lead us on to its completion, namely, to the love of God, wherein we attain unto a blessed acquaintance, fellowship and relationship with the living and true God.

8

Whoever does not wish to hear the voice of the Son of God so as to be made alive again by Him (John 5) is soon put away from before the countenance of the Lord and sealed in the grave of eternal condemnation (as one who is dead), and he comes from this inner, into the outer darkness where there is weeping and gnashing to teeth.

It is also impossible for anyone to preach Christ, the Word of Life, except him who has so experienced, known, seen, heard and handled Him. But these may proclaim Him as much as they like, they will still find as little faith as He Himself found; in short, if one came from heaven or arose from the dead, the dead (sinners) would still not hear. The Father testified; the Son testified; the Holy Ghost testified, but this three-fold testimony is not sufficient to convince the world.

## Chapter IV

## The Connecting Link

May 19, 1840 (Tuesday); Evening Meeting; I John 1:1 ff.

Just as the male and female (generation and conception) must together contribute toward the birth of a new life, so it is also with the birth of Christ in us: by the Word (Seed) the generative power is the Spirit of Truth, by faith conception is the heart of man. For sin Christ took on our *human* nature and died in it so as to give us His *divine* nature in its stead in order that we might live in it unto God (John 6; Hebrews 2). All divine life flows forth from Christ (the Vine) and for connecting organisms He uses His chosen apostles (the branches), His eye-and-ear witnesses.

Each spiritual regeneration for a new birth, from beginning to end, is brought about by the Gospel. Upon the generative power of the apostles' testimony of Christ, upon their word, He has established it. Christ is with them until the end of the world and nothing of their testimony can be changed if it shall produce divine fruit. All believers (children of God) are their fruit (John 15) by the Holy Ghost.

If a teacher should come today and speak another word than their word and by another spirit than they spoke by, he is a deceiver, a liar and a seducer. But the devil does not like their way and the world will not listen to it because it leads to life. Therefore the devil introduced tradition in place of the apostles' word in his church (infant baptism, etc.), which contradicts the Word of God, and men themselves become what the seed (word) which they receive, is. They are the exact reflection and expression of that which they have heard and accepted, for in every word lies a spirit which passes over them and becomes active. Now, if it is not the spirit of God, which gives life, then it is the spirit of the world, which causes death. Therefore one needs only to measure the false nominal Christians by the measuring stick of the apostolic word to know that they are the seed of a false teaching, not the teaching of Christ.

Therefore Christ *exclusively* is called the *Word* of God because He also is the Spirit of God, Which alone begets divine life. But whoever does not believe the truth must believe the lie. As John had received his teaching from Christ, thus has . . . . learned his from the devil. But a contrived system and a dead orthodoxy are of no account here; here it must be the Spirit of Truth and of Life that engenders that it may give life. We must therefore pay attention to that which we preach and hear; for as the preacher is responsible for what he preaches in order that it may be the pure, unadulterated Word of God, so also is the hearer of the same responsible if he does not accept it as such, but doubts whether it has to be taken so literally and wishes to modify, change and regulate it according to his carnal mind.

There indeed is preaching in the world too, but the fruit proves that it is not the Word of God. Indeed the more exactly a teacher follows the pattern of the apostolic teaching, the more he is persecuted and accused of heresy in the world, and all who are quickened by the Word of Truth would have to be called new believers because the true believer is news and a curiosity in the world—namely, the living Christ— for salvation from sin is promised to everyone who calls upon the Lord: but the calling depends upon faith, faith however upon hearing; the hearing however upon preaching; the preaching however (not upon man) upon God and the Word of His Grace. So men remain in the principality of darkness because the Word of God is not preached unto them and even where it is preached, only the fewest accept it so as to be saved (Romans 10).

May 21, 1840 (Thursday); Evening Meeting; I John 1:1 ff.

The remarkable thing about this passage is the repetition of the words, "which we have *seen* and *heard*." John emphasizes this especially because all depends upon faith in this mystery of the appearance of the Only Begotten Son of God in the flesh and in the world: for whom else shall we believe in the most important thing upon which our eternal welfare depends and which, for all that, is contested by the whole world, than the aforetime-elected witnesses upon whose foundation and testimony Christ will build His house (Hebrews 3; Ephesians 2)? for the apostles stand in the same direct and inseparable relationship to Christ as Christ stands to the Father; He ordained them and sent them in His name, as He Himself came in His (the Father's) name; the Father gave them to Him that they should be one with Him (John 17) as branches are with the vine.

They are His visible representatives on earth and their testimony has a continuous generative power until the end of the world, just as we according to the flesh descend from Adam. All those who believe and are saved, first enter a relationship with the apostles and *only by them* a relationship with Christ as the fruit of the Vine, and it indeed is the ultimate goal that there be many of them, but the increase does not come about in a carnal way as it is done in the world.

He who does not accept the Word of Truth, does not by the testimony of the apostles become an entirely new creature of God: that one does not stand in fellowship with Christ and does not belong to the house of God, even though he belongs to a party or sect here. They must all harmonize with Christ, must have His life in them, for the body of Christ consists of nothing but individual members, but there is no blot on the entire body: this is the fellowship of the saints, this is the house of God wherein Christ is as the Son.

As each individual one is so also is the whole. Every single one, by the Spirit, becomes a dwelling-place of God and all, together, build a holy temple in the Lord. Therefore we must search ourselves to determine whether Christ by faith dwells and reigns in our hearts so that we *also* belong to the community of the saints. —For even though the world builds a temple as beautiful and as dazzling as the one in Jerusalem, if it is not the spiritual and living one built up of only new and sanctified men, then one stone will still not remain upon the other; the twenty-fourth chapter of Matthew must first be fulfilled against it *before Christ can come* to build a new temple in its place in which He may dwell and reveal His glory.

# Chapter V

## "Come and See"

May 24, 1840 (Sunday); Morning Meeting; I John 1:1 ff.
(with light and power)

> "That which was from the beginning, which we have
> heard, which we have seen with our eyes, which we have
> looked upon, and our hands have handled, of the Word
> of life;
> "(For the life was manifested, and we have seen it,
> and bear witness, and shew unto you that eternal life,
> which was with the Father, and was manifested unto us;)
> "That which we have seen and heard declare we unto
> you, that ye also may have fellowship with us: and truly
> our fellowship is with the Father, and with his Son Jesus
> Christ."

The words remind one of John 1:35 ff., "Come and see."

> "And again the next day after John stood, and two
> of his disciples;
> "And looking upon Jesus as he walked, he saith, Be-
> hold the Lamb of God!
> "And the two disciples heard him speak, and they
> followed Jesus.
> "Then Jesus turned, and saw them following, and
> saith unto them, What seek ye? They said unto him,
> Rabbi, (which is to say, being interpreted, Master,)
> where dwellest thou?
> "He saith unto them, Come and see. . . . "

The elderly John still proclaims the gospel (good news) of the Incarnate
Son of God to his brethren in Christ, just as newly and as joyfully lain
hold upon as when he as a young man had for the first time found and
recognized Christ by John the Baptist's testimony of him. One said to
the other, "We have found the Messiah." (Without doubt John himself
was one of the two disciples who first beheld Him.) He could not be
silent about that of which his heart was full and wherein he had become
so greatly blessed. He wished to make others blessed, together with
himself, by the good news of this joy, which alone deserves the name.

12

With this news we could indeed not bring as much joy to carnal men as when, for instance, we would announce to them that they had drawn the lucky number, and the like, for as the mind of man is, so also is his joy and his sorrow: it must be something earthly and carnal if it shall make them rejoice or make them sad. The glad tidings of Christ does not touch them for they do not know their misery; because of all the other idols, they have no room left within them for the living God; they are already full, namely, of the devil and all unrighteousness, wickedness, greed, etc. (Romans 1:29 ff.).

> "Being filled with all unrighteousness, fornication, wickedness, covetousness, maliciousness; full of envy, murder, debate, deceit, malignity; whisperers,
> "Backbiters, haters of God, despiteful, proud, boasters, inventors of evil things, disobedient to parents,
> "Without understanding, covenantbreakers, without natural affection, implacable, unmerciful:
> "Who knowing the judgment of God, that they which commit such things are worthy of death, not only do the same, but have pleasure in them that do them."

Yes, they are filled therewith to overflowing; that is the condition of all natural men and none know or believe it. But each one who learns to know himself is shocked and made sorrowful (Matthew 5:4; II Corinthians 7:9 ff.).

> "Blessed are they that mourn: for they shall be comforted."

---

> "Now I rejoice, not that ye were made sorry, but that ye sorrowed to repentance: for ye were made sorry after a godly manner, that ye might receive damage by us in nothing.
> "For godly sorrow worketh repentance to salvation not to be repented of: but the sorrow of the world worketh death."

Therefore, Christ Himself cannot come direct to men as He would like and the Gospel is not the first thing that should be preached, but He sends John the Baptist before Him with his preaching of repentance, "O generation of vipers," etc., and all those who therein recognize the justice of God and condemn themselves as sinners are being prepared for the coming of Christ. The old hearts and stone temples of the idols

13

must first be shattered to pieces by this hard hammer in order that the poison of the old serpent may not any longer flow over instead of under, but is completely obstructed altogether, that Christ may form new vessels of His glory into which He can then pour His new Spirit, for Christ does not mend the old, neither does He mix the new with the old (Matthew 9:14 ff.; Psalm 51).

"Then came to him the disciples of John, saying, Why do we and the Pharisees fast oft, but thy disciples fast not?

"And Jesus said unto them, Can the children of the bridechamber mourn, as long as the bridegroom is with them? but the days will come, when the bridegroom shall be taken from them, and then shall they fast.

"No man putteth a piece of new cloth unto an old garment, for that which is put in to fill it up taketh from the garment, and the rent is made worse.

"Neither do men put new wine into old bottles: else the bottles break, and the wine runneth out, and the bottles perish: but they put new wine into new bottles, and both are preserved."

Those however who will not let their old hearts be broken because, in their own eyes, they are already right and good, like the Pharisees (Luke 7:29 ff.), will afterwards be dashed to pieces as vessels of wrath.

"And all the people that heard him, and the publicans, justified God, being baptized with the baptism of John.

"But the Pharisees and lawyers rejected the counsel of God against themselves, being not baptized of him."

As we by nature were filled by the devil so that his poison of unrighteousness flowed out from us at every hand, thus must we by the grace of Christ become full of the living and true God that rivers of living water flow forth from us (John 7:38 ff.).

"He that believeth on me, as the scripture hath said, out of his belly shall flow rivers of living water.

"(But this spake he of the Spirit, which they that believe on him should receive: for the Holy Ghost was not yet given; because that Jesus was not yet glorified.)"

# Chapter VI

## The Eternal Way

May 24, 1840 (Sunday); Afternoon Meeting; I John 1:1 ff.

The divine designation and true blessedness of man subsists in his reunion and spiritual fellowship with the living God through Christ, Who has come for the purpose that *eternal life* may take its beginning in us now, for blessedness in this world can consist only in those things in which there is eternal blessedness.

Men are therefore very unhappy and restless in themselves here because they do not have the living God and they do not seek Him and His fellowship because their spirit, by darkness and the love of vanity, is entirely removed from its goal. They are all dead, mad, regular fools, just as those are from a social standpoint who are locked up in insane asylums. Like madmen, all run and pursue after the possession and enjoyment of deceptive phantoms and let Christ the Eternal Life and Substantial Good, Who is so near to all, stand outside (Romans 10:6).

"But the righteousness which is of faith speaketh on this wise, Say not in thine heart, Who shall ascend into heaven? (that is, to bring Christ down from above:)"

Their life is vain imagining and deception (Ephesians 4); they never come to themselves, to understanding or to their senses (Psalm 14). If a person has a fine home and fine clothes he thinks he is rich and distinguished and does not know that he is poor and miserable and God says to him, "Thou fool (Luke 12)." Another imagines he is wise and yet he is proud, covetous, sensual, etc., and does not know that he is a fool (Romans 1:22; Proverbs 28:26).

"Professing themselves to be wise, they became fools,"

---

"He that trusteth in his own heart is a fool: but whoso walketh wisely, he shall be delivered."

Another imagines himself powerful and mighty (John 19:10 ff.) and does not think his breath is in his nostrils.

"Then saith Pilate unto him, Speaketh thou not unto me? knowest thou not that I have power to crucify thee, and have power to release thee?

15

> "Jesus answered, Thou couldest have no power at
> all against me, except it were given thee from above:
> therefore he that delivered me unto thee hath the greater
> sin."

Thus all seek what is vain and not the living God. They would like to
live well and fare sumptuously and when they are filled their soul is still
empty and dissatisfied and the desolation of the spirit remains unfilled
in spite of all earthly things, for they have all been deceived by the
devil, since only in God are all true things—fulness, contentment and
blessedness. He makes us truly rich, strong and wise, that we can
glory in Him by knowing Him (I Corinthians 1; Jeremiah 9:23 ff.;
Psalm 119:98 ff.).

> "Thus saith the Lord, Let not the wise man glory in
> his wisdom, neither let the mighty man glory in his
> might, let not the rich man glory in his riches:
> "But let him that glorieth glory in this, that he under-
> standeth and knoweth me, that I am the Lord which
> exercise lovingkindness, judgment, and righteousness,
> in the earth: for in these things I delight, saith the Lord."

------

> "Thou through thy commandments hast made me
> wiser than mine enemies: for they are ever with me.
> "I have more understanding than all my teachers: for
> thy testimonies are my meditation.
> "I understand more than the ancients, because I
> keep thy precepts."

This is good cheer, joy, peace, righteousness; not imagination, delusion, confusion, intoxication of the senses. More than this, with the
living God we cannot sink even though the waters surge and roll
(Psalm 46). Christ teaches us to walk on the water, to tread on serpents
and scorpions (Luke 10:19).

> "Behold, I give unto you power to tread on serpents
> and scorpions, and over all the power of the enemy: and
> nothing shall by any means hurt you."

But if we live and walk according to Christ, the world cries, "Look
at those fools!" This is the greatest foolishness of fools, that they consider themselves wise and the wise according to divine things, fools.
Besides, they crown their insanity with this, that they still *in this time*
think God dwells in temples made with hands, as was the pattern in the

Old Testament. They do not know that we ourselves *in the Spirit* must be the temple of God, as a community of saints. Any other worship than this is nothing but idolatry. The old stone temple must first be destroyed before Christ can build His new one (Acts 6 and 7). We must however take heed that we are not removed from the fortification of God, for there are many evil spirits all around us who tempt us in all kinds of ways to stir us up to anger.

## May 26, 1840 (Tuesday); Evening Meeting; I John 1:1 ff.

John cites the blessedness which subsists in the fellowship of the living and true God. Without this, man may have or find whatever he will, he is still unhappy in himself. But the longing, desire and inclination for vain things is implanted in all by nature and where this would not yet be enough, one helps the other to destruction: " . . . evil men and seducers shall wax worse and worse, deceiving, and being deceived (II Timothy 3:13)." Blind leaders offer themselves to the blind and so both fall into the ditch.

The devil uses the earthly for a bait, which he fastens to his fishing line, and because delusioned men eagerly seize and devour it, they are caught and the most of them are lost beyond recovery — unless God takes wondrous pity on them and releases them from the snare of the devil (Matthew 19; I Timothy 6), "For the love of money is the root of all evil;" and is not reconcilable with the love and service to God (Matthew 6). Men indeed seek happiness but not in God and the devil cannot give them any joy for he has none. They are of the opinion and hope that they will also be saved, but they do not take the only road to it and therefore cannot reach the goal. They have gone astray and will not be shown the right way of life and peace.

By nature, there is no inclination or disposition in man toward God, but much more a disinclination to Him and enmity against Him. One sees that in children already in their youth, how tedious and annoying it is to them to hear about God and this increases with their age, how glad they are as soon as their so-called divine worship is over, how much more are they inclined to the joys of this world. For God and His salvation they are, by far, less knowing than the beasts (Isaiah 1). They mockingly say of true godliness, "Yes, one has eaten if one prays much," and the like. Anything that they cannot see with their eyes and touch with their hands has no attraction for or value with them.

Now, one can indeed not see the living God with one's eyes nor touch Him with one's hands and His joys are not carnal, nor are they

17

for the carnal minded. For this reason His witnesses, who reconcile us, come, saying: "We have seen with our eyes and our hands have handled the Word of Life—yes, Eternal Life—and our blessedness is unspeakable. Come now and join us so that you also, together *with* us, may be blessed in the fellowship of the Father and His Son Jesus Christ." But men are so unsusceptible and so indifferent that it requires the greatest effort and labor until one believes, and these, for the most part, are not from the high and noble of this world but from the poor and lowly.

No one at all knows God and His Gift except him who has himself received, experienced and enjoyed it and if each one would examine himself according to the Word of God, he would find out how far he still is from God and His kingdom and would earnestly inquire after the eternal way on which *alone* we can come to God and find Him.

## Chapter VII

### Fellowship in the Spirit

May 28, 1840 (Ascension Day); Morning Meeting; I John 1:3 ff.

> "That which we have seen and heard declare we unto you, that ye also may have fellowship with us: and truly our fellowship is with the Father, and with His Son Jesus Christ.
>
> "And these things write we unto you, that your joy may be full.
>
> "This then is the message which we have heard of him, and declare unto you, that God is light, and in him is no darkness at all."

The invitation of John to "fellowship with us" refers to the Christian church or congregation that is the body of Christ, whose Head He is in heaven at the right hand of the Father, whither He has ascended so that He might fill all by His Spirit and His fulness is the church (His body), which is also with Him in heaven, for what He is and has, that He is and has for it. It is a fellowship of the Spirit and the saints (not of the flesh); it, to be sure, is also a fellowship of the body, but this body of Christ, as well, is spiritual and holy as He Himself is. However it is *one* body and *one* Spirit in the entire body and *one* hope for all the members (Ephesians 4):

" . . . When he ascended up on high, he led captivity
captive, and gave gifts [of His Spirit] unto [believing]
men.
"(Now that he ascended, what is it but that he also
descended first into the lower parts of the earth?" —

and appeared in our human and a servant's form so as to take, indeed
as the Son of man, His prey away from the strong one so that the devil
could not complain about the might and injustice.

Yes, up to this time, Christ leaves it to everyone's free choice
whether he wishes to become converted or would prefer to remain in
Satan's power. Therefore Christ lets the Gospel be proclaimed and
each one must choose and decide his eternal destiny for himself. No
one is forced to be saved or to be condemned, but because all belong to
the devil by nature, none are incorporated in Christ without conversion
(John 6). Christ has indeed bound and overcome the strong one, but
only for the obedient (the believers); for the others, the devil is not
bound, but loose, as can be seen in all the world. Who then can be saved
and what must we do to be saved and not be condemned with the world?

But the world in this respect is careless and secure and takes a
chance on it until death. They then all hope to be saved, but wrongly so
and without foundation, for the world is unsaved and shall be condemned. But we must be sure about the matter as it concerns us ourselves; here no uncertainty is permitted: it is a question of eternal
salvation or eternal damnation and everyone faces one or the other
(Hebrews 9:27 ff.).

"And as it is appointed unto men once to die, but
after this the judgment:
"So Christ was once offered to bear the sins of many;
and unto them that look for him shall he appear the
second time without sin unto salvation."

Therefore we must ask in earnest and must know who will and who
cannot be saved. John gives us the right answer: Whoever has fellowship (in the Spirit) with the living God (Father and Son) will be
saved and is already saved and has eternal life in him.

However, no one enters into fellowship with God according to the
flesh, but according to the Spirit, as a new creature, and the condition
thereunto is faith in the Gospel of the apostles, upon which baptism
follows (Matthew 28; Acts 2). The way to God has not changed in
1,800 years, that one could now come into His fellowship according to

the flesh, and every modification which occurs in the way is not from God but from the devil. Each one must himself answer the question, whether he belongs to Christ and has His life in him so as to be saved, and any preacher who cannot rightly solve the question, who will be saved and who damned, is a deceiver and the blood of the lost is upon him; but he who answers it so plainly that everyone can understand it and choose, has saved his soul.

May 28, 1840 (Ascension Day); Afternoon Meeting; I John 1:3 ff.

As Christ, the Head, is holy, thus also is His body, the church, holy; yes, also invisible and hidden with Him (Colossians 3:1 ff.) (below), for what there is *on earth* of it (visible) is an insignificant part of the true Christians.

> "If ye then be risen with Christ, seek those things which are above, where Christ sitteth on the right hand of God.
> "Set your affections on things above, not on things on the earth.
> "For ye are dead, and your life is hid with Christ in God.
> "When Christ, who is our life, shall appear, then shall ye also appear with him in glory."

All the called saints are strangers and pilgrims here below who are scarcely tolerated and pass through hardly. They are from above and strive after that which is above and attain thereunto. Where some of them meet in this strange land, there is rejoicing and they have the *fellowship of the saints;* there God stands over them; there we find a Bethel (house of God).

An unsanctified Christian is an inner contradiction. Whoever is not holy (a new creation) is not a Christian, for Christ is holy and the Father is holy and His Spirit sanctifies us and without that we do not belong to Christ. Therefore the so-called Christian church of the world is not the body nor the church of Christ because its members are not holy. With their worship they are under the law and they snap at and smite those who would show them the way to God.

One is accepted into the fellowship of their church through the flesh and the law, compulsorily: "What those of old sang the younger ones learn too." They have left the order of Christ and the apostles, and as many as have been called and chosen (separated from the world) by God—walk according to this standard—are hit by the world's scorn and hatred and must be called queer people, hypocrites, the sanctimonious, new believers, etc. All manner of evil is said of them because they (like Christ) are not of the world and they no longer do as it does and *by that* they condemn all in the false church.

On the contrary, one attains unto fellowship with the body of Christ only through fellowship with His Spirit (not inversely); that is, we must first have become participant of Christ before we can be accepted into His church. The seal of the forgiveness of the former sins is sanctification (Hebrews 10:14 ff.).

> "For by one offering he hath perfected for ever them that are sanctified.
> "Whereof the Holy Ghost also is a witness to us: for after that he had said before,
> "This is the covenant that I will make with them after those days, saith the Lord, I will put my laws into their hearts, and in their minds will I write them;
> "And their sins and iniquities will I remember no more.
> "Now where remission of these is, there is no more offering for sin."

Therefore the unbelievers have no forgiveness of their sins.

## CHAPTER VIII

### SPIRITUAL BLINDNESS

May 31, 1840 (Sunday); Morning Meeting; I John 1:3 ff.

> "That which we have seen and heard declare we unto you, that ye also may have fellowship with us: and truly our fellowship is with the Father, and with His Son Jesus Christ.
> "And these things write we unto you, that your joy may be full.
> "This then is the message which we have heard of him, and declare unto you, that God is light, and in him is no darkness at all."

The purpose of the apostle in this writing is a two-fold one:*

---

*The second purpose is meditated upon in the afternoon meeting.

21

The *first* is *fellowship with God,* which is lacking in men and about which they neither trouble themselves nor worry. *We* however shall not forget or underestimate it for it is our destiny and the call of God. Unconverted men live without God (ungodly) and without hope in the world because they are not called or do not accept the call, as such who think they are already right; the called of God however thirst after the living God and He is their Light and Salvation and the Strength of their Life and so they are unafraid (Psalms 27 and 42). David longed for fellowship with God all his life as king of Israel and as a shepherd, but Saul gave way to obstinacy and disobedience (self-elevation and self-confidence) and was rejected on that account. All unconverted men and those not rightly converted in the world are like that. Their (inner) darkness is so great that they induce themselves to believe that there is no God and therefore He does not see them—as if they could hide themselves from Him or at least excuse themselves—but God will punish them and set their sins in order before their eyes (Psalm 50). This darkness already is an unblessed state (death and damnation), but they do not yet feel what it means to be separated from God because they *love* darkness; however they shall feel it in eternity when they shall reap what they have sown. Thus the walk in the light (fellowship with God) is a blessing (eternal life) now already.

The recognition of sin and confession thereof is the return to fellowship with God. The first foolishness of man is the sin he commits; the second, greater foolishness is the lie (denial of sin); the third is the greatest, that he imagines, by reason of his denial, he remains unpunishable, when even a proverb says, *"Es ist nichts so fein gesponnen, es kommt endlich an die Sonnen."* (Everything comes to light in the end.) Now, God knows very well indeed that we are sinners and His Word testifies on every page that we sin from our youth, and that is not to be wondered at either since we descend from Adam; and we ourselves also know when we have sinned or we would not immediately take refuge in a lie and deny it so that we should not be punished (John 3:20).

> "For every one that doeth evil hateth the light, neither cometh to the light, lest his deeds should be reproved."

But what one must be astonished at is this blindness! How one can persuade himself that God, Whose testimony he surely has in his conscience, does *not* know it and he is *punished* just on account of this second greater sin (the lie), for even though a person had sinned, if he would confess it remorsefully, it would certainly be forgiven him. But what *is* unpardonable is that a sinner would still wish to cover his wickedness by lying and justify himself, for he thereby hardens his conscience, the testimony of which should make his return to God and his being forgiven, easier and in this way he becomes flames of hell.

A child of God can also err in some way, but he is sorry and does not conceal it; instead, he confesses it to the Father in order that he may be healed by His forgiveness, for he knows God and is upright before Him, like David (Psalm 32). Therefore he who wishes to have his life and soundness of the Spirit (fellowship with God) must not spare his old man but unclothe him to nakedness and hang him in the sun (like Christ on the cross) that he must be ashamed. He however who *himself* wishes to cover his sin shall nevermore be freed or forgiven of it—eternally.

An upright confession is the mark of a converted man and is the difference between him and a hypocrite, for it is not necessary that one hide what is not right in darkness as liars do, who first hide themselves and then blame others, like Adam. Fellowship with God and the walk in the light impress themselves upon our entire life. Here, then, is no falsity, no lie, no wickedness, no darkness, etc.

May 31, 1840 (Sunday); Afternoon Meeting

The *second* purpose of this writing is that the *joy of the believers* be fulfilled by fellowship with God. Aside from this, the Gospel already is joyful news to those whom it concerns; that is, the poor, heavy-laden and laboring sinners who sorrow over their death in sin (Matthew 5:4; 11:28; Luke 2:10 ff.).

"Blessed are they that mourn: for they shall be comforted."

---

"Come unto me, all ye that labour and are heavy laden, and I will give you rest."

---

"And the angel said unto them, Fear not: for, behold, I bring you good tidings of great joy, which shall be to all people.

"For unto you is born this day in the city of David a Saviour, which is Christ the Lord."

Their heart is revived by the proclaiming of Christ the Crucified, but their joy is not yet made full by that, for what is Christ to me if He is preached to me as a dead Savior, the Crucified One, only and if the message is only fulfilled in my ears and not in my heart as well, that Christ may become my life? The world has a dead, according-to-the-letter Christ too, Who is outside of and not in them as Eternal Life and they are and remain dead in sin. Indeed it is the world which still crucifies and kills Christ anew in the members of His body, in whom His Spirit, that is, He Himself, lives, and without His Spirit we are not Christians (Romans 8:9).

> "But ye are not in the flesh, but in the Spirit, if so be that the Spirit of God dwell in you. Now if any man have not the Spirit of Christ, he is none of his."

Now, the declaring of the Man Christ belongs to the first things (I Corinthians 15:1 ff.) (below), but the *Christ living within us is the true One,* and by our spirit-fellowship with Him and the Father *our joy is made full.* This is the final aim of the entire Gospel.

> "Moreover, brethren, I declare unto you the gospel which I preached unto you, which also ye have received, and wherein ye stand;
> "By which also ye are saved, if ye keep in memory what I preached unto you, unless ye have believed in vain.
> "For I delivered unto you first of all that which I also received, how that Christ died for our sins according to the scriptures;
> "And that he was buried, and that he rose again the third day according to the scriptures:
> "And that he was seen of Cephas, then of the twelve:
> "After that, he was seen of above five hundred brethren at once; of whom the greater part remain unto this present, but some are fallen asleep.
> "After that, he was seen of James; then of all the apostles.
> "And last of all he was seen of me also, as of one born out of due time.
> "For I am the least of the apostles, that am not meet to be called an apostle, because I persecuted the church of God.
> "But by the grace of God I am what I am: and his grace which was bestowed upon me was not in vain; but

I laboured more abundantly than they all: yet not I, but the grace of God which was with me.

"Therefore whether it were I or they, so we preach, and so ye believed.

"Now if Christ be preached that he rose from the dead, how say some among you that there is no resurrection of the dead?

"But if there be no resurrection of the dead, then is Christ not risen:

"And if Christ be not risen, then is our preaching vain, and your faith is also vain.

"Yea, and we are found false witnesses of God; because we have testified of God that he raised up Christ: whom he raised not up, if so be that the dead rise not.

"For if the dead rise not, then is not Christ raised:

"And if Christ be not raised, your faith is vain; ye are yet in your sins."

But as soon as we have the living Christ in us through the Spirit and are no longer contented with the dead One, we are called fools, visionaries, fanatics, etc. by the world. It is so certain that men neither have nor know the true Christ because they neither have nor know His Spirit. Therefore we find no fellowship of saints in the world where one suffers with another and rejoices with another in the Lord, but only selfishness. But the joy in the Holy Ghost must necessarily increase in us in just the same degree as we receive a fuller fellowship with the Father and the Son and learn to know the living God by a holy walk.

## CHAPTER IX

### THE JOY IN THE HOLY GHOST

June 2, 1840 (Tuesday); Evening Meeting; I John 1:4

"And these things write we unto you, that your joy may be full."

With deepest feeling and from convincing experience, John shows us the way to that which all men would willingly possess, but which is nevertheless not to be found in this world except in God; namely, to a true and abiding joy in God and His Holy Spirit, for earthly joy is not of an eternal nature but vain and transient. Whoever drinks of this cloudy water will thirst again and never be filled. Christ however

25

gives us everlasting living water as a continuous, inexhaustible fountain of joy, that we shall never, eternally, thirst again (John 4), for it is a part of the inner kingdom of God, but is to be found only where righteousness and peace prevail (Romans 14:17).

"For the kingdom of God is not meat and drink; but righteousness, and peace, and joy in the Holy Ghost."

The real joy in the Holy Ghost lies in the continuous awareness and divine assurance that the righteous God is not only our God but at the same time our Father also in Christ and that we are His children and His heirs with Christ. This is such an unspeakably great and unsearchably deep mystery that, when we consider ourselves and understand that we are nothing, we cannot wonder and rejoice enough in the Spirit that God is thus mindful of us and visits us. Yes, for a little while, we have to be forsaken by God in order that He may crown us afterwards with everlasting glory and honor (Psalm 8; Hebrews 2).

But we must take heed that this fountain of joy be not stopped up; that is to say, this knowing God as our Father must not only inspire us with joy but with confidence and patience also, that we may be satisfied with the grace of God, even though an angel of Satan smite us and at the same time all other comforts and times of refreshing be withdrawn and wither on earth, for the Upper Wellspring can still never fail us, and so we continue to flourish and to be fruitful even when a year of drought comes (Jeremiah 17; I Corinthians 12). Be it affliction or consolation, we must be independent of every earthly spring, and the living God alone, as our Highest Good and Eternal Portion, must be sufficient for us (Psalm 73).

Satan, as our accuser, withstands us as though our faith and confidence in God were dependent upon our personal well-being and in order that this may be shown and proved, God is forced to strip us of every temporal comfort; and even if blow upon blow comes, God and His joy must ever remain unto us, to persuade us that He loves us and that He alone is wise, that He has the most perfect right to all things and still does not permit us to be tempted beyond our endurance, that there is nothing that can harm us or be taken from us that can be compared to the future glory: and if we cling firmly to God in trials and temptations of this kind, our faith shall be established as true and crowned like that of Job, David and others (James 1:12; 5:11), for the very God Who lets us descend into this deep pit is mighty also to save us again out of it.

26

"Blessed is the man that endureth temptation: for when he is tried, he shall receive the crown of life, which the Lord hath promised to them that love him."

---

"Behold, we count them happy which endure. Ye have heard of the patience of Job, and have seen the end of the Lord; that the Lord is very pitiful, and of tender mercy."

So if we know from experience and have tasted how kind the Lord is, we shall also abide in Him and our joy will then be fulfilled.

## June 4, 1840 (Thursday)

The apostle wishes the believers a full, consummate and perfect joy in God and His Holy Spirit. He is not and they shall not be content either with a small or half-measure of this joy, for it stands in equal proportion to the knowledge and fellowship of God and to the love to God. If we know from experience what we have in God—if Christ and His Spirit is our life—our heart must then pulsate for love and leap for joy as David sang and sprang when he rejoiced exceedingly in his God (11 Samuel 6).

Far be it indeed from us that outer afflictions and persecutions for righteousness' sake would be able to dampen this spiritual joy; rather, they are the best means to heighten it and to enrapture the heart with effervescence and joyousness, just as fire brings cold water to a boiling point, for the tasting of God's kindness and the foretaste of eternal glory then first become very precious to us (Matthew 5; Romans 8; James 1), and that then really enrages the devil and the world that they heat their furnace seven times hotter still. Since carnally minded men have not the faintest idea of spiritual joy, it is most incomprehensible to them that we can still rejoice in the midst of the heat of affliction and persecution and that is proof to them that it is all ardor and exaltation of mind with us, just as they, on the other hand, consider it madness if one in the beginning of his conversion is saddened unto death. In no way is one able to suit them (Matthew 11:16 ff.).

"But whereunto shall I liken this generation? It is like unto children sitting in the markets, and calling unto their fellows,

"And saying, We have piped unto you, and ye have not danced; we have mourned unto you, and ye have not lamented.

27

"For John came neither eating nor drinking, and they say, He hath a devil.

"The Son of man came eating and drinking, and they say, Behold a man gluttonous, and a wine-bibber, a friend of publicans and sinners. But wisdom is justified of her children."

Yes, the wisdom of God is justified by her children.

It is not a good witnessing of a believer if he is not exuberant with joy in his God and Savior, and Christ has not deserved it from us that we be lukewarm and drowsy toward Him. The lukewarm are so unbearable to Him that He will spew them out of His mouth (Revelation 3). It is false judgment on the part of the false Christians who feign something of faith in Christ and yet do not wish to be offensive to the world by an abounding joy in the Holy Spirit, so as not to be considered fools. They seem to have something of Christ and yet it is nothing. They are a hybrid, not entirely cold like the critical enemies of Christ and still less than entirely warm, as is befitting of the friends of Christ, that they be fervent in the Spirit (Romans 12), for as one knows a dead person by his being cold, so ought one also to know a living one in Christ by the warmth and fervency of love and joy in the Spirit; but a lukewarm person one does not rightly know where he belongs, whether to God or to the devil.

On account of the lukewarm, the name of God is being blasphemed among the heathen, and just as we must not be guided by the judgment of the world, which understands nothing of the Spirit of God, so also must we not present ourselves as being lukewarm or we also shall be rejected. Christians who are not ashamed to belong entirely to Christ and to walk as His own in the world are scarce and they have in themselves more of the consummate joy of the Spirit than one at first glance may think.

## Chapter X

## Faith, The Only Bridge to God

June 7, 1840 (Sunday); Afternoon Meeting; I John 1:3 ff.

The apostle testifies of what they have seen and heard of the hidden, heavenly and divine mysteries, with the same certitude and confidence as Jesus Himself had testified, Who, as an eye-and-ear Witness, had descended from the Father and men did not believe Him (John 3:11 ff., 25 ff.):

28

"Verily, verily, I say unto thee, We speak that we do know, and testify that we have seen; and ye receive not our witness.

"If I have told you earthly things, and ye believe not, how shall ye believe, if I tell you of heavenly things?

"And no man hath ascended up to heaven, but he that came down from heaven, even the Son of man which is in heaven.

"And as Moses lifted up the serpent in the wilderness, even so must the Son of man be lifted up:

"That whosoever believeth in him should not perish, but have eternal life."

---

"Then there arose a question between some of John's disciples and the Jews about purifying.

"And they came unto John, and said unto him, Rabbi, he that was with thee beyond Jordan, to whom thou barest witness, behold, the same baptizeth, and all men come to him.

"John answered and said, A man can receive nothing, except it be given him from heaven.

"Ye yourselves bear me witness, that I said, I am not the Christ, but that I am sent before him."

for they had not believed nor understood Moses, whose pattern- and shadow-presentations, in comparison to the reality which appeared in Christ, are what the terrestrial is to the celestial. There, it was a visible sanctuary, made with hands; but here is the true one into which Christ has entered with His own blood, after He Himself had accomplished the cleansing of it.

So we must learn to be loosed from the visible and outer so as to also enter into the invisible and inner; namely, the fellowship of the Father and His Son, by the renewing of the Holy Spirit, which the apostles witness of and proclaim to us and to which they invite us. Not that they themselves had ascended into heaven, but, for that purpose, the Holy Spirit, as Christ's Representative, had descended to proclaim all things to them and to glorify Christ as the Eternal Life in them: for as long as Christ was with them outwardly only and taught them, they grasped it only outwardly and imperfectly in their minds, but it was not yet glorified in them as the Life of God Himself. The departure of Christ therefore was expedient to them, that the Spirit of Truth might come in His stead and thus place them here like Christ Himself, and it must also happen thus with all believers so that it may be a fellowship of saints, where God Himself stands over them and the ladder descends from heaven unto the earth; there, then, is a house of God.

What little fruit is brought forth where the Gospel is accomplished in the ears only of men, we can see in the inhabitants of Nazareth, as it filled them with wrath instead of with joy because they took offense at the person of Jesus and rejected His proclamation. However, where the Word of God is accomplished in the hearts of the hearers as well, there they also become filled with joy in the Holy Ghost so that they cannot conceal what they have received, for where Christ lights a light in the darkness of this world, there it shall not be kept hidden but shall shine forth to the glory of God. Therefore, when the disciples of John announced to him that Jesus had a greater following than he, he was gladdened by the report and testified (John 3:29 ff.):

> "He that hath the bride is the bridegroom: but the friend of the bridegroom, which standeth and heareth him, rejoiceth greatly because of the bridegroom's voice: this my joy therefore is fulfilled.
> "He must increase, but I must decrease."

Now, as Christ grows when many are converted to Him—united with Him as His bride and share His divine nature—we dare not let Christ stand outside and know Him only outwardly according to the flesh and the letter, but we must receive Him Himself in us by His Spirit of Life so that *our* joy may be fulfilled also in a much higher degree and meaning, in that we belong to His bride as children of God, taught by God Himself and having His living law written in our heart in order that we may, at all times, not only know but also joyfully do His good, acceptable and perfect will, so that the doing of the good becomes as natural and easy for us (as our other, divine nature) as the evil—which one did not need to teach us—formerly was. Surely, just as full-fledged villains on their cots already ponder evil things, thus also shall the children of God, day and night, meditate upon the good until they become perfected in it.

June 8, 1840 (Pentecost Monday); Afternoon Meeting; I John 1:5

> "This then is the message which we have heard of him, and declare unto you, that God is light, and in him is no darkness at all."

The apostle more closely approaches his aim and more clearly explains what he means: This is the message which we have heard of

30

Him and in return declare it unto you. The apostles did with the Word of Life as with the bread they received blessed from the hand of the Lord and again handed over to the people until all the hungry were filled. In this way millions already have been filled by the Lord through the apostles' word unto eternal life and the abundance of His blessings is still here, but there is little hunger here for this food when we hear their message, "that God is light, and in him is no darkness at all." This is no welcome news for those who love the darkness and would not like to have their works revealed and punished. They assiduously hide themselves in darkness, just as Adam avoided the light of the presence of God and fled after he had sinned and fallen into darkness, and all who have bad consciences are doing the same thing.

The Holy Ghost uses a figure of speech with respect to God so as to describe His nature and being to us, which is known to all who were not born blind: "light," the opposite of darkness; and this emblem of God, taken from Nature, is all the more necessary to reascend to the true knowledge of God since we by nature were all born blind with respect to the spiritual and know God in His nature as little as Adam knew sin before he had sinned, or as little as we would have an idea of darkness if it were always day. Now, no mortal eye is able to endure looking at the sun in its brightness without becoming blind and a sinner can just as little endure beholding the glory of God, and all who have not become qualified therefor *here* by faith will flee from before Him in eternity.

Faith in the Son of God is the only bridge for crossing over from the realm of the darkness of the devil into the realm of the light of God, and after the bridge has once been demolished, there is left no way of crossing over the great gulf fixed between by God Himself (Luke 16; John 8), namely, between the children of God and those of the devil. The difference between the two is the *latter* with their spirit are a darkness in the night, but for the *former* Christ, as the Light of the World, is shining and He illuminates them that they walk as in broad daylight and without stumbling, knowing whither they go. They do indeed not yet see Christ, the Sun, face to face, but through faith and love they have fellowship with Him and know Him, and with the light beaming from Him, they are enabled to understand and discern things, as far as their horizon reaches, more or less definitely as by daylight. They must first use their enlightenment for the searching knowledge and purification of themselves—not like the Pharisees who could indeed see keenly as far as others were concerned but were blind in respect to themselves—and if they are not conscious of any impurity in themselves, they may then give light to others also and show them the way, on which account however they are hated and persecuted by the world, like Christ, because they punish the darkness and its unfruitful works by their light.

June 11, 1840 (Thursday); Evening Meeting; I John 1:5

> "This then is the message which we have heard of him, and declare unto you, that God is light, and in him is no darkness at all."

"This then is the message." Remarkable! John sums up the whole Gospel in one word, which we would not have thought of, "that God is light." The Gospel has two aspects, namely:

Insofar as it is proclaimed to the unconverted, it is a message from the Son of God, because He has appeared in the flesh as the Light of the World and the Dayspring from on High, to give light to them that sit in darkness and the shadow of death (Luke 1) and to take sin away, destroy the works of the devil by His substitutional obedience unto death on the cross; but as far as it is proclaimed to the converted believer, it is a message from God the Father as to how we shall know Him, have fellowship with Him and walk in the light.

The former is the means by which we shall not continue to remain, not make the purpose of it merely to hear and say that Christ has come and died, or we reverse the Gospel (as if we considered the tool as the work that shall be accomplished by it). The latter however is the final aim of the whole Gospel for which Christ came into the world: to bring us to the Father as new men of God; for if we could have found and known God by ourselves and could have come to Him (were not sinners), Christ would not have appeared in the flesh.

For the natural man there is a double hindrance standing in the way of knowing God and having fellowship with Him: (1) the *darkness which the devil has spread over the whole world by the fall of Adam,* and this has been lifted by the first appearance of Christ as the Light of the World, however not unconditionally and for everyone, but only for the believers who receive and follow Him (John 1 and 8), the second hindrance (namely (2) following) remaining still, in addition, for the unbelievers and disobedient who love darkness more than the light; (2), the *inner darkness,* the blindness of the heart, by which men are estranged from God (Ephesians 4:18; Matthew 6:22 ff.) and live in sin, unchastity and unrighteousness (Romans 1).

"Having the understanding darkened, being alienated from the life of God through the ignorance that is in them, because of the blindness of their heart:"

---

"The light of the body is the eye: if therefore thine eye be single, thy whole body shall be full of light.
"But if thine eye be evil, thy whole body shall be full of darkness. If therefore the light that is in thee be darkness, how great is that darkness!"

## Chapter XI

### Seeing Eyes

Darkness, it is true, originates from the absence of light, and as soon as light appears the darkness must vanish, for the light (as God Himself) is more powerful than the darkness (of the devil). But without enlightened (seeing) eyes, even the brightest light does not help us, and the first message of Christ's appearance in the flesh did not help those who did not become converted by the Word so as to be enlightened by Him—as little as a blind man sees by reason of my telling him, "The sun is shining."

Now, all men are blind and dead for God by nature and it is clear from this that they do not see or know God: for as I must *see light* if I but have *open* eyes, so must I also *see God* if I have *enlightened* eyes or a pure heart (Matthew 5:8; Acts 15:9):

"Blessed are the pure in heart: for they shall see God."

---

"And put no difference between us and them, purifying their hearts by faith."

and every enlightened Christian can say with Christ, "I have set the Lord always before me (Psalm 16)."

So Christ must then not only be the outer daylight for us by which we see, but also the inner eyesight by which we see all things. Only then has He become the Way to the Father for us, and we must then take heed that our inner eye is not contaminated, clouded or darkened again by sin, as, surely, a sound eye can endure no uncleanness; for if we are always in the light (have God before our eyes and in our hearts), we then are careful to avoid sin so that the light will not be extinguished for us.

33

June 14, 1840 (Sunday); Morning Meeting; I John 1:5 (with joy)

> "This then is the message which we have heard of
> him, and declare unto you, that God is light, and in him
> is no darkness at all."

One should think one could bring no greater joy to poor, blind, darkened men than the message: "God is light and has appeared for the purpose of taking your darkness away." But one brings them no great joy with this message because their hatred of the light is just as great as their love of the darkness. Therefore, because the world in its wisdom did not acknowledge God in His wisdom, it pleased God well to redeem the believers by the foolishness of the preaching of Christ (I Corinthians 1). The wisdom of this world—of which it boasts so much—is just as much foolishness in the sight of God as the wisdom of God is foolishness to the world. Just on this account God punishes and plagues the unbelieving world with preaching which appears foolish, to provoke them therewith, just as He by Moses announced to disobedient Old Israel that He would move them to anger and jealousy with a foolish, silly people who were not a people, because they had moved Him to jealousy with a god which was not God.

And so it happened when Christ appeared as the Light of the World, that the Jews, on account of their self-righteousness, were offended by Him and killed Him; but, by reason of this, the light broke forth for the Gentiles as it went out and became night for the Jews (N.B. the Jews begin their day in the evening), and what the Jews had rejected, the Gentiles now accepted, joyfully, and were enlightened and became a people of God, of whom the Jews had said in their pride, "Nothing will ever become of them; they are excluded and rejected." (N.B. the Jews and the Gentiles are like the two . . . . . .) From then on, up to now, the day of the Gentiles continues until the fulness of them has entered in, that is, as long as the entering in is done by faith.

But this foolish preaching will please the so-called Christians less and less, compared to their own wisdom—a heathenish culture—the longer it continues. Soon there will be no more saints and consequently no more true believers (Psalm 12) as the believers and the saints are the same. The saints have become an object of derision and it is ridiculous to a false Christian that they should not be Christians of themselves and that they should first have to become believers.

As the Jews had fulfilled their time and sins 1800 years ago by the rejection and crucifixion of Christ in the flesh, that of them all just blood shed on earth from Abel to Christ has been demanded, and as punishment therefor, they, since then, must wander about in the world like sheep without a shepherd, like a curse and wonderment to all nations, on account of their false, blind zeal for their own righteousness, opposing the righteousness of God. So also must the false, nominal Christians, on the other hand, fulfill their time and sins by the rejection and crucifixion of Christ in the Spirit (namely in His true members if any still remain), on account of their false, blind zeal for their own wisdom of this world, and this eradication of Christ in the Spirit must come to pass before Christ returns in glory and, with it, the time of the Jews (the morning of the New Day), when the receiving of Him will no longer be done by faith, but instantly by the beholding and knowing face to face (Matthew 23:39; Revelation 1:7).

"For I say unto you, Ye shall not see me henceforth, till ye shall say, Blessed is he that cometh in the name of the Lord."

———————

"Behold, he cometh with clouds; and every eye shall see him, and they also which pierced him: and all kindreds of the earth shall wail because of him. Even so, Amen."

Now, as much greater as the sin of the falsely called Christians is than the sin of the Jews, so much greater also is their punishment, namely, an eternal rejection, for their own wisdom is a still greater and a more abominable idol than their own righteousness; and wherever the righteous Christ nowadays appears in His Word and Spirit, He is scorned, ridiculed, scourged and crucified and here the patience and faith of the saints is necessary. (Compare Luke 17:25 with 21:12.)

"But first must he suffer many things, and be rejected of this generation."

———————

"But before all these [signs], they shall lay their hands on you, and persecute you, delivering you up to the synagogues, and into prisons, being brought before kings and rulers for my name's sake."

# Chapter XII

## The Goal of Salvation

June 14, 1840 (Sunday); Afternoon Meeting

If John calls God a pure, unadulterated light, the darkness then, as His opposite, is the devil, and as the light of God, where it is received in faith, becomes the life of man, so also has the dark power of the devil, through faith in the lie and disobedience to God, become death in all men by nature. Now, this death and all sins arising therefrom are indeed undeserved on our part and God accordingly forgives them freely for Christ's sake to the whole world. This is the voluntary offer which God makes to all men (Romans 3; II Corinthians 5), but the rejection of this love of God and grace of Christ, the non-acceptance of this light and life, is man's own guilt and condemns him (John 3).

Now, because the end in view of this Gospel and the appearance of Christ is our fellowship with God and this subsists only in a walk in the light, we have a choice between two things only, for whoever walks in darkness has no fellowship with God. The devil as the prince of this world reigns with full power over the unbelievers through his darkness; his kingdom is in them by reason of sin: but over the believers also, because and as long as they are still in the world, he, by God's wiser permission, exercises a definite power through all kinds of temptations (or vexations), so as to rob and kill them again, where possible, just as he tempted Adam and even Christ Himself.

Yet Adam did not fall accidentally; he was warned, and on just that side the devil attacks. The flesh is ever inclined on the side of sin (of the devil), but most of all in temptation, which does indeed not come from God but is permitted for our proving (James 1). Therefore we must unceasingly be on our guard with weapons of light—watching, sobriety and prayer—that we enter not into the temptation of the devil but resist him through the Spirit of Christ (Matthew 26:41; I Peter 5:8 ff.).

"Watch and pray, that ye enter not into temptation: the spirit indeed is willing, but the flesh is weak."

---

"Be sober, be vigilant; because your adversary the devil, as a roaring lion, walketh about, seeking whom he may devour:

> "Whom resist stedfast in the faith, knowing that the
> same afflictions are accomplished in your brethren that
> are in the world."

The devil tempts us in the very way against which God warns us. He puts a thought in our mind, as in David's (II Samuel 24:1 (below); I Chronicles 21), and if we are not careful and do not weigh it on the scales, we will then be deceived by the flesh.

> "And again the anger of the Lord was kindled against
> Israel, and he moved David against them to say, Go,
> number Israel and Judah."

We must indeed be tempted in this way (and only the believers can be tempted), so that it may be revealed whether Christ is our Life in the Spirit. However, because God reduces the temptation according to our ability, we still need not fall in it but can overcome. Every temptation arises from darkness (that is to say from the devil) and withal, it is often so heavy and dark within that we think we no longer stand in the light ourselves; but just this anxiety is a proof that our spirit is in the light, only we dare not, besides, become discouraged or doubt, but shall quench the fiery darts of Satan by the shield of faith and consider that we shall be crowned after a short conflict.

June 16, 1840 (Tuesday); Evening Meeting; I John 1:5 ff.

> "This then is the message which we have heard of
> him, and declare unto you, that God is light, and in him
> is no darkness at all.
> "If we say that we have fellowship with him, and
> walk in darkness, we lie, and do not the truth:"

The apostle (verse 3) (below) has indeed invited the believers to fellowship with God as the goal of the salvation accomplished by Christ.

> "That which we have seen and heard declare we unto
> you, that ye also may have fellowship with us: and truly
> our fellowship is with the Father, and with his Son
> Jesus Christ."

But so as to warn us in this respect of a common self-deception, he shows us the only condition in which a fellowship with God is possible. We shall not lie ourselves into this fellowship of God, not ascribe to ourselves falsely and without grounds something which we nevertheless do not have, for that would not help but only harm us, because he who satisfies himself in this respect with mere imagination is a hypocrite and does not further strive for that which he does not have; and this is the worst darkness, self-deception.

We shall unbiasedly examine and judge ourselves according to the Word of God, whether we have a real or an imaginary fellowship with God, for if we say we have fellowship with Him and, besides, still walk in darkness and deny Him by our works (Titus 1:15 ff.), we are liars.

> "Unto the pure all things are pure: but unto them that are defiled and unbelieving is nothing pure; but even their mind and conscience is defiled.
> "They profess that they know God; but in works they deny him, being abominable, and disobedient, and unto every good work reprobate."

The children of God cannot testify to or prove their light-nature and relationship to God otherwise than by a walk in the light. They are sure of the matter themselves, like Christ (John 8), for they bear and feel the light and life of God in them and take note of all their inner emotions, whether these agree with the divine nature or not. They do indeed not boast thereof, but when they are required to testify what they consider themselves to be, they do not deny, but confess, without being abashed or ashamed, that they are children of God. But now, because all men and sinners by nature also consider and claim the same of themselves, foresight is necessary, for, in reference to their relationship to God, all men are *willingly* blind and deceived.

According to the characteristics which the Word of God points out as belonging to the estate of grace and sonship, there is no doubt that the world is full of children of the devil, but who is so honest as to judge himself impartially according to these characteristics and admit that he does not find them in himself and is therefore not a child of God but one of the devil? A real child of God is blessed even though he is condemned by the whole world as an apostate, etc., but the children of the devil could even kill one out of anger if one denies the sonship of God to them (John 8). We have here a choice only between two things: there are only children of God who walk in the light and children of the devil who walk in darkness.

Now, if one has heard this witnessing and realizes and admits that he cannot yet find the character of a child of God in himself and is troubled about it, one must not despair nor doubt but much more believe in Christ the Light, and such impartial self-knowledge and confession is a hungering and thirsting after righteousness, to which satiety is promised (Matthew 5:6):

> "Blessed are they which do hunger and thirst after righteousness: for they shall be filled."

and although this hunger and thirst is not yet repletion, it nevertheless is blessed, for it is the return to the fellowship of God; God lets the upright succeed and to the humble He gives grace. However, a pardoned one shall then take heed that he consider no deviation from the light insignificant, as if this and that could not harm him, but shall preserve and purify himself from all that is unclean which would force itself upon him or he can fall again from grace. Here also self-deception is our worst enemy.

## Chapter XIII

## The Danger of Self-Deception

July 2, 1840 (Thursday); Evening Meeting; I John 1:6

> "If we say that we have fellowship with him, and walk in darkness, we lie, and do not the truth:"

The words, "If we say that we have fellowship with him," deserve our attention especially, for we do not hear the people of the world say this, at least not as a free, joyous admission, but at most as a false assertion, when they are vexed. That, rather, is the real honor of the believing children of God who are actually interested in it and consider fellowship with God an eternal necessity, like to hear it spoken of, perhaps themselves talk about it when they come together.

But there is all the more reason for concern when John even writes about such, who, in spite of their confession of mouth, can still walk in the darkness of their hearts because they have forgotten God in their thoughts and at heart are not turned towards but away from Him and consequently are not enlightened by the light of God but darkened (as the earth is on the side that is turned away from the sun) and, besides, naturally speculate upon and think of, speak and do the things that are incongruous with the fellowship of God and a position in the light. This turning away from God (distraction, absent-mindedness, forgetfulness of Him) is the single darkness of man, and then if God on His part also turns away with His light of grace (which can

39

easily happen) (Jeremiah 2:13; 17:5-13), the darkness is two-fold and replete.

> "For my people have committed two evils; they have forsaken me the fountain of living waters, and hewed them out cisterns, broken cisterns, that can hold no water."

---

> "Thus saith the Lord; Cursed be the man that trusteth in man, and maketh flesh his arm, and whose heart departeth from the Lord.
>
> "For he shall be like the heath in the desert, and shall not see when good cometh; but shall inhabit the parched places in the wilderness, in a salt land and not inhabited.
>
> "Blessed is the man that trusteth in the Lord, and whose hope the Lord is.
>
> "For he shall be as a tree planted by the waters, and that spreadeth out her roots by the river, and shall not see when heat cometh, but her leaf shall be green; and shall not be careful in the year of drought, neither shall cease from yielding fruit.
>
> "The heart is deceitful above all things, and desperately wicked: who can know it?
>
> "I the Lord search the heart, I try the reins, even to give every man according to his ways, and according to the fruit of his doings.
>
> "As the partridge sitteth on eggs, and hatcheth them not; so he that getteth riches, and not by right, shall leave them in the midst of his days, and at his end shall be a fool.
>
> "A glorious high throne from the beginning is the place of our sanctuary.
>
> "O Lord, the hope of Israel, all that forsake thee shall be ashamed, and they that depart from me shall be written in the earth, because they have forsaken the Lord, the fountain of living waters."

Men consult with themselves and others, seek comfort and help from the creature instead of from the living God and thus fall from one foolishness and sin into another.

But how much more blessed and better counselled is the man who, in all his concerns, turns direct to God in prayer and supplication and confidence (Psalm 16) without burdening his own heart with vain sorrows, for God at all times is near those who call upon Him and He accomplishes what His children desire and helps them, and because they walk in the light of His countenance, He cares for them in a fatherly way and does not permit them to fall.

Now, this danger of self-deception demands a most severe self-examination, whether we boast with our lips of fellowship with God and, in spite of it, have darkness in our hearts and therefore also walk in darkness and forget God, for, beside the gross kind of forgetfulness of God of unbelieving men, there indeed is a finer kind of those who otherwise boast of the knowledge of God and this condition of darkness is all the more dangerous where the boasting of fellowship with God is a lie and the walk is reproved by the false confession.

July 5, 1840 (Sunday); Morning Meeting; I John 1:6 ff.

> "If we say that we have fellowship with him, and walk in darkness, we lie, and do not the truth:
> "But if we walk in the light, as he is in the light, we have fellowship one with another, and the blood of Jesus Christ his Son cleanseth us from all sin."

If we say that we have fellowship with God we must then also know Him. Now, as there is a two-fold acquaintance among people, an outward one of word and work (by which one can indeed recognize and judge them after their inner condition also) and an inner (intimate) one which is called friendship in which one then has a free approach and open access and shares things in common, so is there also a two-fold knowledge of God in which He reveals Himself and His invisible existence to men; the one is outward, by the works of the creation, by which He already speaks to the heathen (Romans 1), the other, in part, by His word, which He has entrusted especially to the Jews (Romans 3:1 ff.).

> "What advantage then hath the Jew? or what profit is there of circumcision?
> "Much every way: chiefly, because that unto them were committed the oracles of God.
> "For what if some did not believe? shall their unbelief make the faith of God without effect?
> "God forbid: yea, let God be true, but every man a liar; as it is written, That thou mightest be justified in thy sayings, and mightest overcome when thou art judged."

41

From these two sources combined, one can draw a vast knowledge of God if one would esteem them, and many people think if they thus (outwardly) know God, they are already believers, but from there to fellowship with God is still a great distance and such an outward knowledge is insufficient for salvation. Others, again, deny the one or the other of these sources of knowledge, or both (atheists, free-thinkers, naturalists, etc.). The outward knowledge of God is however the lowest step of attainment unto the real, inner or spiritual fellowship with Him.

As an acquaintance with a person is not yet a familiarity with him —either the outward conditions or the inner dispositions are too unequal—so it is also between God and men: they are either too high in their own estimation for Him (an abomination, Luke 16:15):

> "And he said unto them, Ye are they which justify yourselves before men; but God knoweth your hearts: for that which is highly esteemed among men is abomination in the sight of God."

or too deeply sunk; or He is too high for them, that they do not come together, and the inequality can be reconciled only in Christ, in that He makes us participant of His divine nature and holy, as He is holy. But to be holy and to appear holy are entirely different things. A Pharisee imagines that he is better than another sinner and yet he is no better and thus hypocrites are the worst sinners in the sight of God. But the children of God must be holy in the deed and in mind and walk— throughout—different from all other men. If they are not and do not live entirely the opposite of the world, they are not in fellowship with God.

The children of God and the children of the devil are as different as light and darkness, which have nothing in common. On earth they are like antipodes for the ones have day and the others night. The world, of course, cannot endure that; therefore it hates and persecutes the children of God, as Cain hated and persecuted Abel. That frightens many away; so they conform to the world as much as possible, deny the light (a holy life) and by that fall into hypocrisy and lying if they say they have fellowship with God. It indeed is not a little thing to be and to be called a child of God in this world which is entirely of the devil.

# Chapter XIV

## Sin and Righteousness

July 5, 1840 (Sunday); Afternoon Meeting

Two things are irreconcilable: to walk in darkness and to have fellowship with God. Darkness is sin and death (the devil's power), which entered into all men by the fall of Adam. For this, the Son of God appeared with His mediation to inaugurate a new way to fellowship between God and us. Without His mediation it is impossible to come unto God. But this mediation is brought about in a two-fold way: by Christ's death on the cross and by His life with the Father. If Christ does not stand intermediately with His reconciliation for our union with God, sin with the condemning law stands there as a partition-wall and separation from God, for indeed Moses was also a mediator, of the Old Testament (Galatians 3:19 ff.) (below), not for reconciliation and union however, but for a severance and separation because the hearts are uncircumcised.

> "Wherefore then serveth the law? It was added because of transgressions, till the seed should come to whom the promise was made; and it was ordained by angels in the hand of a mediator.
> "Now a mediator is not a mediator of one, but God is one."

The cause of the separation, again, is two-fold: (a) the original sin descending from Adam *without our guilt* as the indwelling mother-sin and (b) the many sins arising from the law *through man's own guilt* (for it is *not necessary* for one to commit adultery, steal, kill, etc.; Adam is not responsible for that and he also who committed nothing of all this—which the law forbids—would still be a sinner through Adam). Now, the cause of damnation, of course, is original sin as the fruitful mother, but her many fruits increase the condemnation because they are committed voluntarily.

But Christ died also in this two-fold way and purpose: to abolish Adam's guilt as well as the curse of the law, and the many committed sins are indeed forgiven and wiped out by the blood He shed and faith alone; but the original sin cannot be forgiven (for we are not guilty of it): it must instead be killed and eradicated from the heart, and that

43

does not come about by the blood of Christ, nor by faith, but by His death on the cross or broken body and by baptism into His death, after the many committed sins (according to the law) have previously been forgiven through faith.

There is a difference between Christ's death and His blood. Also, Christ died on the cross before His side was opened and blood and water flowed out. His broken body (flesh) is the door (passageway) to our reunion with God. Original sin (the first death) only there constitutes and remains to be the cause of damnation where no forgiveness of the many sins committed has been sought or found; however the forgiveness of these sins only is not yet sufficient for salvation (we dare not depend upon the instance of the pardoned robber as upon a divine precept; he is a rare exception among thousands who in the anguish of death have promised to turn back, hardly one of whom keeps his promise), but the abolition and destruction of the mother-sin must also take place in order that man may sin no more afterwards.

Then, in place of the old original or mother sin, new original or mother righteousness enters by faith in Christ. However, this as well may not remain alone, but as the mother-sin in Adam has yielded much fruit, so also must the mother-righteousness in Christ yield much fruit, and as the many committed sins follow the condemned, stand at his side and raise their thousand-fold cry against him, so also must the many works of righteousness follow and stand at the side of the pardoned one unto his glorification before the judgment seat of Christ. Whatever good or evil anyone has done here, that he has done for himself (on his own account) and he shall receive it from the Lord. That is the divine ruling and order.

July 7, 1840 (Tuesday)

The assertion of one that he has fellowship with God is still no sure proof of the truth of the matter itself, because, with it, a walk in darkness is still possible and *then* one does not know the condition of one's heart for darkness has blinded his eyes. But the unmistakable proof of a true fellowship with God is a walk in the light; that is, such a faithful guarding and watching over one's self that one, through all and at all times, does that which is the acceptable will of God and avoids whatever is against it. This is the necessary consequence of the new birth from God, and by it the Divine Life and Image (Christ) grows in us to its full stature. It depends however upon the once-accomplished forgiveness or cleansing of our former sins by the blood of Christ and because this occurs only there, where the body of sin ( the old man) is broken and laid aside, it is easy to presume that new sins cannot occur if one walks faithfully according to the rule of the Spirit or the new creature.

And although some instances of deviation can happen, yet a gradual turning back to the flesh is a falling away from the living God and a crucifixion of Christ, from which there is no rising again, because Christ did not die and shed His blood for that and Christ does not die a second time. These are those who have died twice—uprooted trees—for whom an eternal darkness is reserved.

July 9, 1840 (Thursday); Evening Meeting; I John 1:7 ff.

> "But if we walk in the light, as he is in the light, we have fellowship one with another, and the blood of Jesus Christ his Son cleanseth us from all sin.
> "If we say that we have no sin, we deceive ourselves, and the truth is not in us."

This passage is very greatly misunderstood and misused as a cloak for the wickedness of those who willingly abide in sin, as if John had here given a continuous consolation and assurance of forgiveness by the blood of Christ, when he nevertheless says exactly the opposite: (a) continual sinning (walking in darkness) is incongruous with a walk in the light (fellowship with God); (b) the blood of the Son of God cleanses us from *all* sin and indeed entirely, once (John 13:10):

> "Jesus saith to him, He that is washed needeth not save to wash his feet, but is clean every whit: and ye are clean, but not all."

and only once in a life, namely at the time of conversion through faith, in reference to the past life of ignorance (Romans 3). He who is so washed and cleansed stands *entirely clean* before God and shall consider himself a saint, that he henceforth guard himself from new defilement of this new garment (Revelation 3:4; I Corinthians 6:11).

> "Thou hast a few names even in Sardis which have not defiled their garments; and they shall walk with me in white: for they are worthy."

---

> "And such were some of you: but ye are washed, but ye are sanctified, but ye are justified in the name of the Lord Jesus, and by the Spirit of our God."

It is indeed possible that sins can be committeed again after the pardoning (for all unrighteousness is also sin, Galatians 6:1):

> "Brethren, if a man be overtaken in a fault, ye which are spiritual, restore such an one in the spirit of meekness; considering thyself, lest thou also be tempted."

but these are not cleansed by the blood of Christ: for if they are not sins unto death, they do not deserve death (the blood of Christ), do not draw death after them, but one shall confess them and pray that they may be forgiven (not keep them until the judgment). However, if they are sins unto death, there is no other sacrifice and no forgiveness for them, for Christ's sacrifice did not occur for these sins, but only for the sins of the time of man's ignorance and powerlessness.

But him, whom God has forgiven these former sins, He has also healed by the wounds of Christ and restored to health, now to walk in a holy life, free and loosed from sin; and whoever does not have the power of the life of Christ, does likewise not have the forgiveness of his sins, for where this has occurred, there the death of the old man has also occurred, so that he can no longer bear the fruit he bore before: for the subsequent faults, deviations and trespasses of the standard of the new creature are not malicious nor habitual sins, but momentary ones of overhaste, caused by inattention, which, again, are also momentarily repented for, confessed and laid aside, and the more faithful one is in this, the more also will he watch over himself and the less seldom will they occur.

July 12, 1840 (Sunday); Morning Meeting; I John 1:8 ff.

> "If we say that we have no sin, we deceive ourselves, and the truth is not in us.
> "If we confess our sins, he is faithful and just to forgive us our sins, and to cleanse us from all unrighteousness.
> "If we say that we have not sinned, we make him a liar, and his word is not in us."

Compare Hebrews 10:14 ff.:

> "For by one offering he hath perfected for ever them that are sanctified.
> "Whereof the Holy Ghost also is a witness to us: for after that he had said before,

"This is the covenant that I will make with them after those days, saith the Lord, I will put my laws into their hearts, and in their minds will I write them;

"And their sins and iniquities will I remember no more.

"Now where remission of these is, there is no more offering for sin."

Where the forgiveness or cleansing of sin has once taken place, there is no further sacrifice for sin(s), for Christ has perfected the saints forever by a *single* sacrifice, and in place of the old indwelling sin, the pardoned one receives a new law of the Spirit, written by God into his heart and mind, so as to *preserve* the received cleansing by the doing of righteousness (Romans 6).

The blood of Christ does not have a continuous power of cleansing from sin unto the end of one's life, for the man in Christ (a child of God) shall sin no more unto the end of his life, for if it were a matter of indifference to God whether we sinned all our life long, He would not have put the cleansing of the former sins committed during the time of ignorance, at the beginning or entrance, but at the end of life, as it was actually done at one time (in the third and fourth centuries). The false opinion and reversed practice of the church was to save baptism until the end of life because they meant by that to let all committed sins be washed away at *one* time (as for instance Emperor Constantine who in that time did not have his baptismal garment removed until he died), so as to then appear clean before God.

But that is a mistake, for baptism is not in reference to the *committed sins,* but in reference to the *indwelling-mother* or *original sin,* after the committed sins, by faith in the blood of Christ, have previously been blotted out, forgiven and washed away. For that reason also, infant baptism, in every respect, is wrong, non-sensical and purposeless: for even supposing that the baptism of Christ (like the baptism of John) would be for the forgiveness of the former sins, the former sins could not be forgiven to infants because they have not yet committed any and baptism is not a remission of punishment for sins yet to follow, but a killing off of the old man; but that, again, is neither the case with infants, nor possible, because they have *not believed* and the life that follows proves sufficiently that their old man (inherited sin) is not dead but alive.

God has therefore put the cleansing from sin neither at the beginning nor at the end of our earthly life, but at the beginning of our spiritual life, namely, at the time of one's conversion, when he becomes a believer in Christ, and because God has placed the only cleansing from sin at *this* beginning, that also proves that it is the will of God that the cleansed shall henceforth live holily and blamelessly in this world and not commit further sins nor make more debts since there is no more sacrifice for them. Therefore all who would extend the power of the cleansing of the blood of Christ over the entire life for their consolation in sinning, reverse the truth, so that they really never become clean because they never become free from sin itself; they are the sort who think they are clean and are not washed of their defilement (Titus 1 and 2), etc.

## Chapter XV

## Carnal Boasting and False Claims

July 12, 1840 (Sunday); Afternoon Meeting

Now, if we put verses 8-10 and 6 and 7 together for comparison, is there not a contradiction between them? Does "to walk in darkness" not mean as much as to commit sin (to sin) and "to walk in the light" as much as to lead a holy and godly life (without sin)? Does John not call *him* a *liar* who says that he has fellowship with God and yet does not walk in the light but in darkness? Do verses 6 and 7 not constitute a definite antithesis to verses 8-10?

So we ask: Whence then come the sins (verse 8: "If we say that we have no sin ... "), if a child of God shall sin no more? We reply: Verse 6 and verse 8, it is true, constitute an antithesis, but, jointly, no contradiction, for the meaning is altogether different.

John does not utter two contradictory statements in one breath, but there is nothing said either that John took verse 8 back and allowed what he avowed in verse 6:

He who says that he has fellowship with God and nevertheless walks in darkness lies and does not the truth (John 3:21):

("But he that doeth truth cometh to the light, that his deeds may be made manifest, that they are wrought in God.")

and he who says that he has no sin misleads (deceives) himself and the truth is not in him,

that is, he is still entirely *unconverted* and *outside* of Christ (Who is the

Truth), he is deceived by his imagination, as if he were a Christian and belonged to the church of Christ; he does not yet know the way at all, how one attains unto it, namely, by forgiveness of his sins, with a preceding knowledge of the same and an acknowledgment of his lost and damned condition in Adam and under the law.

But how, now, do those stand who *in this way* were admitted in their pretended fellowship of the Christian Church? Have they ever recognized and confessed themselves as being ungodly and accursed sinners unto the despair of themselves? Have they ever been taught of or put under obligation by this state at their baptism in infancy or at their confirmation? Are they all not already righteous in their own eyes? Do they not say they are without sin? Verse 8 therefore is a test for the false, nominal Christians of which the world is full nowadays, who pretend a fellowship of the Christian church without ever having sought or found the forgiveness of their sins (the entrance thereinto), for it is a hard thing indeed to have to acknowledge that one is a child of the devil and without that no faith and no cleansing from sin is possible; that is, to confess that one has sins.

But John does not require such a confession of true, holy children of God; he much more puts the opposite test (verse 6):

"If we say that we have fellowship with him, and
walk in darkness, we lie, and do not the truth:"

before them by which they shall know themselves.

We notice moreover:

(a) *Not to do* the truth and *not to have* the truth (or God's Word) in one's self are two different things. These, of verse 6, could do the truth because it presupposes real believers, who were once actually converted and cleansed but who forgot the cleansing from their former sins (II Peter 1), and in such a condition lie about a fellowship with God. On the other hand, those, of verse 8, are not even *able to do the truth* because they do not have it in them, because they have never been converted and, accordingly, it is an evil sign if a believer would apply verse 8 ff. in his favor as being consistent with the state of grace (which John however denies).

(b) In just the same way, it is something different *to have* sin and *to do* sin, for he who does sin is from the devil and has never as yet known Christ; but whoever admits that he has sin (or has sinned (verse 10) which is the elucidation of verse 8) is a contrite sinner who seeks forgiveness and obtains his cleansing in the blood of Christ.

49

Therefore, everyone who says that he has no sin (has not sinned) makes God a liar because *He has not sacrificed His Son in vain for the sin of the world* and because the death of Christ was not a heroic self-sacrifice or even wild imagining, of which the unbelievers say He should rather have left it undone and have yielded, but His death was *necessary* for our reconciliation from sin.

A believer cannot make God a liar by that which he as a child of God shall not do. As he is a liar who, without conversion and the cleansing of his sins, claims fellowship with the church of Christ, so also is he a liar who, *after* his conversion and cleansing, does not walk in the light and still pretends to have fellowship with God. This therefore is just the opposite and accordingly, by verse 8 ff., John cuts off all carnal boasting and every false claim of men to sonship of God and church fellowship, for each one who has attained thereunto knows that he has gained this right, not by nature nor the law, but only by the call of God (John 1:12 ff.) (below), with the open confession that he formerly was no Christian or child of God but a child of the devil and of wrath.

"But as many as received him, to them gave he power to become the sons of God, even to them that believe on his name:

"Which were born, not of blood, nor of the will of the flesh, nor of the will of man, but of God."

John, by verse 8 ff., therefore refers just as much to an *earlier* condition as Paul does in Romans 7, in that he describes the way of the beginning of conversion, upon which we attained to fellowship with God and the church of Christ. Verse 6 however shows us how we shall make manifest and preserve the fellowship of the saints.

## Chapter XVI

### Characteristics of a Child of God

July 21, 1840 (Tuesday); Evening Meeting; I John 2:1

"My little children, these things write I unto you, that ye sin not."

By this, John points back to the foregoing (as in verse 4 already):

("And these things write we unto you, that your joy may be full.")

and indeed to verses 5-7 as convincing testimony:

> "This then is the message which we have heard of him, and declare unto you, that God is light, and in him is no darkness at all.
>
> "If we say that we have fellowship with him, and walk in darkness, we lie, and do not the truth:
>
> "But if we walk in the light, as he is in the light, we have fellowship one with another, and the blood of Jesus Christ his Son cleanseth us from all sin."

between which verses and our text, verses 8-10:

> "If we say that we have no sin, we deceive ourselves, and the truth is not in us.
>
> "If we confess our sins, he is faithful and just to forgive us our sins, and to cleanse us from all unrighteousness.
>
> "If we say that we have not sinned, we make him a liar, and his word is not in us."

serve only as elucidation, how one may attain unto the cleansing of his former sins and unto fellowship with God—be he a Jew or a heathen or a nominal Christian—and not at all as an abrogation or a retraction of what was said before. The standard for a converted and believing Christian who extols the forgiveness of his sins in the blood of Christ and fellowship with God is always firmly based upon this, *that he shall sin no more.*

This is the only authentic mark of a child of God, who, by the indwelling of Christ, has become participant of the divine nature, for sin as a continuous practice is the old man and is from the devil, servitude and not freedom; sin and the curse are always inseparable. A sinner is still under the law, not in Christ under grace, for anyone who is no longer under the law has been loosed and made free from sin (Romans 6).

It is impossible that sin could be a trifling and harmless thing for a child of God as the wrath of God comes over the children of disobedience (over the unbelievers) for that very reason. Now, what preference would we have in Christ over the unbelievers out of Christ if we should still continue to sin as they? We, as regenerated children of God, are only a lantern and the Spirit of Life in Christ Jesus is the Light of God and of the Truth, which shall shine forth from us on every side, and by it we shall not, for ourselves alone, walk unblamably and inoffensively,

51

but shall also be a shining light for the others all around us in darkness and the shadow of death.

This is our calling and designation from God and in all that we do and think, the rule of the Spirit, the holy commandment, which has been given to us in Christ, shall guide us that we sin not but keep ourselves as such who must give account of every idle word we have spoken, and only he who does not fail in a single word is a perfect man. This perfection shall be our constant thought and aspiration because it is the will of God to usward. We shall never be forgetful or so conduct ourselves or walk as if there were no God or as if we did not believe in God.

John indeed admits the possibility of a sin in a believer, but with such restriction that nothing can be said of it as being a general rule or necessity. The restriction of sin is two-fold:

(a) "if even" (in case it should happen, that—) and

(b) "perhaps one" (not everyone or "we");

and just for the reason that it can even overtake us unawares, we shall watch over ourselves that we sin not carelessly from wickedness nor from habit. It is enough that it perhaps can even happen otherwise, when it should indeed never happen at all, and we shall implore the forgiveness of God also for our secret faults.

July 23, 1840 (Thursday); Evening Meeting; I John 2:1

"My little children!" This expression of motherly love and care shows whom John had in mind by the admonition, "that ye sin not," to wit: the saints and believers in Christ. From that, it is not merely an exhortation simply made to men who, of course, would not be equal to it, but to reborn children of God, who have received the power to keep themselves from sin by the indwelling of Christ or His Representative of the Spirit of Truth (as . . . . . , Bystander, Interceder and Advocate), Whose office it is to lead them into all truth and to sanctify them therein. The Holy Spirit pleads for the children of God in all things, as well in prayer to the Father in the name of the Son as in their responsibility of the truth before men and against the attacks of the devil.

But just as the lie is not merely a conception or spoken word of falsehood but the devil himself in the flesh and death in man, so also is the truth not a mere idea or word but Christ in the flesh and the true, divine life in man. Hence every offense against the truth, that is to say, against a divine life, is an actual sin and a staining of the inner man, which a child of God should not permit himself to be guilty of because the light or the seed of God is in him, by which he can and shall walk inoffensively, unblamably and irreprovably in this world.

For as full as this present world is of pitfalls, snares and rocks of offense, it nevertheless is not necessary for a child of God to fall into or over them like the blind, who, beside the outer, have the inner darkness also and do not see their way or where they tread, who, on that account, make little of sin when they step into puddles of mud and besmirch themselves, just so they do not fall head first and full length into them. They consider nothing sin except, perhaps, adultery, theft, murder, etc. (gross sins against the law), and if they are only not revealed in them they are already satisfied, though they are much more keen-sighted for the faults of the believers and in this even strain at gnats and swallow camels (yes even elephants). Therefore the children of God shall not be influenced in their judgment as to what is or is not sin by the people of the world for they have an entirely different law.

The characteristics of a child of God are purity and truth, far from every lie and all hypocrisy. He needs not cover or hide himself from man, for all things are revealed to God and what God may know and see (Who sees much better than all eyes), that men also may see and know. A true believer is transparent (luminiferous) like clear glass, like the city of God (Revelation 21:18, 21).

> "And the building of the wall of it was of jasper: and the city was pure gold, like unto clear glass."

---

> "And the twelve gates were twelve pearls: every several gate was of one pearl: and the street of the city was pure gold, as it were transparent glass."

That too which the ungodly do not only not consider sin but something even delightful, worthy of their love, and the manners and usages of good society, is not at all befitting of a saint and is sin to him (Ephesians 5). An offense painfully injures a faithful, exact, careful child of God even if he does not fall.

The children of God therefore are careful in their walk so as not to stumble and bemire themselves since the Spirit of Truth leads them; and John for their comfort says that they have Jesus Christ as their Advocate with the Father so that they may not lose heart over eventual divergences. Thus we have a two-fold Representative or Paraclete, the Holy Spirit with us in our hearts on earth and the Son with the Father in heaven.

# Chapter XVII

## Zealous Children of God

July 26, 1840 (Sunday); Morning Meeting; I John 2:1 ff.

> "My little children, these things write I unto you, that ye sin not. And if any man sin, we have an advocate with the Father, Jesus Christ the righteous:
>
> "And he is the propitiation for our sins: and not for our's only, but also for the sins of the whole world.
>
> "And hereby we do know that we know him, if we keep his commandments.
>
> "He that saith, I know him, and keepeth not his commandments, is a liar, and the truth is not in him.
>
> "But whoso keepeth his word, in him verily is the love of God perfected: hereby know we that we are in him."

It depends upon to whom the Gospel is proclaimed, whether to the unconverted who are still outside or to the converted who are already in Christ. For the former it is a proclamation of reconciliation with God through Christ; for the latter however, a challenge to a holy life. First Christ must be implanted in us and then He brings forth His divine fruit in us by Himself.

The new commandment which He has given us is love and this, in its very nature, is a free-willed impulse, not compulsion. Now, as the unconverted and sinners surely have a common kind of love, falsely imitated, tinctured, carnal and partial however, and what they are resolved to attain they also carry out zealously and have no regrets for the trouble and sacrifice involved because they have an urge in their hearts for it, according to the proverb, *"Lust und Liebe zu einem Ding, macht alle Mueh und Arbeit 'ring"* (Desire and love for anything, makes all trouble and work as nothing); so also is there in the children of God the love and desire wrought by the Holy Ghost to be zealous and untiring for all good things in a godly way. The Spirit of Christ is a pinion to divine activity and the pardoned one does not ascribe the doing of good to himself but to the indwelling of Christ (Galatians 2:20).

> "I am crucified with Christ: nevertheless I live; yet not I, but Christ liveth in me: and the life which I now live in the flesh I live by the faith of the Son of God, who loved me, and gave himself for me."

For pure love is not from man but from God; therefore it can accomplish that which is impossible for natural man (Romans 8:7 ff.) (below) and the honor and praise thereof reverts back to God.

> "Because the carnal mind is enmity against God: for it is not subject to the law of God, neither indeed can be.
> "So then they that are in the flesh cannot please God.
> "But ye are not in the flesh, but in the Spirit, if so be that the Spirit of God dwell in you. Now if any man have not the Spirit of Christ, he is none of his.
> "And if Christ be in you, the body is dead because of sin; but the Spirit is life because of righteousness."

Although the new law of Christ is always only one law—love—it still has two sides or tables like the old law, according to what it is applied toward. In reference to God, it is love with all the heart and with all the soul and with all the mind and with all the strength, and he who knows God and the nature of the New Covenant does not find this is asking too much but is most reasonable and blessed, for the inclination of the heart must ever be just *one*, not divided between God and the devil (Matthew 6). Therefore, a person who does not love God undividedly and wholly cannot love Him at all, and the best proof of this is that even the best and most pious men out of Christ (namely those under the law), do not really love God but only fear Him and avoid the evil for fear of punishment and condemnation, with which the law threatens the transgressor. But there is no fear in love; instead joy and a willingness unto all good things, and perfect love casts out fear for fear has punishment it it and not peace.

But God wishes our whole heart, not the half of it. A whole heart toward God, Christ alone gives us, Who, even in our flesh and blood, as a man and servant indeed, did the will of the Father without any deviation therefrom because He loved the Father, and that He will accomplish in us too if we let Him dwell in us and do not kill Him by the flesh, which happens in the case of the double-minded, who indeed also wish to bring offerings and worship outwardly and after the manner of the law, but not with their hearts, hypocritically like Cain who killed his brother out of hatred and like the Jews who crucified Christ out of enmity against the truth (Matthew 15:7 ff.).

> "Ye hypocrites, well did Esaias prophesy of you saying,

"This people draweth nigh unto me with their mouth, and honoureth me with their lips; but their heart is far from me.

"But in vain they do worship me, teaching for doctrines the commandments of men."

Insofar however as love to our neighbor is concerned, it shall be impartial, like the love of one's self, excluding no one, not even our enemies (Matthew 7:12).

"Therefore all things whatsoever ye would that men should do to you, do ye even so to them: for this is the law and the prophets."

Love is the fulfillment of the law. Whoever does the good does not do the evil. Yet there is a difference between the brotherly love in Christ toward the like-minded in the Spirit and the love to our neighbors in general, toward those who are out of Christ, who stand unequally with us in the spirit and do not return our love; for even God with all His love is nevertheless provoked to wrath over sin and punishes it according to His righteousness: we see that most significantly in the Crucified Christ, and it will happen thus to all those who persist in sin because they do not love God, even though they feign a religious service.

## July 26, 1840 (Sunday); Afternoon Meeting

We see by the word, ". . . we have an advocate with the Father, Jesus Christ the righteous:" that our relationship to the Father is another than that to the Son, because the Father is greater than the Son, and we stand in only an indirect and conditional union with the Father, provided that we safeguard ourselves from sin through the indwelling of Christ: and insofar as Christ is and abides in us, in that degree, of course, our fellowship with the Father is likewise direct, and that is our best and most blessed state. But as soon as we have besmirched ourselves by sin, Christ as our Advocate must enter intermediately and sanctify us; otherwise we would be deprived of our fellowship with God. Hence things are better, not worse, with us if we no longer need Christ in the capacity of an Advocate, for we resemble Him more if we do not sin than if we sin. That is made possible for us by His Spirit of Life.

We shall not think that we do not need Christ at all times if we no longer make use of Him and require Him as an Advocate, for we possess Him all the more completely if we walk innocently: this is His individual nature and this is also the will of God concerning us in order that we may be His children. Christ with His reconciliation is not there for the purpose that He, all our life long, daily wash away and clean our soilure, as a mother washes her little children. It is a poor testimony if we do not grow and mature in Christ and His grace so that we can keep ourselves clean.

He who in his own behalf would refer to Adam in the matter of continual sinning, denies Christ and makes His grace useless, for Christ came for that reason afterwards, that He might remove Adam's guilt from us. Yet if a person prefers to remain in sin, he has the privilege to serve the devil as much as he likes, but he shall not at the same time bear the name of Christ. For if anyone is in Christ, in him again Christ is also, as a new creature of God.

The reconciliation in Christ is only the earnest money which the spiritual recruiter (evangelist) offers all men because Christ died for the reconciliation of all, that He might enlist all. So it's a matter of choice for each one, whether he will allow himself to be enlisted (reconciled) or not. But all who accept the earnest money obligate themselves to obedience and to combatant service for Christ and vow allegiance to henceforth fight against the devil under His banner with weapons of righteousness; and indeed not only a defensive war for the protection of his own life, but an offensive war as well for the taking of other fortresses of the devil, for the rescuing of other men from the principality of darkness, every natural man being a fortress of the devil, barricaded and walled up to the sky with bulwarks of lies, so that it is a real wonder if anyone is truly converted and saved.

July 28, 1840 (Tuesday); Evening Meeting; I John 2:1 ff. (with rejoicing)

"My little children, these things write I unto you, that ye sin not. And if any man sin, we have an advocate with the Father, Jesus Christ the righteous:

"And he is the propitiation for our sins: and not for our's only, but also for the sins of the whole world.

"And hereby we do know that we know him, if we keep his commandments.

"He that saith, I know him, and keepeth not his commandments, is a liar, and the truth is not in him.

"But whoso keepeth his word, in him verily is the love of God perfected: hereby know we that we are in him."

The same Jesus Who first died for the reconciliation of the sins of the whole world is now also our Advocate with the Father, so that we do not fall from grace by a possible unforeseen sin *because sin militates against grace as well as against the nature of God,* and we ourselves, without the mediation of the Son, could not make reparation for the least sin. It was only the intercession of Jesus which avoided Peter in his great fall from falling completely into the abyss (Luke 22:31 ff.) (below) because his heart was still sincere and honest otherwise (not like Judas's).

> "And the Lord said, Simon, Simon, behold, Satan
> hath desired to have you, that he may sift you as wheat:
> "But I have prayed for thee, that thy faith fail not:
> and when thou art converted, strengthen thy brethren."

That is why John also calls Christ a righteous Advocate, One Who knows our hearts—how we mean it—Who has compassion with us and Who does wrong to no one.

However this remark of John is *again* only an interpolation (as already chapter 1:8-10), and so that we do not misuse the intercession of Jesus and think sin could not harm us anyway, he *again* immediately begins with his own text and picks up the thread from 1:5 ff. (see page 51): "And hereby we do know that we know him, if we keep his commandments," and to know God and to have fellowship with Him is the same, just as to keep His commandments and to walk in the light is the same. The former is the proof of the latter. But he who says that he knows God and does not keep His commandments is a liar, just as he is who says that he has fellowship with God and nevertheless walks in darkness.

But men are ever ready to say that they know God even if they do not know Him, for by nature no one knows God, but only by the indwelling of Christ do we learn to know Him, and that is our eternal life (John 17:3).

> "And this is life eternal, that they might know thee
> the only true God, and Jesus Christ, whom thou hast
> sent."

He who lives in sin cannot know God for he is possessed and darkened by the devil, and the devil, who has implanted sin (the spiritual death) in all men, has, by the same, destroyed the order of God and His kingdom in humanity and loosed and torn asunder all the bonds until the time when we are brought thither again by Christ.

# Chapter XVIII

# God's Positive Will

In each person, it is true, there is still a mystical idea or conception of the Diety and there is no people found on earth that did not have a certain kind of religion or divine worship. But each one shapes his God according to his own imagination or according to himself, so that he by it may, without disturbance, do what he desires, and as proof of their falsity they are all antagonistic toward each other and, fundamentally, it is all the same whether their imaginations are represented outwardly in pictures only or if they have them within themselves. When one observes their ungodly life, it is clear that they, all together, do not know the only living, true God (the so-called Christians as little as the heathen), but only deceive themselves with their own imaginations and by their lie sin even more than by their exceedingly evil works.

No natural man has the least conception of God's real nature, holiness and righteousness, etc., that sin militates against Him and that He must punish it. Yes, as the heathen thought of their idols as wrathful, angry, lustful beings who lived in continual warfare with each other, so the so-called Christians also, essentially, do no better with their imagined God, for they sin without fear or wavering and do not think that this is intolerable to the holy and righteous God or that they must be converted from darkness and Satan's power unto God and His light; for only he who leads a holy, godly life knows God and has fellowship with Him, and for this a very distinct (especial) revelation of God to each individual one is required, and in this then all those who made the experience are in complete accord and one.

July 30, 1840 (Thursday); Evening Meeting; I John 2:3 ff. (with power)

> "And hereby we do know that we know him, if we keep his commandments.
> "He that saith, I know him, and keepeth not his commandments, is a liar, and the truth is not in him."

All unconverted people insist that they know God and a customary knowledge of God, one, it is true, cannot disallow of them; but because it is *powerless* to a holy life and godly walk and inadequate to know God in His real nature (as a pure light incongruous with darkness) and to understand Him in His wisdom (I Corinthians 2), it is an imagined (false) knowledge of Him and serves them rather to condemnation than to salvation, that they know of God, and even boast of it (Titus 1:16):

> "They profess that they know God; but in works they deny him, being abominable, and disobedient, and unto every good work reprobate."

but still deny Him by their works and by sin serve another master who militates against God, and even the animals are more thankful in their way than men (Isaiah 1), for whose boasting there is left over nothing except the shame of their thanklessness. It would be better to have no knowledge of God at all than such a one by which He is only derided and mocked.

Now, as ruins, fragments and heaps of wreckage are the silent witnesses of former cities and vanished glory, so also are the confusingly tangled, intricate without order in man, promiscuously-thrown-together, miserable remnants of the knowledge of God the speaking evidences and memorials of a formerly existent glory which men now lack (Romans 3:23),

> "For all have sinned, and come short of the glory of God."

And as one cannot dwell in ruins, can indeed not even build anew thereupon without first removing the old debris—yes, as God has said of Babel and all the accursed cities and lands that henceforth only demons of the field, owls, dragons, serpents and like ominous animality shall inhabit these very places—so also is fallen man no longer a habitation of God but, in His place, evil spirits have made an abode for themselves of him, and all these generations of vipers and ruin must first be removed by Christ before the living and true, holy God may again dwell in the hearts of men in order that all may become new.

Now, whoever boasts of his own wisdom and natural knowledge, boasts of destruction and ruin and of the evil spirits that find an abode therein, against God, and this false boasting in the flesh and imagination of one's self is the greatest hindrance in the way of the restoration of man unto the divine image, because, deceiving himself, he imagines he has something which he nevertheless does not have and is something which he actually is not, and for that reason he does not attain unto the true knowledge of God in which life eternal lies, namely, unto a holy life by the keeping of the commandments of God, and beside all the other sins he adds this one to them: he becomes a liar because he says that he knows God and still does not keep His commandments, like the Jews (John 8:54 ff.).

> "Jesus answered, If I honour myself, my honour is nothing: it is my Father that honoureth me; of whom we say, that he is your God:
> "Yet ye have not known him; but I know him: and if I should say, I know him not, I shall be a liar like unto you: but I know him, and keep his saying."

Therefore, the complete life of Jesus Christ in us (the love to God) is required of us so as to boast truthfully of the knowledge of God. To that end, there is contained in the expression of John's, "And hereby we do know that we know [or have learned to know] him," the definite indication that this true knowledge of God is in no one by nature but is only later (at an appointed time, Galatians 4:2):

> "But is under tutors and governors until the time appointed of the father."

attained by grace, so that no flesh may glory before God; but he who would glory, let him glory only in the Lord through revelation from God and in this knowledge of God, God Himself dwells as in His spiritual house.

August 2, 1840 (Sunday); Morning Meeting; I John 2:3 ff.

> "And hereby we do know that we know him, if we keep his commandments.
> "He that saith, I know him, and keepeth not his commandments, is a liar, and the truth is not in him.
> "But whoso keepeth his word, in him verily is the love of God perfected: hereby know we that we are in him.
> "He that saith he abideth in him ought himself also so to walk, even as he walked."

The knowing of the commandments of God is the concern of the mind; the keeping of them, that of the will. Therefore, where the mind is enlightened by God, there the heart also must be directed toward God, but where the latter is missing there the former also is missing. Now, with respect to this knowing, everyone makes claim upon the truth and yet he is of the lie and of darkness if he does not at heart love God to the extent of doing His will. Thus there is a contradiction in man: he knows that there is a God and yet he does not serve and thank and honor Him, but the devil instead who has all in his power. Even the Only One, over Whom he had no power, he wanted to tempt to apostasy from God, but Jesus smote him with the words, "Thou shalt worship the Lord thy God and him only shalt thou serve."

Now, we cannot serve God with works unless we love Him with all our heart and keep His Word as proof that we have received redemption from the power of the devil, through Christ, because the doing of His will is our life as the doing of sin is our death, since God can have no fellowship with sinners but must condemn them. For if an outward, divine service combined with the serving of sin could have pleased God, the old law and Israel would have been sufficient and Christ as the Mediator of a new covenant would have been unnecessary. He however had not only to take our sins away by His death, but also to set up a new law and life by His resurrection.

The commandments of God, which we as His children must do, like Christ, are His *positive will,* unlike the old law which forbade sin only; by it, accordingly, no actual righteousness ever came forth. So much higher is the New Testament than the Old Testament. However, at the present time, most people are not even Pharisees (hypocrites) with an appearance of godliness but live openly in sin, and, in view of this, whatever they would do as a divine worship is a dead formality and habit, the most irrational thing that one can think of, because they do not sanctify their whole life as a sacrifice unto God.

No one, it is true, has ever seen God, but whoever is reconciled to Him by Christ and united with Him in the Spirit, his heart surely can cling fixedly to God and associate with Him in perfect love. For all those who are from God ever return to Him with all desires, just as those who are from the world strive after the things that are from beneath (John 8). Where the treasure is, there the heart of man is also and since all men are darkness by nature, one can easily know who has become a light in Christ or a child of God: the light shines in the darkness and the life of the children of God is a complete contrast to the life of the children of the devil.

August 2, 1840 (Sunday); Afternoon Meeting

The real difference between the Old and the New Testaments and what pertains to either, consists in this only: that there, all is done by compulsion and fear, here however by love and good will, for the inwardly written law of the Spirit teaches us not only the entire good will of God, but *at the same time* also gives us the strength and joy to fulfill it, and it must be Christ Himself Who does it within us. In this, we shall take no man as a pattern except Christ Himself, in all His holy, sinless life, or craftiness is ever ready to refer us to these and those people who indeed are not even perfected, not as the apostle said, "Brethren, be followers together of me, and mark them which walk so as ye have us for an ensample (Philippians 3:17)."

And even if we could not now find such, that would still not be an excuse for the impossibility of it, for it is written that even if a believer sins, it is not to be justified by reason of that, since it always happens from forgetfulness of God and if he would use aright the strength and grace he received and love God with all his heart, he would *never* sin but always do the will of God with pleasure. Indeed, not that the flesh would be so willing and would not resist, but we shall restrain it by the Spirit and force it to obedience, that we yield not to its inclinations. *Its way is by slothfulness in the doing of good and where one once gives place to that, there the doing of evil and the suffocation of the Spirit very soon follow.*

There is something wrong with a believer if one must always be after him with the rod and punishment and the Spirit of Christ does not Itself teach and impel him. For over him who is in Christ, the devil no longer has power unto sin and no believer dare blame the devil or hide behind him like Eve if he has sinned, for by that he only reveals his shame, that he has not preserved himself. Now a Christian (who is *in* Christ) is known by this, that he keeps the commandments of God and walks even as Christ walked on earth. But he who, under the name of Christ, lives in conformity to the world, is banished from and rejected in the church of Christ; one shall have no fellowship with him, for we cannot judge sin in the world, only the sinners in the church, *so that we do not become conformable to the world (I Corinthians 5).*

## Chapter XIX

### Knowing God Aright

August 4, 1840 (Tuesday); Evening Meeting; I John 2:3 ff. (with rejoicing)

> "And hereby we do know that we know him, if we keep his commandments.
> "He that saith, I know him, and keepeth not his commandments, is a liar, and the truth is not in him.

"But whoso keepeth his word, in him verily is the love of God perfected: hereby know we that we are in him.
"He that saith he abideth in him ought himself also so to walk, even as he walked."

To know God means to evermore walk in His light, in His presence, to love Him and to do His will joyfully (in which alone is blessedness), not to avoid sin merely out of fear of punishment, but to do the good out of love to God so as to be acceptable to Him (I John 3:21 ff.; 5:3).

"Beloved, if our heart condemn us not, then have we confidence toward God.
"And whatsoever we ask, we receive of him, because we keep his commandments, and do those things that are pleasing in his sight."

"For this is the love of God, that we keep his commandments: and his commandments are not grievous."

This affords us great joyousness in God, Whom we know to be not only *all around us* (we in Him), but Whom we bear and feel *in us* as well. This blessed fellowship with God and the doing of His good pleasure vouchsafe the great advantage that one does not commit sin (how that is possible no one knows without making the experience himself).

Herein the state of grace is entirely different from that of the law, where one has to think only about repulsing sin (a defensive system), and with that is so occupied with the continual struggle against sin that he does not come to the doing of the acceptable will of God. The ship of the law leaks on all sides. The water (sin) forces its way in everywhere. If one would stop up one hole another opens. All pumping and work is in vain. For the possible preservation of life one must finally decide to throw the cargo overboard and at last even the ship itself is wrecked and despairing man must be glad if he is saved with his bare life.

But with just this shipwreck of the law, the true blessedness and salvation of the soul unto eternal life is bound. The believer in Christ then receives a new, sound ship for crossing over through the tempestuous sea of this world to the shore of eternity. In this ship of faith, the rescued one needs not fear that he could sink, for Christ Himself is within as its Pilot and *by hope* its anchor is already entering on the other side.

But if we have faith and hope in God, we must then also work for Him in love and contemplate for ourselves a ship of faith laden with a rich cargo of good works so that we do not have to appear empty-handed and naked before God; for what we do in faith and love, in hope upon the Lord, that we really do to our own advantage—we shall receive it from the Lord and the more abundantly we have sown, the more abundantly also shall we reap, even though mercenariness does not lie at the bottom of it but a pure impulse of divine love (John 1:17 ff.; I Thessalonians 1:3; I Corinthians 13:13).

> "For the law was given by Moses, but grace and truth came by Jesus Christ.
> "No man hath seen God at any time; the only gotten Son which is in the bosom of the Father, he hath declared him."

> "Remembering without ceasing your work of faith, and labour of love, and patience of hope in our Lord Jesus Christ, in the sight of God and our Father;"

> "And now abideth faith, hope, charity, these three; but the greatest of these is charity."

August 6, 1840 (Thursday); Evening Meeting; I John 2:5 ff.

> "But whoso keepeth his word, in him verily is the love of God perfected: hereby know we that we are in him.
> "He that saith he abideth in him ought himself also so to walk, even as he walked."

"Hereby know we that we are in him." That is to say, if we keep His commandments and do not sin. John mentions sign after sign by which we shall recognize those who are in Christ (real Christians) and distinguish them from the false Christians, who have nothing of Christ but the name and thereby misuse this name and deceive themselves. The second deception is still worse than the first one in Adam, since by it the only possible salvation for men is frustrated and made to naught and their damnation is unavoidable, for the redemption in Christ consists only in a liberation from sin and the power of Satan, and from this, those, as well, are not excepted who maintain that they believe in the reconciliation of sin by the death of Christ and, besides, still abide in sin and deny Him by their deeds and make Him unnecessary.

To be a Christian in the mind of the world and *to be in Christ* in the meaning of the language of the apostles are certainly two entirely different things; the former has become an empty title for appearance' sake, the latter however signifies the nature of a believer. To be in Christ means to be in God and God in the believer as the Eternal Life by means of a new creation, and just because the Holy Spirit had foreknown that the devil in the course of time would turn even the salvation of Christ into a mere title and appearance for men, He therefore by the apostles has indicated so clearly and so plainly, in advance, the true and real nature of a Christian that we could measure all men by this standard, and we should write these words over our doors so that we never forget them: Consider no one a Christian except him who keeps the commandments of God and does His will in all things. Anyone else is a liar if he claims the name and salvation of Christ.

But, besides, we should be careful not to consider walking strictly according to the commandments of God a burden (Jeremiah 23:33 ff.) (below), as a hard, grievous, sour, troublesome, annoying thing, as if God wished only to trouble, oppress, tempt and enslave us, when, by the accomplishment of His acceptable will, He has only our true blessedness in mind—just as the committing of sin and the doing of the evil will of the devil are our real destruction.

> "And when this people, or the prophet, or a priest, shall ask thee, saying, What is the burden of the Lord? thou shalt say unto them, What burden? I will even forsake you, saith the Lord.
>
> "And as for the prophet, and the priest, and the people, that shall say, The burden of the Lord, I will even punish that man and his house.
>
> "Thus shall ye say every one to his neighbour, and every one to his brother, What hath the Lord answered? and, What hath the Lord spoken?
>
> "And the burden of the Lord shall ye mention no more: for every man's word shall be his burden; for ye have perverted the words of the living God, of the Lord of hosts our God.
>
> "Thus shalt thou say to the prophet, What hath the Lord answered thee? and, What hath the Lord spoken?
>
> "But since ye say, The burden of the Lord; therefore thus saith the Lord; Because ye say this word, The burden of the Lord, and I have sent unto you, saying, Ye shall not say, The burden of the Lord;
>
> "Therefore, behold, I, even I, will utterly forget you, and I will forsake you, and the city that I gave you and your fathers, and cast you out of my presence:
>
> "And I will bring an everlasting reproach upon you, and a perpetual shame, which shall not be forgotten."

The power to do the will of God lies in Christ, and if the strength for this fails, then one has not put Christ on and does not stand in the right relationship to Him: for as death has reigned in Adam, so must life now, much more, reign in Christ because grace has become more powerful than sin was. Whoever does not acknowledge and believe that, does likewise not know Christ and does not believe the Gospel. Man is capable of both, according to whether Christ or the devil reigns in him and he gives himself over to the one or the other; but it is all the more shameful if we would still serve sin (the devil) after life and the power of righteousness have appeared so abundantly in Christ.

## Chapter XX

## The Amazing and Adorable Mystery of the Gospel

August 9, 1840 (Sunday); Morning Meeting; I John 2:4 ff.

"He that saith, I know him, and keepeth not his commandments, is a liar, and the truth is not in him.

"But whoso keepeth his word, in him verily is the love of God perfected: hereby know we that we are in him.

"He that saith he abideth in him ought himself also so to walk, even as he walked."

John places the knowledge of God and the keeping of His commandments in such a necessary juncture, that he calls him who maintains of himself the former and does not do the latter, a liar. The true knowledge of God attests itself by odebience to His will and both are one. That natural men do not live according to the commandments of God is no wonder because they do not know Him, but that there are men who make claim to the knowledge of God (and who would deny such a claim with respect to himself?) and still *with it* do not do the will of God but the will of the devil (the evil), that *is* to be wondered at, that they do not notice the deception, for the true, living knowledge of God does not originate from our nature or reasoning but only from the direct revelation of God Himself in the heart of man.

It is true that He also employs the means of preaching by His messengers, and as often as we assemble about the Word of God, it is with no other intention than to always learn to know God and His will better, so as to live according to it; but still it is not with the intention of learning something by heart (the memory also belongs to the ruins of the former glory of man) and of reciting prayer thoughtlessly and without devotion as, for instance, one teaches children from their youth to repeat the Lord's Prayer, etc. from memory without their comprehending it, and so also is the knowledge of God in all men which is not associated with obedience to His will. All such knowledge is imaginary and false.

What then does "to know God" mean? He says (Jeremiah 9:24a), "But let him that glorieth glory in this, that he understandeth and knoweth me, that I am the Lord . . . ," and again He says (Malachi 1:6a), "A son honoureth his father, and a servant his master: if then I be a father, where is mine honour? and if I be a master, where is my fear?" Therefore he who says that he has known Christ and the Father, must acknowledge Him as a Lord of All and also as his Lord, so as to serve and obey Him, else one mocks Him, as He says of the false Christians who would not have Him to reign over them (Luke 19:14), although they call themselves after His name.

Now, Paul, it is true, says (I Corinthians 12) that no one can call Jesus the Lord except by the Holy Ghost, but he says this only of the true confession of Christ of those who are taught by the Holy Ghost and to whom it is a heartfelt necessity to worship and call upon Jesus as their only Lord and bend their knees to Him in secret (Philippians 2), but not of the lying "Lord, Lord" saying of those who, in spite of that, deny Him by their works because they do not serve Him and therefore will not enter into the kingdom of God (Matthew 7).

Just this is the amazing and adorable mystery of the Gospel, that the Lord of Heaven, the Only Begotten of the Father, left, took off and laid down His sovereignty and glory and put on the form of a servant in its place so as to serve as a *servant* for us for several more than thirty years in obedience and to give His life as a ransom for many—for our salvation or redemption from the devil's dark power of sin, which directly opposes the acceptable, holy will of God and makes us His enemies. But he who now hears this message of the love of God toward us should become converted and let himself be reconciled to God (relinquish the enmity) and, as a reborn child of God, subject himself in voluntary obedience to Christ as the only Lord (Romans 6). For Christ will have no forced servants; He leaves the choice to each one, whether he would prefer to serve the devil in sin rather than God in righteousness. He tolerates His enemies in His patience a long time already, until they are ripe for judgment, because they despise salvation.

68

Further, the contrast between verses 4 and 5 is to be noted. Of him who does not keep the commandments of God, John says, "the truth is not in him," but of him who keeps the Word of God, he says, "in him verily is the love of God perfected." Thus, in a certain measure, truth and love are one and the same and yet there is a difference, as between a tree and its fruit. As the truth is, thus it manifests itself by love; it passes over into love by faith. What the truth is in us, that love is outwardly. In one way, truth is the counterpart of the lie (in an unconverted person) and, in another, grace (in a converted one) (John 1:17).

> "For the law was given by Moses, but grace and truth
> came by Jesus Christ."

Now, as the lie is the personal, living devil revealed by sin, thus is the truth the personal, living Christ revealed by love. Christ is the Truth (Ephesians 4:20 ff.):

> "But ye have not so learned Christ;
> "If so be that ye have heard him, and have been
> taught by him, as the truth is in Jesus:
> "That ye put off concerning the former conversation
> the old man, which is corrupt according to the deceitful
> lusts;
> "And be renewed in the spirit of your mind;
> "And that ye put on the new man, which after God
> is created in righteousness and true holiness."

that is to say, a holy, godly life and restoration of the Divine Image, and consists herein, that the old man with his works has been put off and in his stead the new man in righteousness and the holiness of truth has been put on, where there no longer is Jew, Greek, etc., but Christ is All in all. In Him all are one, one body, though many members; that is what the truth (Christ) is and accomplishes in us, which does not permit itself to be separated from the right grace.

But those who wish only grace from Christ for the forgiveness of sins, without truth for the restoration of the Divine Image and Life, would like to divide Christ and by that themselves fall again into the lie of the devil. For the truth is much more important for us than grace, since the latter does not save without the former. The two are in the same relation to each other as the two brazen columns of Solomon's temple, Jochin (he will raise up) and Boas (in him is strength).

The truth was what Jesus promised His disciples and on which account He went to the Father, so as to send the Spirit of Truth in His stead, with the great, double advantage that He would be in them and with them unto eternity. This Spirit of Christ in us is the right Teacher and Guide into all truth, so as to make all the will of God known to us, to which oral preaching shall only incite and inspire us. But he in whom the inner witnessing of the Spirit is wanting is no child of God and him the outer word does not help either, for he is a forgetful hearer and no doer of the Word, but the children of God must walk in the truth (11 and III John; John 4). Truth and love are divine twins; where one would speak only of love without truth or at the expense of truth, there the love of God is not to be found and so it is also, inversely, with the truth.

## CHAPTER XXI

## THE PAINTED DELUSION OF THE DEVIL

August 11, 1840 (Tuesday); Evening Meeting; I John 2:5 ff.

"But whoso keepeth his word, in him verily is the love of God perfected: hereby know we that we are in him.
"He that saith he abideth in him ought himself also so to walk, even as he walked."

The doing of the good is the fruit and the evidence of perfect love to God; and that is the only unerring mark which shows that we are in Christ, know Him in the Spirit and have put Him on in His divine nature, as a child of God. If the law of the Spirit of Life in Christ is thus in us—has freed us from the law of sin and death—we then descend from the same Father and God that the Son descended from and there is then no other difference between us and Christ except that He is the Firstborn among many brethren and therefore He is not ashamed to call us His brethren (Hebrews 2), and the necessary result is that we also walk as He walked, namely, like saints.

And as Christ did not seek His own honor on earth but the honor of the Father, thus must we as children of God also live to the honor of God in all things, that is, altogether do that which pleases Him and avoid what displeases Him and defiles us, namely, sin, which was not to be found in Christ (John 8; I Peter 2). If we should think that this is not attainable for us, we shall then know and consider that the Spirit of Christ is effectual in us and that we are not Christians without that, for what the world calls Christendom is nothing but a painted delusion of the devil, with which he deceives men.

Christendom does not know Christ in the Spirit, but according to the flesh and the letter only, what He has done and suffered in the world (as one beholds and knows a painting) and does not know that in these things He is only our Pattern Whom we shall resemble. And when John says that he who abides in Him ought himself to walk even so as He walked, we shall then not think, "Yes, if only we knew how He was, if only we had seen Him." —That is not necessary if we know Him in the Spirit, for the same Spirit works in us just as it worked in Him and glorifies Him in us: the Word is not far off, but in our mouths and hearts, that we do it.

A holy, sinless life is the will of the Father and the ultimate purpose of the appearance of Christ in the world (II Corinthians 5) and if that is not found in one (as a believer) he has forgotten the cleansing of his former sins and is blind. Only he makes his calling and election sure who diligently endeavors to live the holy life of Christ and to him then the portals into the kingdom of glory are opened wide (II Peter 1).

He who knows God (as His Father) must as well love Him and he who loves God will also honor Him by obedience to His will and gladden His heart. Even in our earthly relations, the love of children to their parents is something natural and the opposite is unnatural and against nature (even when sin is still in man). Also, the only positive command of the old law is: "Honor thy father and thy mother," with the appended promise [in the New Testament] (Ephesians 6:1):

> "Children, obey your parents in the Lord: for this is right."

How much more must the love to their Heavenly Father and Savior then be something *natural* in the children of God *after* their heart has been cleansed from sin! And just as faithful, loving children who would willingly gladden rather than sadden their parents' hearts, do everything they can see and read in their eyes, thus the children of God also, at all times, behold the face of their Father in Heaven in the Spirit, so as to do those things by which they may please and honor Him and avoid those which might grieve Him. For them, His gracious good pleasure surpasses all else.

71

August 13, 1840 (Thursday); Evening Meeting; I John 2:6 ff.

> "He that saith he abideth in him ought himself also
> so to walk, even as he walked.
> "Brethren, I write no new commandment unto you,
> but an old commandment which ye had from the begin-
> ning. The old commandment is the word which ye have
> heard from the beginning."

"Brethren, I write no new commandment unto you, but an old commandment, which ye had from the beginning." What is this old commandment? It is the word that is in verse 6, that a true Christian ought
himself to walk even so as Christ walked on earth. It was an old well-
known, foregone conclusion with the believers of that time, that no one
can lay claim to the name of Christ except him who has His holy, sinless
life in the Spirit, follows step by step in His footprints (I Peter 2:21 ff.).

> "For even hereunto were ye called: because Christ
> also suffered for us, leaving us an example, that ye should
> follow his steps:
> "Who did no sin, neither was guile found in his
> mouth:
> "Who, when he was reviled, reviled not again; when
> he suffered, he threatened not; but committed himself to
> him that judgeth righteously:
> "Who his own self bare our sins in his own body on
> the tree, that we, being dead to sins, should live unto
> righteousness: by whose stripes ye were healed."

Ask, now, and hear what the present-day Christians know about
this. They not only know nothing of it, that that constitutes a Christian,
but they even consider it an abominably false doctrine, as if the
apostles had preached lies; however it much more remains that God
alone is truthful and all men are liars, that they deny, falsify and tread
underfoot the old commandment of Christ. So unknown and unheard
of has it now become, that if one no longer walks according to the world
but according to Christ, he is hated, slandered and persecuted as a
fool, a fanatic, a sectarian and an apostate person by all, and while
they plague and crucify one in the most unjust manner until one's soul
fairly departs (I Peter 4), they say, mockingly, "It happens rightly
to you, you queer people. Why do you condemn all others (by a holy
walk in Christ)? Live like the others and you will fare like the
others!" etc.

If we here look upon the visible and do as the world does, it will then certainly happen to us as it happens to the world, which lies in wickedness and which will be condemned in the world to come (I Corinthians 11:32).

> "But when we are judged, we are chastened of the
> Lord, that we should not be condemned with the world."

But if we fare in the present world as Christ and His Church fared from the beginning, we nevertheless are still favored with blessings and can rejoice in tribulation for Christ's sake. For, just because a holy life is not from men but from Christ, suffering on account thereof is also suffering for Christ, by which God is glorified and we are sanctified and favored.

Here we dare measure ourselves by no man: Christ Himself, alone, is the Measure and Pattern and as *this*, on the one side of imitation, makes it not only . . . . , but impossible for the natural man, so just *this* makes the matter easy for the spiritual man, because Christ Himself dwells and walks in him and this also bars every excuse of its being impossible, for he who has not put Christ on in the Spirit has no part in Him at all, because real Christendom consists not in the mere name and outward form but in the following after Him and conformity to His life.

But it is now also true that he who bears the name of Christ *without having His Spirit* is not only deceived but is as well an anti-Christian; that is to say, he, first of all, is an institutional Christian (a false instead of a true one) and such a one then, at the same time, takes on the character of enmity against Christ and becomes an oppositionist-Christian. In the apostles' time already this spirit had taken root and now the whole world is full of institutional- and oppositionist-Christians.

## CHAPTER XXII

### THE POWER OF HIS LIFE

August 16, 1840 (Sunday); Morning Meeting; I John 2:7

> "Brethren, I write no new commandment unto you,
> but an old commandment which ye had from the begin-
> ning. The old commandment is the word which ye have
> heard from the beginning."

The old commandment is the love of God (or to God, chapter 5; verse 3):

"For this is the love of God, that we keep his commandments: and his commandments are not grievous."

and thence the keeping of His commandments. Already under the Household of the Old Testament, this was the principal point and summation: "Thou shalt love the Lord thy God with all thine heart," etc., and this has not *decreased* but *increased* under the Household of Grace and has become perfect in Christ: for if *there* already, each transgression received its just recompense, how should we *here* escape if we neglect such a salvation as this (Hebrews 2 and 10)!

Love to God without the doing of His will is a contradiction, and a religion of outer sacrifices without love and obedience of the heart is hypocrisy: for by Christ's death the former impossibility is removed and by His resurrection the possibility is accomplished (Romans 8) and every excuse has fallen away. God has reconciled the world with Himself and the giving of His Only Begotten Son for us is such an astounding proof of His love that a doubter of His ready willingness to help and to save us from sin and the power of the devil is an ungodly person.

But even if men do not doubt this act of love and reconciliation on the part of God toward a sinful world, they still *on their part* do not enter into reconciliation with God but remain in enmity against Him, namely, in sin and the disposition of the flesh, which is death, for only those who let themselves be delivered and freed from sin by Christ, actually and truly let themselves be reconciled with God. Why did Christ sacrifice Himself and become a curse, but for the fulfilling of the will of the Father, that is, to take sin away and to redeem us from it? But men are loath to reconcile themselves with God because they really love darkness more than the light and hate God, and when the Gospel offers them the choice of salvation, they nevertheless choose the devil and therefore must also inherit damnation with him, because they reject God's loving offer. If anyone is inseparable from the devil in this world, he is then in eternity also.

The non-acceptance of reconciliation with God is a self-willed disobedience and resistance, man's own choice. God in Himself was already reconciled to men (full of love and pity) *before* He gave His Son (otherwise He would not have given Him) and the purpose of the death of Christ, consequently, is not a purchasing of the good will of God toward us, but His death occurred for the purchase and salvation of the sinner from the power of the devil, which takes place immediately *(unmittelbar)*, after man on his part lets himself be reconciled with

74

God; so real salvation from sin is the earnest of our reconciliation with God.

Now, if the death of Christ is mighty enough to destroy the dominion of sin, how much mightier then is His life to establish divine obedience in us as the necessary consequence of the knowledge and love of God, which is the old commandment! But in the Old Testament, love to God was not the foundational impulse of human conduct, single instances excepted, for example, David's (Psalm 18, etc.), and even in his case not absolutely, although his knowledge of God lifted him over the boundaries (Psalm 51) and over the viewpoint of others.

August 16, 1840 (Sunday); Afternoon Meeting.

The love to God is the first and old commandment. If we have become His children through Christ, everything is in order and we love God anew and keep His word, so that it is sweeter and more precious to us than all else (Psalm 19)—if we can do God's good, acceptable and perfect will. But for this we must know Him; that is, the eyes of our heart, with which we can see God and the invisible things, must have been enlightened, for the reason why sinners do not love God and the things that are His, is their inner eyes have been blinded and darkened by the devil. They all chase after the phantom, that which one sees with the physical eye, that which is perishable, wherewith they are deceived, because in the end they must leave it all behind and the real existence which is in Christ, they pass by for they have no eyes for it, being blind for the glory of God.

The dear Lord must uphold the whole world and keep it occupied, to prove that we have no other gods (idols) beside Him and then we can lose nothing, much more possess all things in Him and indeed eternally. We shall not love our life in this world more than Him for it also belongs to the perishable and deceptive phantoms with which the devil makes fools of men. Yet we should love ourselves also in a rightful and godly manner, namely as God loves us, that we may be saved eternally by the sanctification of the Spirit in obedience unto the truth, for if there were no right self-love we then could not love or would not need to love our neighbors as ourselves. For the sinner does not love himself but the devil instead, because if he loved himself he would not serve sin, which hurls into eternal damnation and by which one destroys the other, as they stand in each other's way, in that all run after the same phantom, for, in the world of men at least, the devil reigns by nothing but confusion and destruction and none live according to the rule which each one has written in his heart: "What you wish (or do not wish) that others shall do unto you, that do (or do not do) unto them."

Man himself, of course, is not sin but entirely different from it (Romans 7), yet whoever commits sin is also penetrated and stained by it (a sinner). Accordingly, God's wrath is not upon man as man, but upon sin: but he who does not let himself be separated from sin by the death of Christ, on him the lot of the wrath of God falls.

As many, now, as have been converted unto God by faith in Christ —are reconciled, united and at peace with God—have the same aim, namely, the love of God, and just as *with them* nothing further rivals with the love of God (they no longer love anything idolatrously but sacrifice all visible things to God), they vie not one with another in chasing after the phantom and no longer devilishly hate, envy and subordinate anyone, but love all in a divine way with the desire to save them. And this love to our neighbor is the second and new commandment of God, which is real (in power) in Christ and in His believers and saints because in them the darkness is past and the true light shines.

## CHAPTER XXIII

### THE HIDDEN, INVISIBLE LOVE TO GOD

August 18, 1840 (Tuesday); Evening Meeting; I John 2:8 ff.

> "Again, a new commandment I write unto you, which thing is true in him and in you: because the darkness is past, and the true light now shineth.
> "He that saith he is in the light, and hateth his brother, is in darkness even until now.
> "He that loveth his brother abideth in the light, and there is none occasion of stumbling in him."

It is probable that John understands the same thing by the old and new commandment (as for instance Gassner thinks the old must ever again be renewed), but as the old refers to God, so the new refers to the brethren (mankind). Both commandments, of course, stand in a very close connection to each other, and as one feels a person's pulse to determine whether he is alive, so also is the love of the brethren the proof of the love of God or that one stands in fellowship with God and has a spiritual life. The love to God is within, invisible and hidden, but the love to the brethren is the outward, manifest sign of life: "That he who loveth God love his brother also (chapter 4:20 ff.)."

> "If a man say, I love God, and hateth his brother, he is a liar: for he that loveth not his brother whom he hath seen, how can he love God whom he hath not seen?
> "And this commandment have we from him, That he who loveth God love his brother also."

All men are indeed not children of God nor brethren in Christ, but our love shall nevertheless be unrestricted and impartial toward all because we are still brethren according to the flesh, just as God loved all men when they were still His enemies and wished to see that all might be helped from their fall in Adam (I Timothy 2), and he who has himself been saved has the intention and love also to save others together with himself. Divine love seeks all men in all things in order that everywhere some may be saved (I Corinthians 9).

Love bears no hatred according to the flesh, not even against those who hate us without cause, simply because we belong to Christ and have His life in us. If the world hates us on that account, as it hated Christ, we are innocent, but if we ourselves are a stumblingblock and offense to men, we have not the mind of Christ and walk not in the light but in darkness and there is then no fellowship of the Spirit or of the saints either, where the name of *brother* is defiled (I Corinthians 5). But we shall take heed that the cause of the stumbling and offense is not in us ourselves, that we are not easily and willingly offended and annoyed about things that are only human weaknesses in others and not sin, on account of which the main thing (in which all ought to agree) is so often neglected, forgotten and suppressed. Such are like butting and easily provoked goats and have indeed never quite left the former darkness and they make demands on others which they themselves do not fulfill.

Each one, rather, should begin with himself and strive to be perfect. He then will not be offended and vexed so easily by others and innocent things, will not on that account deny love and himself become offensive and annoying to others instead of helping along on building up the body of Christ, as ought to be the case among those who are children of one Father, members of one Body, filled with one Spirit and called to one Hope. Here, every insignificant, secondary matter and personal interest, with which the devil very willingly disturbs the peace and unity of the Spirit among the children of God, ought to yield. True love is concerned with the removal of all stumblingblocks of offense (I Corinthians 10:32 ff.).

> "Give none offence, neither to the Jews, nor to the Gentiles, nor to the church of God:
> "Even as I please all men in all things, not seeking mine own profit, but the profit of many, that they may be saved."

August 20, 1840 (Thursday); Evening Meeting; I John 2:9 ff.

"He that saith he is in the light [has been divinely enlightened; he knows God and has fellowship with Him], and hateth his brother, is in darkness even until now." —The old devilish darkness has not yet passed away in him in spite of his assertion that he is in the light and his enlightenment therefore is not genuine either.

John has a manner of teaching and demonstration altogether peculiar to himself, so simple and yet so decidedly sharp and piercing, like a two-edged sword. He contrasts the half with the whole—that is to say, the false and the true Christians—and thereby puts us in such a tight place—as the angel put Balaam in—that there is no escape. Already for the third or fourth time he puts himself with his sword in our way (chapter 1:6; 2:*4, 6, 9*):

> "If we say that we have fellowship with him, and walk in darkness, we lie, and do not the truth:"

---

> "He that saith, I know him, and keepeth not his commandments, is a liar, and the truth is not in him."

---

> "He that saith he abideth in him ought himself also so to walk, even as he walked."

---

> "He that saith he is in the light, and hateth his brother, is in darkness even until now."

and, besides, he takes us at our own word, and even if we have avoided him two or three times (like Balaam), still, in the end, there is no more fleeing from him and we must come to a standstill and examine ourselves before God and learn to know ourselves.

More than this, we shall be alarmed about it, for we must once be revealed as we are, and just on that account John does not acknowledge anything " half" (counterfeit) in Christ, as it is worthless and has no value before God. And if we are not yet as we should be, we ought to seek all the more earnestly, for Christ is rich unto all who call upon Him. It is better that we learn to know ourselves rightly *now*, than first in eternity, for nothing is more usual and more dangerous besides, than the self-deception of an only half-existence in Christ, and John is referring only to those who, themselves, say that they are Christians (enlightened). Here, then it must be something complete—perfected— or John denies us everything, and Christ also makes it just as emphatic when He says (Matthew 13:12):

> "For whosoever hath, to him shall be given, and he
> shall have more abundance: but whosoever hath not, from
> him shall be taken away even that he hath."

It is very possible that one hears, believes and approves the Word of Truth, the Gospel of our Salvation, is enlightened by his understanding and can speak of it like a book, without having his heart enlightened, broken, torn asunder and renewed to a godly life and an image of Christ; he can know all truth and yet let sin and darkness dwell in his heart with hatred and wrath, etc. Such half- and false Christians are very usual, and whoever will measure and judge himself according to them, will never come to the true life of Christ, as the only Pattern for all. These are the "who hath not" ones (who do not let the Word of God enter their heart so as to cleanse it from sin) and from whom, therefore, shall even that which they have, be taken away (the knowledge of the truth as the enlightenment of the understanding, II Peter 2). Such fall away again and become worse than before, dogs and swine, blasphemers, etc.

There is a terrible contradiction in those whose understanding is definitely enlightened by the Word and whose heart is still darkened. Although the enlightenment of the understanding is the first step toward the redemption of man, if the understanding of the scriptures is opened by the lighted lamp of the preached word (Acts 17:11):

> "These were more noble than those in Thessalonica,
> in that they received the word with all readiness of mind,
> and searched the scriptures daily, whether those things
> were so."

yet this enlightenment is nevertheless much more to one's condemnation than to one's salvation if the heart remains unchanged (Acts 2). It is something entirely different to *know* the Word of Reconciliation (believingly understand it) or truly accept Christ into the heart through deeper knowledge of one's lost condition for the purpose of commencing a new life: that then is the right enlightenment and whoever gives his heart away in this wise is the one "who hath" and to whom shall be given that he may have abundance; he shall be filled with Christ to overflowing in word and works. Here, all things are in accord: what the mouth of our mind has masticated, that the stomach of our heart digests and divides so that the Word of God passes over into power and life.

## Chapter XXIV

### Brotherly Love

August 23, 1840 (Sunday); Morning Meeting; I John 2:9 ff.

"He that saith he is in the light, and hateth his brother, is in darkness even until now.

"He that loveth his brother abideth in the light, and there is none occasion of stumbling in him."

John speaks of a light indeed, in contrast to a false, lying, imitation light, between which there is a difference as between the sunlight, which at once radiates heat and fructifies and penetrates all things, and every other light which men make artificially and which has a radiance too, but gives no warmth or life. The true Light is Christ Himself, Who not only enlightens the understanding with the knowledge of the truth, but also warms the heart and makes it fruitful with His love. Now, he who makes a science only of the divine truth, without letting it penetrate his heart so as to lead a godly and holy life in Christ, is deceived by a false light and brightness and he does not yet know at all as one ought to know. Knowledge by itself puffs up but love edifies (I Corinthians 8). With a dead, cold knowledge, one has the name that he lives and yet he is dead.

With respect to the truth of faith, people can reciprocally become angry, can wrangle, quarrel, snap at and destroy one another, so that they forget and deny the most important thing in the kingdom of God— love—and tear down rather than build up. I Corinthians 13 should be taken into consideration here, where Paul, as John here, pronounces a sentence upon all who make a science only of the truth in Christ and carry on idle talk about the grace of God, for Christ did not come into the world and die on the cross merely to originate a new, external form-religion (in place of the old Mosaic one), as is generally supposed and practised in the world, where those who bear His name are not united by His love nor joined in the Spirit, but hate, envy, deceive, curse and help one another to damnation—kill, commit adultery, steal, etc. And although the members of one denomination appear to be united outwardly and hold together against those of another denomination, it is still nothing more than a blind, carnal party-enthusiasm and no bond of holy, brotherly love for the mutual upbuilding of the body of Christ. Thus the aim of salvation is frustrated and the name of Christ misused.

Love, alone, is the light indeed, the bond of perfection, which has a veritable life in itself, that all become one heart and one soul in Christ; and if one then, as far as knowledge is concerned, cannot give an account of things in a systematic way like a learned person, yet his life and walk is an edifying light among men and here a practical knowledge of God is possessed that is to be wondered at.

On the other hand, where one would only talk and debate about the truth without love, there a false light exists and the gift of God (enlightenment of the understanding) is misused to the service of the devil. And one can indeed not expect things to be otherwise with the men of the world (nor does John refer to them) for they do not know God and His Word (even though they are called Christians), else they could not live so ungodly. But even if they have the Word of God, they either do not read it so as to find the whole treasure or they read it mechanically without understanding it (Isaiah 29:16 ff.).

"Surely your turning of things upside down shall be esteemed as the potter's clay: for shall the work say of him that made it, He made me not? or shall the thing framed say of him that framed it, He had no understanding?

"Is it not yet a very little while, and Lebanon shall be turned into a fruitful field, and the fruitful field shall be esteemed as a forest?

"And in that day shall the deaf hear the words of the book, and the eyes of the blind shall see out of obscurity, and out of darkness."

But if we, after having obtained the knowledge of the truth, do not live differently from the world but only quarrel, we are no light in the world but a darkness and an offense. Then our knowledge is false and we belong as little to the church of Christ as the world belongs to it and we shall have to give account to God, for whoever knows his Lord's will and fails to do it, shall receive double punishment and unto whom much is given, of him much is required. Therefore by our love of the brethren we shall be different from the world and all its sects.

## August 23, 1840 (Sunday); Afternoon Meeting

John earnestly wishes to make an impression on the hearts and lives of those who confess the faith: "He that loveth his brother abideth in the light." A true Christian shall not so firmly insist by word on his position in the light as a child of God, as to prove it by his deeds, so as to proclaim the virtues of Him Who has called us from the principality of darkness to His marvelous light.

It is precious indeed to see the zeal of the young, new love where the tongue of the newly converted and redeemed proclaims the praises of their God and Savior and cannot be silent about the great change which God has undertaken in them; as when Christ spoke to the one who was possessed of the devil, as we by nature all are too until Christ makes us free, and it would be a good thing if the first love always remained as fresh as this, as a living testimony to the glory of God and an incentive to the knowledge of Him and His love, among one another. But it is more important still that our entire nature and life testify of the great change which we have undergone—from children of the devil to children of God—so that we no longer hate and destroy but love and edify one another, as is befitting of men who "are made after the similitude of God (James 3)."

It is indeed a sad state of affairs that the people are no longer humane, but brutish, bestial, devilish; yes, even worse than the wild animals, of which we have no example that they tear each other in pieces as men among themselves do: so deeply have they fallen by sin from their original estate and the purpose of their creation by God that they are a disgrace instead of a glory to Him (I Corinthians 10)! For where does one still find something humane in men—in drunkards, usurers, the licentious, the merciless, the proud? Are not all filled by the devil and his darkness and wickedness? Would not the whole earth be a den of murderers if the powers in authority were not here, by the command of God, which bear the sword for the punishment of evil doers? Would one be sure of his life if the wild animals were not restricted by such bonds?

Therefore, we must indeed still thank God for the order of the powers in authority, although the children of God get little comfort therefrom when they have to suffer like evil doers for righteousness' sake. There would not even be a need for the authorities and the law if men were men of God who had the law of the love of God in their hearts. Thus the order of the authorities is only proof of the human depravity and there will come a time when all this will be removed, when Christ will erect a new kingdom of God on the new earth of none but the righteous and all the kingdoms of this world shall be the Lord's.

And we shall now let ourselves be prepared for this, that we may enter that kingdom, and we shall know this: that the saving grace of God, for just this purpose, has appeared in Christ unto all men (by His first appearance), to make us men again by being salvaged from the beastly and the devilish and clothed upon with the divine, that we again live with one another like men and not like animals and devils (Titus 2 and 3). For this only is really humane and befitting of God's men; namely, that we love one another, be at peace with one another, do righteousness, be humble, chaste and godly. For this Christ appeared the first time, for this He planted a church on earth and for it He will come the second time, to unite the obedient and overcomers in God's blessed kingdom of righteousness, peace and joy in the Holy Ghost, who, to the exclusion of everything else, are now becoming qualified for and worthy of it.

## Chapter XXV

## The Divine Simplicity

August 25, 1840 (Tuesday); Evening Meeting; I John 2:10 ff.

"He that loveth his brother abideth in the light, and there is none occasion of stumbling in him.
"But he that hateth his brother is in darkness, and walketh in darkness, and knoweth not whither he goeth, because that darkness hath blinded his eyes."

As he who is in the light loves his brother, so also he who loves his brother abides in the light and grows in the life of Christ. The one indeed is the foundation and condition of the other and for this reason John urges upon those who once were enlightened and became believers, that they now also remain in the light and do not again become darkened and blinded by the devil, that they may not have begun in the Spirit and end up in the flesh, for the beginning is nothing without the completion.

And if one becomes secure and trusts in himself as far as being able to stand is concerned, he is outwitted by the devil and falls by reason of his own security before he realizes it, for the devil is and is called a juggler and those whom he cannot cause to fall by force and tribulation, he seeks to catch by subtlety and the allurements of the flesh, if they do not watch continually over themselves and are not on their guard that their plans and thoughts may not be removed from the simplicity in Christ (II Corinthians 11), like the serpent beguiled Eve with his cunning.

Had Eve remained single-hearted to the Word of God, she would not have longed after the fruit of the forbidden tree, but when the lust had conceived in her, it brought forth sin and after sin had been committed, it brought forth death, which God had threatened and which now—even by nature—reigns in all men, that they are dead for God and still have only the distorted and perverted serpent-way left about them, not the divine simplicity and purity which, without stumbling and offense, continues upon the straight, forward way to the goal of the divine calling that has been laid out for us; as Solomon says that he found God has made man upright, honest and single-hearted, but that they seek many inventions. They are distorted and artful like the serpent by reason of descent.

And it can still happen to all believers who have been raised up and enlightened by Christ (who have come from death unto life and out of darkness into light) as it happened to Eve (who was also in the light and adorned with the image of God), if they begin to subtilize and affect wisdom and in their planning and thinking yield to the magic of the devil, that they fail to remain immovably in the simplicity of Christ, for the devil can accomplish nothing unless they consent; that is, if they remain single-hearted by the Word of God and obey the unction, which leads them on the straight, even way to God. Christ even teaches us that we shall rather use the cunning of the serpent to our advantage against the deceitfulness thereof, however not without the harmlessness of doves, so that we may not become entangled in the net of the lie and seduction.

The divine enlightenment and the unction will teach us all things and remind us when our senses and thoughts stray from the right goal (Christ) and incline towards the side of the flesh, and if we follow the Spirit at all times we shall never stumble or fall. But if we follow the flesh, our light will be darkened and our eyes blinded, that we no longer know ourselves nor find the right way, also accept no further admonition in Christ. So, for this very reason, God still lets the struggle of temptation remain over to us, that our faith may be tried and established as true and revealed whether it is divine or human and that we do not as Eve did, for there is no necessity for eating from the forbidden tree when God offers us enough food so that we do not long for the forbidden kind.

September 1, 1840 (Tuesday); Evening Meeting; I John 2:12

"I write unto you, little children, because your sins are forgiven you for his name's sake."

The forgiveness of sin serves as well to our humiliation as to our comfort: to our humiliation, if we look back upon what we were and whence we came; to our comfort however, if we consider what we have become and to what we are called by the grace of God, namely, new men of God, for with the forgiveness of our sins, the old darkness must have passed away and the power of the devil over us come to an end because he no longer has any claim on us, from which we can conclude that few men have sought and received the forgiveness of their sins, although God offers it to all for Jesus' sake.

For, in that the Son of God appeared in the flesh and was made subject to the law, like a Jew, He came from over the great gulf which is fixed between the lost and the saved (Luke 16), across to us, so as to draw us by His death and resurrection unto Himself on the other side of this great gulf (John 12:32 ff.; 20:17).

"And I, if I be lifted up from the earth, will draw all men unto me.
"This he said, signifying what death he should die."

―――――――

"Jesus saith unto her, Touch me not; for I am not yet ascended to my Father: but go to my brethren, and say unto them, I ascend unto my Father, and your Father; and to my God, and your God."

This passing over takes place now, in this world and time, and the bridge for it is faith, by means of which we, now already, must pass from death over to life and thus we really now *in Christ* stand on the other side and are no longer these of this side (of the world and from beneath, John 8:21 ff.; 5:24; Colossians 3:1 ff.).

"Then said Jesus again unto them, I go my way, and ye shall seek me, and shall die in your sins: whither I go, ye cannot come.

"Then said the Jews, Will he kill himself? because he saith, Whither I go, ye cannot come.

"And he said unto them, Ye are from beneath; I am from above: ye are of this world; I am not of this world."

---

"Verily, verily, I say unto you, He that heareth my word, and believeth on him that sent me, hath everlasting life, and shall not come into condemnation; but is passed from death unto life."

---

"If ye then be risen with Christ, seek those things which are above, where Christ sitteth on the right hand of God.

"Set your affection on things above, not on things on the earth.

"For ye are dead, and your life is hid with Christ in God."

Those who have died and risen with Christ are the real spiritual seed of Abraham, real Hebrews (those who have passed over, those on the other side), and as Abraham, by the call of God, together with his seed, was only a stranger, a foreigner and an alien in the Promised Land, so also are all real children of Abraham and of God in this world. They at most are only suffered here; not native, unknown and yet known, persecuted and accounted as sheep for the slaughter and yet not forsaken. Their daily continuing to stand firm in this world is a daily miracle (Romans 8:35 ff.).

"Who shall separate us from the love of Christ? shall tribulation, or distress, or persecution, or famine, or nakedness, or peril, or sword?

"As it is written, For thy sake we are killed all the day long; we are accounted as sheep for the slaughter.

"Nay, in all these things we are more than conquerors through him that loved us.

"For I am persuaded, that neither death, nor life, nor angels, nor principalities, nor powers, nor things present, nor things to come,

"Nor height, nor depth, nor any other creature, shall be able to separate us from the love of God, which is in Christ Jesus our Lord."

86

And when they are no longer tolerated, they are not sorrowful; they prefer to be at home rather than in this strange land. Now already, all that is the dearest and most precious to them has been brought to safety on the other side; their treasure, their heart, their meditation, walk, citizenship, etc., is above and yonder. When they depart this life, their spirit is snatched away from all the suffering of this time and at their awakening in the last day, their body also will be redeemed from the last power of the enemy and changed in conformity to the transfigured body of Christ (Philippians 3); thereupon their firm hope is based, concerning which they will not come to shame and they let every injustice in this present evil world please them.

And if we should ask why God still lets us remain in this world after He has forgiven us our sins and has accepted us in sonship, the answer is: "Just as Christ, on our account, has come over to us so as to win us, so must we now, on His account, still be here as a testimony so as to save others, together with ourselves, from the principality of darkness," and we shall ever be conscious of our heavenly calling so as to be a light in the name of the Lord.

## Chapter XXVI

### Hatred Is Darkness

August 30, 1840 (Sunday); Morning Meeting (Supplement);
I John 2:11

> "But he that hateth his brother is in darkness, and walketh in darkness, and knoweth not whither he goeth, because that darkness hath blinded his eyes."

Hatred is darkness, the old nature, the devil's kingdom in man; love is light, the new nature, the kingdom of God in man (righteousness, peace, joy). Hatred is a fore-hell; love, a fore-heaven. By hatred, one makes the earthly life, which is already miserable apart from this, unbearable for one another; love however makes it dear and blessed amidst all the sorrows of this time, which are unavoidable and from which no one is exempt, either as a believer or an unbeliever (Psalm 90:10):

> "The days of our years are threescore years and ten; and if by reason of strength they be fourscore years, yet is their strength labour and sorrow; for it is soon cut off, and we fly away."

and even if one lives in splendor and joyfully all his days, he still has a miserable life, full of the fear of death.

The ungodly have no comfort or peace in their sorrows, but the children of God glory in God over the hope of their glory in their tribulations, for they walk in the light and know whither they go; they always have their goal in sight, and from there the jewel to which they hasten, sparkles. This is their mark of distinction, that they love the appearing of the Lord without having to be fearful of it. They would prefer to depart if they did not know that their life and the suffering of this time yielded the fruit of glory. Therefore they are contented with things as they are, for the duration of their suffering is short, and they make life and the tribulation of this time as bearable and as blessed as possible for one another by mutual love. Love has changed them back into men and brethren, as Christ died that He might transfer us from darkness to light, from hatred to love.

But true love is not carnal and blind that it would not punish the sins which destroy men. The blinded world considers the right divine love for the salvation of the lost, hatred toward men, uncharitableness and a condemnatory passion because we deny them life and hope in their unconverted state. However it is not love if I see someone in danger of perishing, who is unaware of it because he is blind, and I do not warn him so as to save him, and if men perish in this way and the watchmen are silent, the blood of the lost will be demanded of them (Ezekiel 3:17 ff.).

> "Son of man, I have made thee a watchman unto the house of Israel: therefore hear the word at my mouth, and give them warning from me.
> "When I say unto the wicked, Thou shalt surely die; and thou givest him not warning, nor speakest to warn the wicked from his wicked way, to save his life; the same wicked man shall die in his iniquity; but his blood will I require at thine hand."

No unconverted man knows himself. All by nature are deceived about their condition. They imagine to be from God and to go to Him and do not know that they are of the devil and are going to him; they are in darkness (for they hate one another) and walk in darkness and know not whither they go. The end of their way is hidden from them like their origin, for what man really believes that he is of the devil (from beneath)?

Truly, one perhaps asks, "Whence am I?" or, "For what purpose am

I here?" but it is not answered according to the truth and therefore he does not become converted. Men are none the less of the devil because they do *not know* or believe it, but all the more so. It is no wonder that the world hates the children of God for it does not know God (Love). But the children of God must love one another—serve, bear and help one another, esteem the other higher than himself—and thus fulfill the law of Christ; and, because they have recognized and experienced the purpose of the sending of Christ, they also love all men in a divine way (for their salvation's sake) and hate no one, for hatred is from the devil but love is from God.

## Chapter XXVII

### The Seed of Life

August 30, 1840 (Sunday); Afternoon Meeting; I John 2:12

"I write unto you, little children, because your sins
are forgiven you for his name's sake."

In what connection does this stand with the foregoing? One might think this an old, unnecessary matter to remind believers of, and yet John writes it very solemnly and indeed for a good reason, just because the forgiveness of sins is taken so lightly, as if it were understandable of itself because Christ died for all men, but only the fewest know what it comprises within itself and how the forgiveness of sin is brought about.

Some would put it at the beginning of life and for that reason baptize infants for the forgiveness of sins (which they have not yet committed) so that they may be saved and not damned. Others place it at the end of life and hope for the mercy of God when they are dead. Others take the Lord's Supper from time to time for the forgiveness of their sins. But all that is the deception of the devil and proof that almost no one any longer knows what the forgiveness of sins is and how it is obtained; namely, neither at the beginning nor at the end of life, but at the time when God calls and awakens one from the death in sin to conversion and the sinner becomes obedient to the call of God, recognizes himself as an ungodly person for whom Christ died and as an ungodly one without works of the law, becomes justified by faith in Christ.

Here then, the coarse and the fine sinners are exactly alike (the pious Pharisee is as the ungodly publican). There is no longer any difference for all boasting of the flesh is at an end (Romans 3). For all, there is only one door—through the forgiveness of sin in the blood of Christ—and whoever is too great, too exalted, too proud and unyielding for that, does, of course, not enter in, but instead is satisfied with his own righteousness through works of the law. Thus, almost all—Jews and Greeks—are annoyed and offended by the preaching of the cross of Christ. The entering-in does not suit them; it is too low and too miserable for such important people, yet it is the only entrance to the church of God, and only those whose former sins have been forgiven for His name's sake, become strong from their weakness and healed from their sickness that they need no longer be subject to sin (Isaiah 33-24).

> "And the inhabitant shall not say, I am sick: the people that dwell therein shall be forgiven their iniquity."

For, by that, the seed of life is sown in man, which, from then on, must continue to grow and develop through all the stages of the life of Christ, unto His perfection—children, young men, fathers—and where that is not the case, there the forgiveness of sins has either never been received or it has not been preserved (II Peter 1), for, with the forgiveness of the former sins, a new life in the Spirit must commence. Therefore John reminds the children of God of their beginning and their entering-in, that they may never forget whence they came, that here none has a preference over another (I Corinthians 1), but just as we were ungodly before the forgiveness of our sins, so must we, after the same, be righteous, and indeed have a righteousness of works, for one does not stand still in the beginning and entrance.

## Chapter XXVIII

### The Three Stages in the Believer's Life

September 3, 1840 (Thursday); Evening Meeting; I John 2:12 ff.

> "I write unto you, little children, because your sins are forgiven you for his name's sake.
> "I write unto you, fathers, because ye have known him that is from the beginning. I write unto you, young men, because ye have overcome the wicked one. I write unto you, little children, because ye have known the Father."

All those who have received forgiveness of their sins are "little children," that is, children of God, and no one can grant the forgiveness of sins except Christ Who died for them. But He awards this comfort to those only whom He sees laboring under their sins—the heavy-laden, the sorrowful and the distressed—and if His servants preach forgiveness of sin in His name, it nevertheless is not permitted to be done to comfort wrongly the uncontrite (as men would like to have it), for whoever is not "little" and pure, humble and innocent and continues to so remain, like a little child, comforts himself in vain with the forgiveness of his sins.

And he who, after having obtained forgiveness, does not grow in Christ through all His stages of life, from childhood to the fulness of manhood, still conceals within himself carnal heights and depths which he does not wish to reveal because he is not upright before God. For only by self-humiliation before God and men does one, in Christ, develop in the growing in God and becomes great by being little and insignificant and ever littler still in his own sight, so that he is neither injured nor aroused to indignation over any outward humiliation because he is aware of having received the *forgiveness of his sins* and is therefore nothing by and of himself.

The children of God must ever remain little children as far as they themselves are concerned and in respect to the evil, even if they have grown ever so much as far as Christ and the good is concerned. They are always in school and have never finished learning the wisdom from above that they could say, "Now we are ready and perfect," for as Jesus Himself, as the Son of man, had to grow and develop like another man, so also must we continually grow in the time of grace until we have attained unto full growth and are ripe for the harvest.

Now, if Christ repelled the temptations of the devil (after His baptism) by the Word of God, we shall know that He read and searched the scriptures from His youth in order that He might be able to give answer of what is written. Thus we find Him already as a twelve-year-old boy, "in the temple, sitting in the midst of the doctors, both hearing them, and asking them questions," and the more faithful we are in the employment of the divine means of grace (searching the scriptures, etc.), the stronger we become in the inner man to overcome the wicked one, like Jesus.

The Word of God is like an apothecary shop and an armory of God, provided with every possible prescription and means which could be employed in any case. So we can always find what is the right thing to do if we, like Jesus, are well acquainted with the same, of which the Spirit (the Unction) reminds us, so as to force the devil to quit the field in all his attacks. But if we do not know what is written, how can we know what the will of God is?

September 6, 1840 (Sunday); Morning Meeting; I John 2:13 ff.

> "I write unto you, fathers, because ye have known him that is from the beginning. I write unto you, young men, because ye have overcome the wicked one. I write unto you, little children, because ye have known the Father.
> "I have written unto you, fathers, because ye have known him that is from the beginning. I have written unto you, young men, because ye are strong, and the word of God abideth in you, and ye have overcome the wicked one."

John makes discrimination in the three different stages of the life of believers in Christ, with a distinct designation of each. He who has received the seed of God—is begotten and born of God—must *as well* grow in Christ and, for this, he must be desirous of the sincere milk (I Peter 2). It is a questionable and dangerous condition if one does *not* grow in spiritual life so as to be able to partake of strong meat, for a standstill is retreat and the way to apostasy (Hebrews 5 and 6).

But there, most assuredly, is a difference between a child and an adult: for the young children in Christ are entrusted to the especial care and solicitude of the angels, who must guard and bear them up in their hands that no harm may befall them (Psalm 91), as we see in the case of the Child Jesus; yet, on the other hand, when He had reached the age of manhood, we see also that He would no longer make use thereof to tempt God but instead, in the use of these very words, He recognized a temptation of the devil which He flatly refused by referring to another word of God (Luke 4).

Thus must the young men themselves also enter the battle with Christ and prove their strength for overcoming the temptations of the devil. Then the good days according to the flesh take an end and the evil days come, when many turn back, like Israel in the desert, who, for this very reason, has been set forth as an example of warning to us, that we lust not after the evil, murmur not against God, nor tempt Christ, like those who perished on that account and did not enter the Promised Land because of unbelief and disobedience.

Young manhood, to be sure, is the most dangerous age, for he who has gone through this stage and matured to manhood in it, has also become insusceptible to the fire thereof and stands all the firmer afterwards as a support of the weak and a father of the children. But this intermediate time with its fiery temptations must be fought out so as to prove to the devil that we have become masters of him by the love of Christ. The temptations in the life of Jesus following His baptism were of this kind when He, for His own person as the Son of man, had to overcome the devil, as proof that Adam could have stood the test, and in order to, afterwards, answer for us as a veritable and approved Man and redeem all those who become obedient to Him from the power of the devil, so that we *in the power of grace* may then likewise overcome the wicked one, like Jesus.

For we should not think there is nothing left to be done by us because Jesus overcame, as He has only opened the way for us that we might follow after Him in faith. He, of course, is always the fighting and suffering One in us (for we must put on Christ by baptism and without Him we do not have this suffering—as long as we are of the world and the devil), yet, by this, we are still only those who suffer *with* Him and must indeed be such in order that afterwards we may also be glorified with Him (Romans 8:17; II Timothy 2:11 ff.).

"And if children, then heirs; heirs of God, and joint-heirs with Christ; if so be that we suffer with him, that we may be also glorified together."

--------

"It is a faithful saying: For if we be dead with him, we shall also live with him:

"If we suffer, we shall also reign with him: if we deny him, he also will deny us:"

September 6, 1840 (Sunday); Afternoon Meeting

By "fathers," we have to understand either actual parents or the most experienced and most approved members of the church, especially the elders, who have the stage of young manhood with all its struggles behind them and therefore are also mature (prepared) in their knowledge and in their judgment of spiritual things, to assist others by advice and deed, and themselves again beget spiritual children of God through the Word of Truth.

This *spiritual* age does indeed not depend upon our *physical* age (there can be young people in the church who are older in Christ than other old people), but still it takes years and great faithfulness to attain to manhood in Christ, and no one should be of the opinion that he could quickly be a man and a father; for the beginning of our life in Christ dates from our rebirth and hardly will there be anyone who grows up in divine life as quickly as Jesus grew up, so that, after twelve or thirty years in grace, he would be as Jesus was at that age.

Even if none of the children of God resemble one another according to their spiritual age (but instead are very different), yet *each one* can be perfect according to *his* measure and age if each one attains unto the example of Christ in that age—if, for instance, a child in Christ is just as faithful, humble, obedient and loving as Jesus as a child was in that age. It is a continuous advancement from childhood to youth and from youth to manhood, and Christ shall be fully and entirely represented in a church in all the stages of His life, and he who has not lived through the preceding stage does not reach the following one.

John therefore characterizes the "fathers" by this, that they "have known him that is from the beginning," that is, the Son of God, and this is the highest degree of perfection because, in that age, Christ is completely set forth as in a transfiguration of His life, for this *knowing* is not a scientific one but is gained by experience.

Of the young men however, John says that they are strong and have overcome the wicked one because the word of God abides in them. Their power of overcoming lies herein, that they do the will of God and in each temptation unto evil, like Joseph, say, "That I cannot do because it is against the will and word of God." Through such faithfulness they eventually advance to a perfect life and the fulness of manhood in Christ. Therefore it is good for one to learn to bear the yoke of Christ in one's youth for afterwards it always becomes more difficult.

September 8, 1840 (Tuesday); Evening Meeting; I John 2:13 ff.

John describes the "children" by this, that they know the Father (or have known Him). It, again, however is not a mere knowing, as one can rehearse something of the Heavenly Father to little children without their having a real idea and understanding of the mystery, that and how God is our spiritual Father. Also, John does not write to little children according to the flesh, but to the reborn children according to the Spirit, who truly know God as *their* Father; just as Jesus, as a child already, knew His Father in Heaven and was convincingly aware of having come from God and the purpose for which He had come into the world, without, of course, His guardian parents telling Him of it (for they themselves did not understand the word of His twelfth year, Luke 2:50):

> "And they understood not the saying which he spake unto them."

for Christ, already at His birth, was what we first become by our rebirth, and from then on we must grow as He increased in age and wisdom and grace.

But a reborn child of God can already, in his way, be perfect too, as we surely must believe it to have been the case with Jesus, that He, already as a child, was perfect in humility, simplicity and obedience and avoided sin (if He also was tempted to it in His human nature like other children), because He knew and loved the Father and was ever with Him in secret. He recognized Himself as a servant of God Who should accomplish our salvation from sin and the power of the devil. Thus must all children of God also be aware and certain of their descent from the Father and of their designation so that they run not in uncertainty; and *otherwise* this is not possible, for they have come from darkness to light and have experienced the great change in themselves by which they have entered into fellowship with the Son of God and the Father and, in the knowledge of Him, have received eternal life.

## Chapter XXIX

### Instruction in Self-Examination

We must beware of considering Jesus as our Reconciler by reason of His substitutional obedience only, without at the same time beholding Him in His divine life as our Example, for He died only for the purpose of putting the hindrance (sin) out of the way so that divine life would come, and the representation of the life of Christ in the church and in every individual believer is the main intention of the entire Gospel. We shall meditate thereupon with all diligence, transfer ourselves into it and let ourselves be overwhelmed by it, and in all that we do, ask: "What must I do to imitate Jesus and to be conformable to Him? What would He have done in my circumstances or what would He do in this case?" and if we are really concerned about it the Spirit will enlighten us and answer.

September 10, 1840 (Thursday); Evening Meeting; I John 2:14

John repeats what he said in verse 13 once more and indeed in reference to the young men, with an enlightening additional word: "I have written unto you, young men, *because ye are strong, and the word of God abideth in you,* and ye have overcome the wicked one."

The scriptures designate the devil almost exclusively or by preference by this name, "the wicked one," although there are still many wicked ones, be they in the invisible world of spirits or in the visible world of men, all of whom however have received the wickedness from him and have become it through him; just as it says of God, " . . . none is good, save one, that is God," although there are still many good ones, all of whom however have received the goodness from Him and have become it through Him. The devil, so to speak, is the wicked principal as God is the Source of everything good.

But now, when we consider the great might of the wicked spirit which he exercises over countless causes as an enemy of God, we must indeed be frightened if we believe what the Word of God tells us (and without this divine instruction we do not know it), that he, through the single sin of *one* man (Adam) has received the power of death and darkness over *all* men! And although the ungodly continually raise the name of the devil to their lips and say it and even swear by him (as by a god) and curse their souls to him, they still do not believe that he is in them and reigns over them (else they could not be so wicked and talk so ungodly). And to this inborn wickedness then, for its development, the influences of the wicked spirits become allied—indeed according to the natural tendencies of individual persons in their likings and their susceptibilities—without whose sway and cooperation, men would not be such perfect villains as is actually the case.

Now, as man from the beginning was not created as evil but as good by God and the evil only afterwards came about by man's own choice and disobedience, so must this evil now be separated from us anew by Christ so that we are not lost and damned eternally with the whole world that lies in wickedness. And now, this separation from the evil again takes place by man's free choice and obedience, if the Gospel, this good news of the possibility of our salvation from the power of Satan, is preached to him (Acts 26:18).

> "To open their eyes, and to turn them from darkness to light, and from the power of Satan unto God, that they may receive forgiveness of sins, and inheritance among them which are sanctified by faith that is in me."

Everyone then must decide for himself whether he wishes to remain in the devil and the death of sin or surrender to Christ, the Good Shepherd, and be fully restored by Him. That is the true Gospel which tells us how we ought to be saved from the wicked one and freed by the good One; that, Jesus has indeed done and accomplished for us, and without His intervention it would have been impossible.

But the redeemed one must then also preserve his freedom, that he may not be entangled and caught anew in the snares of the devil, for even though we have once died unto sin through Christ and our body is not sin itself, it still has a relationship with the world, and by its necessities, desires and longings we are exposed to the dangers of the enchantment and victory of the wicked one, who is always our adversary and intent upon bringing us into his power again, after we have escaped from him. Therefore we must ever be on our guard against ourselves and arm ourselves with prayer so that we do not enter into temptation.

Just as it seems as if an evil person still has and does some good, which however in the deed before God is not good and is without merit, simply because it is ambition and self-righteousness, thus it, as well, seems that the good ones (in Christ) also still have and do many things which are not good, which nevertheless are not accounted unto their condemnation if they are faithful and upright to cleanse and preserve themselves. So when a child of God notices that his mind may become interwoven with the earthly and bring the relation of his body with the visible world into danger, he must then unsparingly cut off and sever all such earthly members and bonds so that he may live for God in the Spirit.

September 13, 1840 (Sunday); Morning Meeting; I John 2:14 ff.

"I have written unto you, fathers, because ye have known him that is from the beginning. I have written unto you, young men, because ye are strong, and the word of God abideth in you, and ye have overcome the wicked one.

"Love not the world, neither the things that are in the world. If any man love the world, the love of the Father is not in him.

"For all that is in the world, the lust of the flesh, and the lust of the eyes, and the pride of life, is not of the Father, but is of the world."

It is needful and important that we learn to know ourselves, where we stand and how far we have advanced in the life of Christ. For this, John gives us methodical instruction, for, as the children know the Father, so are the young men strong for overcoming the wicked one (the strong one, Matthew 12:29) through the power and victory of Christ (I Corinthians 15:57):

> "Or else how can one enter into a strong man's house, and spoil his goods, except he first bind the strong man? and then he will spoil his house."

---

> "But thanks be to God, which giveth us the victory through our Lord Jesus Christ."

but otherwise, the devil is strong over all men, that they must serve him as his household furniture and vessels of dishonor and the wrath of God, on which account then Christ had to enter intermediately to redeem us, and even *we* are not strong by ourselves and in this knowledge of our own weakness we shall pray the Father, "Deliver us from evil." The devil has indeed been overcome and disarmed by Christ's victory on the cross for the believers but not for the unbelieving world (II Corinthians 4:4):

> "In whom the god of this world hath blinded the minds of them which believe not, lest the light of the glorious gospel of Christ, who is the image of God, should shine unto them."

and even the believers must fight to overcome him in the following after Christ.

In this respect, there are but two kinds of people, the one kind are for Christ (against the devil), the other, against Christ (for the devil). He who does not gather with Christ scatters. There is no neutrality here in which one might stand for or please neither one of the two and impartially hover midway between them; neither Christ nor the devil would suffer that (II Corinthians 6). He who at heart is not with Christ is already at heart against Him because a decision is necessary here, for the devil militates against Christ and we must overcome him, which is impossible if we do not fight against him.

Besides, this battle has taken on an especial form since Christ's appearance in the flesh, as the devil has set up a new kingdom under the name of Christ and has given his power and his throne to the beast, and the false prophet has made a speaking image for the beast to worship, by which the true believers must be revealed and become conquerors so as to inherit the kingdom of glory with Christ. Now, he who has not decided for Christ is already on the side of the dragon and worships the beast and his image, even though he does not mean it so (for no worshipper of the beast considers himself as such).

Many do not seem to be against Christ but for Him, until He appears in His believers and saints. Then *those* also, whose real nature up to this time had still remained unrevealed, fight against them. He who would be called a Christian and, in spite of it, is not spiritual, but carnal, and lives and conforms to the world and its statutes, belongs to the realm of the beast, which is a concentrated power of the devil on earth, which the whole world clings to in throngs and worships and swears that it is Christ and His church and yet it is the dragon and his kingdom, which fights against the saints and also overcomes them in the flesh, for we must succumb to him outwardly to overcome him inwardly. Anywhere we may live here is right in the midst of Satan's throne (Revelation 2:13):

> "I know thy works, and where thou dwellest, even where Satan's seat is: and thou holdest fast my name, and hast not denied my faith, even in those days wherein Antipas was my faithful martyr, who was slain among you, where Satan dwelleth."

and we must suffer much on account of witnessing for Christ, and if we love the visible in an idolatrous way, we can then not overcome the wicked one for his power of seduction lies in the visible.

What is the beast? It is the lust of the flesh, the lust of the eyes and the pride of life (the opposite of the love of God), under a spiritual appearance, and because the Spirit of God is not in it, it is the spirit of the devil, adorned with Christian formalities so that there is still a semblance of Christ in it or the deception would be entirely too evident. He then who does not definitely go out therefrom and witness of the truth, does not belong to Christ, and he who conforms to the world cannot overcome.

September 13, 1840 (Sunday); Afternoon Meeting; I John 2:14b

> "I have written unto you, young men, because ye are strong, and the word of God abideth in you, and ye have overcome the wicked one."

"I have written unto you, young men, because ye are strong, and the word of God abideth in you." That, John really did not write, but it is comprised as a component part in the last clause, "ye have overcome the wicked one," and he at the same time shows the way thereto: only he who has grown strong in the Spirit can overcome the wicked one, and if the word of God abides in us we become strong.

The word of God is the seed of God, of which His children are begotten and reborn (I Peter 1); it is of divine nature and makes us participant of the same nature. The development is accomplished gradually through three stages, from one clearness to another (Mark 4:26 ff.):

> "And he said, So is the kingdom of God, as if a man
> should cast seed into the ground;
> "And should sleep, and rise night and day, and the
> seed should spring and grow up, he knoweth not how.
> "For the earth bringeth forth fruit of herself; first
> the blade, then the ear, after that the full corn in the ear."

first the green leaf (childhood), then the stalk with the ear (young manhood), then the ripe fruit (manhood).

Truly, the hope of the coming harvest already lies in the seed, but after the first development a wintertide comes, when the green crop lies covered with snow, as Jesus at this age was obscure in Nazareth. During this quiet time, strength must be developed, and if the word of God remains in it, it will then bring forth fruit which lasts unto eternal life, for the word of God, where it is preserved, is an immortal seed. This quiet, inner development is the most important period and he who, in it, has learned and tasted the difference between good and evil, between the servant of sin (Hebrews 11:15) (below) and of righteousness (Romans 6), would never change or turn back.

> "And truly, if they had been mindful of that country
> from whence they came out, they might have had opportunity to have returned."

We however must not only overcome single impulses of the wicked one, but him, the wicked one, himself, and after that, we must then really take heed to be on our guard, that we are not again captured by the love of the world and that which is in the world because we are still in this world and in the body. And even if we are still *tempted* like Jesus, we nevertheless need not yield, but by the love of Christ, we are made invincible and, as it were, invulnerable (like the so-named Siegfried after he had bathed in the blood of the dragon), for whatever is *in* the world, that is also *of* the world and the devil is behind it. That is loose, unsafe, slippery ground and our senses are easily enticed; so we ought to keep ourselves all the more distant from it and fortify ourselves against it, pluck out the right eye and cut off the right hand unsparingly that may lead us to sin, to lust after the evil, so that we may maintain the freedom of the Spirit like Jesus (Matthew 4).

The earth and the fulness thereof, the body and its members are indeed the Lord's; however the world and the flesh are not the Lord's but the devil exercises his might of sin in them, and the *passing over from the earth to the world and from the body to the flesh is imperceptible as soon as lust comes* (I Corinthians 10). Here we must leave to the devil what is his and give to the Lord what belongs to Him and all that we do shall be done to the glory of God, also eating and drinking with thanksgiving, then it will be sanctified. But sin (the flesh and the world) can never be sanctified; do what one will, it is and always remains to be evil, seductive and hostile towards God. It is no art to live carnally—anyone can do that—but it *is* an art to live spiritually, and only a saint can do it.

## Chapter XXX

### "Love Not the World"

September 15, 1840 (Tuesday); Evening Meeting; I John 2:14 ff.

"Love not the world, neither the things that are in the world. If any man love the world, the love of the Father is not in him.

"For all that is in the world, the lust of the flesh, and the lust of the eyes, and the pride of life, is not of the Father, but is of the world.

"And the world passeth away, and the lust thereof: but he that doeth the will of God abideth for ever."

John gives no further instructions to the fathers in Christ with respect to that which concerns this life, because they themselves know Him Who is from the beginning. However he found that the young men needed an admonition, although they are no longer beginners but already stand in Christ's middle age and are strong; yet, right here, admonition is most necessary: "Love not the world, neither the things that are in the world."

*World* in this sense is not the great mass of people, even though they are wicked (for in this respect God loved the world and we also shall love all men as men), but it is the evil in the world, inasmuch as the devil through it draws men unto destruction. Indeed, not all the visible (the earthly, the perishable) is evil in itself, but only becomes so by the misuse that men make of it if they put their love in and lust after it; it indeed is to be used only for our needs and to the glory of God. For love is the innermost impulse (the holiest) of man and if it is bestowed idolatrously and carnally upon anything beside God, it then is the greatest misuse, the most horrible perversion and desecration of the holy (a serving of idols), for our love belongs only to God; and although we shall love our neighbor as ourselves, yet we need not be fearful of an over-measure or rivalry in it with our love to God if we love our neighbor with a spiritual, holy and divine love. But we shall not love the things of this world, our heart shall not cling to them, or the love to God is impossible and we lose possession thereof and are instead possessed by them (mammon).

Thus the rich of this world are not masters but slaves of their riches and those who wish to become rich fall into temptation and the snares of the devil to their own damnation (I Timothy 6). We may indeed have the earthly also and enjoy it in simplicity and with thanksgiving, as much as God gives us of it, but our heart shall be as free therefrom as if we did not have it (I Corinthians 7), so that we could also get along without it and would not give ourselves over to earthly sorrow and death if it were taken from us—yes, even then could thank and praise God, like Job.

*That* Paul had learned, to be content with what he had or did not have (Philippians 4) and we have to learn that too in the school of Christ, and we shall not follow Christ so as to have good days in the flesh. It is still easier to suffer want than to have an abundance and use it rightly. Now just *this* is the art of faith, to possess the earthly without loving it.

We have two wrong ways or errors to avoid in this respect. The one is the idolatrous seeking after the visible, the sensual and the perishable, in all lust of the flesh and of the eyes and the pride of life (ostentation of riches), also the inclination for and aiming after much. On the other side, few indeed stand, but alas! otherwise earnest souls who, through error, fall into the opposite deception, are relentlessly hard on their body, vilify earthly gifts, meats and the stations of life with scornful and remonstrant speech and seek holiness in self-chosen, bodily exercise (mortification) instead of in true godliness (I Timothy 4; Colossians 2), and while they would like to avoid the whirlpool

102

of Charybdis, they are shipwrecked on the cliff of Scylla (I Timothy 1).

Between both of these dangers, the truly godly man directs his course, who is easily satisfied in earthly things without, for that reason, despising them or loving them, because he seeks the Veritable, loves God and would please only Him.

September 17, 1840 (Thursday); Evening Meeting; I John 2:15 ff.

If one would say to the natural man, "Love not the world, neither the things that are in the world," it is preached to deaf ears. They can neither grasp this nor comply to it because a carnal mind is inseparably united and grown together with that which is in the world and cannot possibly love God. The lust and the love of world is his life and this life must first die with Christ before the life of God can come forth in the souls (Romans 8).

The unconverted man has no mind for God at all, but is dead and an enemy of His because he is an idolater, as one who seeks and loves only the sensual and is never sated with it. He offers up all his time and strength, body and soul, to this idol of the world and if he dies in that way, he is eternally lost and poor because he lived like a fool (Luke 12). In all eternity he cannot see everlasting life because he does not have his delight and pleasure in God, but is and walks in darkness; for eternal life begins in children of God in this time.

The first step toward eternal life therefore is the knowledge that one is dead and lost by nature and the conviction that he must be converted from the power of Satan to be redeemed and saved: for men are not first lost after they have spent their entire life in the service of sin and vanity, but they serve the lust of the world *because they are already lost.* Because God does not wish the death of the sinner but that he should be converted and live (Ezekiel 33) is the reason why God lets us be warned so faithfully, and whoever will not be warned will simply have to be lost eternally. He who will not let himself be counseled is not to be helped.

Therefore the commandment, "Love not the world," is not the first but the last one; it is given to the young men in Christ, who are strong enough to do it. The mere reminding them suffices; they then already know what they have to do; they need not be told twice so as to be acceptable to God: for if the children in Christ already know the Father, how much more then the young men who have already grown in Christ! But if we love God with all our heart, we then also know how to appraise all other things according to their true worth, without despising the creature or putting him in the place of God.

Moreover, how endlessly great is the difference between the children of God and the children of this world! The former *have* the living God and possess all things in Him; to Him they commend all things; they have nothing to fear and nothing to lose in this world; without His will not one hair falls from their head (Matthew 28:18):

> "And Jesus came and spake unto them, saying, All power is given unto me in heaven and in earth."

whether they live or die they are the Lord's. They know the answer to the question, "What is your only comfort in life and in death?" by their own experience. —But the children of this world are the opposite of this; they have no God and no anchor for their souls; they are dead in life and lost in death.

## Chapter XXXI

## The Alluring Fruits

September 20, 1840 (Sunday); Morning Meeting; I John 2:15 ff.

> "Love not the world, neither the things that are in the world. If any man love the world, the love of the Father is not in him.
> "For all that is in the world, the lust of the flesh, and the lust of the eyes, and the pride of life, is not of the Father, but is of the world.
> "And the world passeth away, and the lust thereof: but he that doeth the will of God abideth for ever."

The love of the world is dangerous and a hard battle is required to overcome it: (a) because it is our natural life; and (b) because the love of God cannot subsist with it and man cannot be saved, for where one's treasure is there one's heart is also. If one is lost it is on account of the love to the world. Some are not freed from these snares of the devil all their life long and others return again to this slavery, like Demas. The entire aim and inclination of natural man is wrong.

The tree of sin is already implanted in all by nature and should be done battle with and uprooted in one's youth by a bringing up in the Lord, but, instead of that, it is still more zealously taken care of in the world by the wrong education and bad examples and watered by the lust of the eyes and of the flesh and the pride of life. For that reason it is not to be wondered at that the young people are so unruly and "of no account." However we shall have no regrets for spending so much effort in combating the sensuous inclinations; it will be abundantly rewarded.

The love of the world and of that which is in and of the world is an idolatrous service; that is, a worshipping of the devil (according to I Corinthians 10:20).

> "But I say, that the things which the Gentiles sacrifice, they sacrifice to devils, and not to God: and I would not that ye should have fellowship with devils."

Here man is in darkness; and after we, by Christ, have come into the light again and have become children of God, we stand in trial and temptation like Adam. The forbidden tree of knowledge is the world. God, here, speaks very determinately to us, "Do not love it." This tree stretches its ravishing branches and alluring fruits out everywhere—we need not reach far—and the devil, the old serpent, sits in it, and says, "Fear not to eat of it; you will not die." But whoever eats thereof will die again (Romans 8; II Peter 2). Adam indeed died for *all* and all are dead by nature on account of his evil desire. But now, whoever has eaten of the Tree of Life and afterwards allows himself to lust after the evil again and eats of the forbidden tree of the world, dies *for himself alone,* but eternally, for he again turns to his own vomit and again wallows in the mud, after he has been washed.

Both of these, the washing away of our former sins on the part of God and the vomiting up of the same on the part of man, constitute the conversion by which one comes from darkness to the light; that is, comes to the knowledge of God and no longer turns his back on, but his eyes toward, God so as to be enlightened and made alive by Him. And the more fully man turns to God, the more will he be enlightened, even unto high noon. But the devil reigns in darkness (in the lust and love of the world) and whoever has never as yet vomited and detested that, that one is not yet converted at all from Satan's power unto God. There are many, too, who do not even wish to be converted.

Now, if we think we would have done better in Adam's place than he did, we can make the test of it as long as God allows us to remain in this world after our rebirth. Besides, we still have an advantage over Adam as far as overcoming is concerned, for, before the fall, he did not know what death, which was threatened to him, was. But we know it because we were first in death and only afterwards came unto life, so that the difference between the two should teach us to choose the good and reject the evil, for the eating of the Tree of Life saves us and shall also bring us so far that we become dead and have died for all other desire, even though hard fighting is required for this. Adam and Eve had the longing only and fell. Therefore we must guard ourselves from the first impulses of the desire for evil so that we may not fall as they fell.

## Chapter XXXII

### Enemies of the Cross of Christ

September 20, 1840 (Sunday); Afternoon Meeting

The confusion of men and their turning away from God shows itself nowhere more horribly than in the choice of the pleasures in which they seek gratification of their lust, in things that are vain, perishable, foolish, unreasonable, inhumane, bestial and devilish, that a real man of God must be ashamed and have a disgust and abhorrence of them, and pity the poor creatures that are called men and should be of the image of God, destined for fellowship with Him, and yet find pleasure in such miserable, shameful lusts and besides wish to be called wise! By this one can see how deeply man has fallen and indeed the higher he stands in the world, the more deeply he is sunk in his pleasures, the more foolish his joy. As man is, so is his pleasure and as his lust, so is he himself. No trace of the image of God remains over where one can have one's heart in such dissolute pleasure in which a man of God could take no part at all in any of it (I Peter 4): however for him it is no denial, to him it is no privation.

The lust and pleasure of the world is just as much foolishness to the children of God as the joy in the Holy Ghost is foolishness to the men of the world, for as righteousness, peace and joy in the Holy Ghost is the kingdom of God, so also is the lust of the flesh and the lust of the eyes and the pride of life the kingdom of the devil, in man. Therefore everyone who wishes to become wise in God must become a fool in the world, and in the end the men of the world are the real fools because they have not had God and His kingdom; and when one advises them to save their souls, it seems ridiculous to them (Genesis 19:14).

> "And Lot went out, and spake unto his sons in law,
> which married his daughters, and said, Up, get you out
> of this place; for the Lord will destroy this city. But he
> seemed as one that mocked unto his sons in law."

The fact that men seek their desire and gratification in the world is proof that they are in the devil and serve him—do his will—during which time they imagine they are doing what *they* want to do and are free: for we see by Christ (Matthew 4) that the devil gives the pleasures and glory of the world only to those who worship him as God: then they are his vassals.

The children of God, of course, still dwell in the mortal body and on this account are exposed to the temptations of the world and the devil; but, on the other hand, they, as well, bear the kingdom of God within them (Luke 17) and have received the power in Christ to rule over themselves, so that they do not even do what *they wish,* much less that which the devil wishes (Galatians 5). This is the great difference between the children of God and the children of the devil: the children of God are vassals of God.

Christ took over the realm in their hearts after He had destroyed the realm of the devil in them and He gives and entrusts it to them to govern in His name (Psalm 8; Hebrews 2); they bridle their tongue; they have made a covenant with their eyes (Job 31:1) (below); they lock their doors and windows when they notice that death would like to force itself in through evil lusting; they do not serve their palate and belly but the living God with body and soul.

> "I made a covenant with mine eyes; why then should
> I think upon a maid?"

These are the signs of the lordship of the *indwelling* kingdom of God, and after they have thus walked for a time in faith and as forsaken of God (II Corinthians 5) and are found faithful in the least in the government of the inner kingdom of God, they are later set over much in the revelation of the kingdom and glory of God unto His children.

Sin and worldly pleasures are far beneath the dignity of men. Whoever has learned to respect and value himself after a godly manner, whereunto we are destined according to the will of God, can no longer devote himself to and stain himself with them. However he who does so, brings shame upon himself and upon his human dignity . . . . .

The children of the world and of the devil are very ingenious and adroit in the gratification of their carnal lusts and desires, so as to drive tediousness away and to waste their precious time of grace in pleasure and miserable child's play and nonsense. In that they possess unbelievable skill. They consider what the children of God do for the salvation of their souls a useless waste of time, but their own foolishness and vanity they do not consider as such. The devil flattered the first men with this, that their eyes would be opened if they ate from the forbidden tree. But in opposition to this, the Gospel of Christ comes so that man's eyes may be opened in order that he may again know God.

September 22, 1840 (Tuesday); Evening Meeting; I John 2:15-17

> "Love not the world, neither the things that are in the world. If any man love the world, the love of the Father is not in him.
> "For all that is in the world, the lust of the flesh, and the lust of the eyes, and the pride of life, is not of the Father, but is of the world.
> "And the world passeth away, and the lust thereof: but he that doeth the will of God abideth for ever."

John contrasts that which is of the Father and that which is of the world and indeed so, that he who has the one in his heart and mind, cannot, at the same time, seek and love the other because no one can serve two masters, God and the world (mammon) (Matthew 6). One can likewise not satsify both, for, him who would cling to God and please Him only, the world hates and persecutes (II Timothy 3:12).

> "Yea, and all that will live godly in Christ Jesus shall suffer persecution."

But whoever loves the world and what is in it, is an enemy of the cross of Christ and of God, although he himself may perhaps not intend to be that, just because the heart cannot be divided; for when Paul, with tears, writes (Philippians 3) of such enemies of the cross of Christ, he does not at all mean the Jews or the heathen—it is not to be wondered at that they take offense at the Word from the Cross—but he says it of the members of the church who flee the cross and are ashamed of the reproach of Christ because, fundamentally, they are earthly minded and their belly is their god and therefore their end is damnation.

Now, the more shocking this thought is, the more carefully must we examine our hearts to see whether we are in the faith, whether Jesus Christ is in us and our walk is in heaven, so that we do not become objectionable and disqualified for the future kingdom of glory. For as the entire life of those who care and are minded for the earthly is lost together with them themselves, thus, on the other hand, the soul of those who do the will of God is saved together with their work so that both remain in eternity.

However, that we may be aware of what the will of God is, we must *first* know the will of God and then *secondly* be enlightened by the Spirit of God and led into all truth so as to *at all times* do that which is acceptable before God, to prove what is good and evil, so that the good may be chosen and the evil rejected and when we are devoted only to that which is of the Father, His kingdom and His righteousness, we then have the promise also that He will never leave nor forsake us, so we are unafraid (Hebrews 13:5, 6 and 13 ff.).

"Let your conversation be without covetousness; and be content with such things as ye have: for he hath said, I will never leave thee, nor forsake thee.

"So that we may boldly say, The Lord is my helper, and I will not fear what man shall do unto me."

---

"Let us go forth therefore unto him without the camp, bearing his reproach.

"For here have we no continuing city, but we seek one to come.

"By him therefore let us offer the sacrifice of praise to God continually, that is, the fruit of our lips giving thanks to his name."

But if we walk so faithfully according to the rule of the Spirit as to always do the will of God that He so knows our heart, we shall then not fear the unjust criticism of men, who are not able to know how we are minded, when even brothers would misinterpret and misjudge us (I Corinthians 4:1 ff.).

"Let a man so account of us, as of the ministers of Christ, and stewards of the mysteries of God.

"Moreover it is required in stewards, that a man be found faithful.

"But with me it is a very small thing that I should be judged of you, or of man's judgment: yea, I judge not mine own self.

"For I know nothing by myself; yet am I not hereby justified: but he that judgeth me is the Lord.

"Therefore judge nothing before the time, until the Lord come, who both will bring to light the hidden things of darkness, and will make manifest the counsels of the hearts: and then shall every man have praise of God."

In this we shall not be hasty in our judgment of others but wait until the Lord comes, Who will bring to light the hidden things and reveal the counsels of the hearts and each one shall then receive his praise of God; but where the mind is manifestly earthly and the walk carnal, there we also can and shall judge and punish.

## Chapter XXXIII

### The Mirror of the Word of God

September 24, 1840 (Thursday); Evening Meeting; 1 John 2:15 ff.

Has the admonition of the apostle now accomplished its purpose on us that we are healed from the love of the world? For we do not reflect upon the Word of God that it may pass by us without bearing fruit; instead we look into it as into a bright mirror to behold how we ourselves are fashioned before God (James 1), for if we do not do so, the Word shall then not save but condemn us.

Now, when John takes as his reason for wishing to make the love of the world sickening to us the fact that the world and its lust passes away, it is not meant as all men themselves *already know* that all visible things are perishable (they also say, "Let us eat and drink for tomorrow we die"), but because the love of the world disqualifies us for the love, fellowship and salvation of God and accordingly hurls us into damnation. For the love of the world is the first death in Adam and he who is not awakened from it and healed by Christ (converted) in the time of grace, abides in the second death eternally because he has lived without God and without hope in the world, in that he continued to remain captured by the earthly as by a lime twig of the devil. So he, whom the beholding and knowledge of the vanity and perishableness of all visible things does not make wiser unto salvation for the purpose of seeking the Veritable and Eternally-abiding, is still a fool, nonsensical (Titus 3:3) (below), as we by nature all are, and still walks on the wrong ways of sin (Ecclesiastes).

> "For we ourselves also were sometimes foolish, disobedient, deceived, serving divers lusts and pleasures, living in malice and envy, hateful, and hating one another."

And everyone, who, by the mirror of the Word of God, comes to the knowledge of himself, must grieve over his death and perdition and the time he lost, the fruit of which he must now be ashamed of (Matthew 5; Romans 6), and he then begins to hunger and thirst after righteousness until he is comforted and filled by the Gospel of Christ, for Christ came that His sheep might have life and all fulness. These then see and confess that nothing beside God is able to quiet and satisfy the necessity and longing of our spirit.

It is just this emptiness, desolation and bewilderment—this longing, gnawing and burning of the human spirit—which drives one about everywhere in the world, restlessly seeking rest and contentment without finding it. Like butterflies on flowers, wandering men settle themselves on earthly pleasures and sensual joys and ever remain empty. Yes, as wine and gambling only urge those who yield to them further on, so it is also with every sensual enjoyment: their servants are ever bound more tightly so that they can no longer do otherwise. In whatever one sins by that he is punished. For all the contention in the world is caused by the carnal lusts and one is a devil to the other; and if they then die in that condition without having found and tasted the living God, their gnawing worm does not die and their burning fire is unquenchable (Mark 9). Just for this reason, Jesus invites the miserable, wretched, straying ones to come unto Him and find rest for their poor souls (Matthew 11).

We shall, by no means, consider conversion to God a grievous matter, by reason of which one could have no further joy and becomes awry, gloomy and useless. The devil actually says this to those who do not know what conversion is, to frighten them away. But the spirit of man finds its right element, peace and joy, only in God—just that which it lacks, which he seeks and which is not to be found in the world. Therefore we must turn our back to the world and its perishable, vain lusts and our face to God; then we are helped.

September 27, 1840 (Sunday); Morning Meeting; I John 2:16 ff.

> "For all that is in the world, the lust of the flesh, and the lust of the eyes, and the pride of life, is not of the Father, but is of the world.
> "And the world passeth away, and the lust thereof: but he that doeth the will of God abideth for ever."

To observe the standard which John gives us is dependent upon our learning to discern what is good and evil; namely, what is of the Father and what is not of the Father but of the world (Hebrews 5). But no natural man can do that; they judge all this reversely, call the good (which is of God) evil and the evil (which is of the world and the devil) good, and *in this* the highest in this world are stricken with the same blindness as the lowest and must pass away in their false wisdom (Isaiah 5; I Corinthians 2). That is why their eyes must be opened and enlightened, but in a different way from that which the serpent had promised; at that time they were enchanted and now they must be disenchanted; for the mind of the flesh is enmity against God and death, but the mind of the Spirit is life and joy.

The mark of the unconverted man is his proneness to that which is in and of the world. All things first touch the outer senses of man, until he, through extremity and misery, begins to reflect and returns to (enters into) himself so as to find God anew and let His kingdom be set up in his heart (Luke 15). Then we shall no longer conform to this world but shall be changed by the renewing of our mind, to prove what the good, acceptable and perfect will of God is (Romans 12). What we would accept must have the stamp of the Father in Heaven if we are to become rich in God. If the people of the world fumble money over two or three times and look it over to determine whether it is counterfeit so as not to be deceived, we ought to be much more cautious and take things exact in spiritual matters. The earthly is only for our needs, not for pleasure; we shall not strive after temporal riches, honor and good living, in which is only restlessness for this present time and condemnation thereafter.

Every good and every perfect gift comes down to us from above, from the Father of Lights; in them is rest, joy, peace and invariableness; in God we have everything; godliness is the greatest gain (James 1; I Timothy 4). God does not permit His children to die of hunger in the world if they presently strive not after the earthly but the heavenly, although Paul had to suffer hunger and nakedness, but God has put His servants in the nethermost place in the church as those destined to die. For that reason, so many decline with thanks to be followers of Christ under the cross and prefer to have things comfortable according to the flesh. But the man of God shuns that which is of the world and pursues after righteousness, godliness, faith, etc., so as to lay hold on eternal life (I Timothy 6:10 ff.).

"For the love of money is the root of all evil: which while some coveted after, they have erred from the faith, and pierced themselves through with many sorrows.

"But thou, O man of God, flee these things; and follow after righteousness, godliness, faith, love, patience, meekness.

"Fight the good fight of faith, lay hold on eternal life, whereunto thou art also called, and hast professed a good profession before many witnesses."

That is why John calls to the young men, "Be on your guard for counterfeit money. Investigate everything carefully to ascertain whether it is of the Father or of the world!" Now, he who strives only for the things of God is considered a fool in the world, but the fools do not know that they themselves are fools (Luke 12:20).

"But God said unto him, Thou fool, this night thy soul shall be required of thee: then whose shall those things be, which thou hast provided?"

## Chapter XXXIV

### The Anti-Christ

September 27, 1840 (Sunday); Afternoon Meeting; I John 2:18 ff.

"Little children, it is the last time: and as ye have heard that anti-christ shall come, even now are there many anti-christs; whereby we know that it is the last time.

"They went out from us, but they were not of us; for if they had been of us, they would no doubt have continued with us: but they went out, that they might be made manifest that they were not all of us."

The apostle now turns to the children in Christ and speaks to them of the future, to warn them of another danger which however comes from the same source, namely, from the disposition of the flesh, in a spiritual garb. "Children, it is the last hour; and, as you have heard, the anti-christ is coming and even now there are many anti-christs."

If the last hour of the world began already 1,800 years ago, what still remains of it now? And if there were already *at that time* many anti-Christs in the *church,* then the world is filled with anti-Christs now, and if the personal anti-Christ was to be expected at that time, then, by now, he has come already, long ago.

**113**

His spirit was in the world long before him and prepared his kingdom for him and now it is so general and extended that we must take heed that we ourselves do not belong to it or are infected by his spirit, while we are of the opinion that we are *Christians*. For there are no anti- or institutional-Christians other than those who bear and wish to bear the name Christian: for, as there is only *one Christ,* but by His Spirit He has set up a dwelling-place in many who, by it, have become Christians, so also is there only *one anti-Christ* but his spirit is in many, who keep his commandments.

An anti-Christ is anyone who has the name of Christ but does not have His Spirit and Life, who, with His name, is carnally and earthly minded, for the spirit of the anti-Christ is precisely the same spirit that is in the world, only that it has taken on a new stamp or character, and each institutional-Christian is also an oppositionist-Christian because *thereby* the kingdom of God is reversed into an outward form, concerning which the worshippers of the beast are very obstinate and hate and persecute the real Christians.

This spirit was at work already in the time of the apostles. More and more feigned and half-confused members continually forced their way into the church of Christ and leavened the whole of it, up to the time of Constantine, 300 years later, out of which then the Roman bishop went forth as a pope and head, who set himself above and rose up against all gods and lords of the earth (II Thessalonians 2), in that the dragon, under the name of Christ (viceroy of Christ), gave him his throne and great might.

For that reason, we shall be fearful not only of the anti-Christ who will come at a future time, but of the real one whose kingdom is actually in the world, that we obey not his human commands, by which he has displaced and weakened the commandments of Christ. These have to do with that which is within, with a holy life; those, with that which is outward. Now, if one has that which is outward, practises and accepts it and does not have the life of Christ, he is an anti-Christ, appear he as lovely as ever he will.


September 29, 1840 (Tuesday); Evening Meeting; I John 2:18

If God let us be told, "It is the last hour," what would we think? Would we not have to consider it a summons and an alarm: "Prepare yourselves, hold yourselves in readiness, the Lord is coming!" (Compare Luke 12:35 ff.)

"Let your loins be girded about, and your lights burning;

"And ye yourselves like unto men that wait for their lord, when he will return from the wedding; that when he cometh and knocketh, they may open unto him immediately.

"Blessed are those servants, whom the lord when he cometh shall find watching: verily I say unto you, that he shall gird himself, and make them to sit down to meat, and will come forth and serve them.

"And if he shall come in the second watch, or come in the third watch, and find them so, blessed are those servants.

"And this know, that if the goodman of the house had known what hour the thief would come, he would have watched, and not have suffered his house to be broken through.

"Be ye therefore ready also: for the Son of man cometh at an hour when ye think not."

The coming of Christ is certain, but the time thereof is uncertain and for that reason we must ever expect it, watch and be prepared (I Thessalonians 5). But the day of Christ could not come unless apostasy from Christ—general unbelief—had preceded it, when men lie buried in carnal security as in the time of the flood. That is the surest sign of the approaching appearance of Christ. He comes for the world as a thief in the night, unawaited and suddenly, that there is no more escape, for when He comes, He comes for judgment of the unbelieving world and for the deliverance of His oppressed believers, who cry to Him day and night (Luke 18; II Thessalonians 1 and 2).

If we do not believe that the world is full of anti-Christians, that we live in the midst of anti-Christendom, we can then not earnestly believe in the coming of Christ either, let alone prepare ourselves for it, and we are as secure as if there were no danger! The more mockers that arise, saying, "Where is the promise of his coming?" etc., the nearer it is (II Peter 3:4 ff.).

"And saying, Where is the promise of his coming? for since the fathers fell asleep, all things continue as they were from the beginning of the creation.

"For this they willingly are ignorant of, that by the word of God the heavens were of old, and the earth standing out of the water and in the water:

"Whereby the world that then was, being over-flowed with water, perished:

"But the heavens and the earth, which are now, by the same word are kept in store, reserved unto fire against the day of judgment and perdition of ungodly men.

"But, beloved, be not ignorant of this one thing, that one day is with the Lord as a thousand years, and a thousand years as one day.

"The Lord is not slack concerning his promise, as some men count slackness; but is longsuffering to us-ward, not willing that any should perish, but that all should come to repentance.

"But the day of the Lord will come as a thief in the night; in the which the heavens shall pass away with a great noise, and the elements shall melt with fervent heat, the earth also and the works that are therein shall be burned up.

"Seeing then that all these things shall be dissolved, what manner of persons ought ye to be in all holy conversation and godliness,

"Looking for and hasting unto the coming of the day of God, wherein the heavens being on fire shall be dissolved, and the elements shall melt with fervent heat?

"Nevertheless we, according to his promise, look for new heavens and a new earth, wherein dwelleth righteousness.

"Wherefore, beloved, seeing that ye look for such things, be diligent that ye may be found of him in peace, without spot, and blameless.

"And account that the longsuffering of our Lord is salvation; even as our beloved brother Paul also according to the wisdom given unto him hath written unto you;

"As also in all his epistles, speaking in them of these things; in which are some things hard to be understood, which they that are unlearned and unstable wrest, as they do also the other scriptures, unto their own destruction.

"Ye therefore, beloved, seeing ye know these things before, beware lest ye also, being led away with the error of the wicked, fall from your own stedfastness."

From now on, until the return of Christ, there will be but few believers who have Christ's Spirit and Life, but all the more false Christians. It is just as though the present world had been given over to the anti-Christ, where he reigns with authority and unrighteousness and privileges all manner of sin under the name of Christ.

That is why the true Christians must leave the modern world to the anti-Christians and be resigned to suffer in order that they may inherit the future one, the new earth in which righteousness dwells, on which also the whole creation will be put back into its original paradisaical state of freedom. From the beginning, this thousand-year kingdom was the exclusive hope of the saints, but now it has become a mockery (Chiliads, etc.); and as this unbelief is a just judgment of God over the world, they can thereby not detain the coming of Christ but only hasten it.

October 1, 1840 (Thursday); Evening Meeting; I John 2:18 ff.

"Ye have heard that anti-christ shall come, . . . " Thus this, at that time, was a sure thing and a teaching for warning the believers against allowing themselves to be led astray by false spirits. But for this, one must be able to prove and discern the spirits, which is possible only if one has and knows the Spirit of Christ, so as to set the truth and the lie up against each other. All others are not only exposed to every seducer, but they have already been led astray and deceived, for actually no one can be misled except him who walks on the right way. That the false so-called Christians are not on the right way to eternal life is revealed by their ungodly walk, for the kingdom of God does not subsist in the knowing but in the doing.

But now, the false Christians, who have never seen nor known Christ, think that they, in and by themselves by nature and birth, are Christians, that they need not further trouble and worry themselves about it—they shall not come amiss—and that they have to guard themselves of nothing as much as from the seduction of a new teaching and conversion to a new faith. They will adhere firmly to the old so as to, by no means, become renewed in Christ, and do not know that just the old itself is the mark and seal of the anti-Christ. They fear and warn only of Christ and conversion to Him in apprehension of being enlightened from their darkness. Yes, they are so certain in the matter, that their wrong is right, that they blaspheme, spit at and crucify Christ wherever they may find Him in His members and believers; that is why it is so difficult for anyone to be converted.

Even as much as the apostles suffered on this account at the hands of the Jews and the heathen, it is still much harder now than at that time because of the deception in which all have been caught by believing that they are Christians *without conversion;* for who at present believes that there is an anti-Christ in the world and that he reigns? Yes, and

117

who of all of them thinks with regard to himself that he is an anti-Christian? Is the world any the less full of anti-Christians for that reason? (Because of the many trees the anti-Christians do not see the forest (Paul's complaint II Corinthians 11:4.).)

> "For if he that cometh preacheth another Jesus, whom we have not preached, or if ye receive another spirit, which ye have not received, or another gospel, which ye have not accepted, ye might well bear with him."

For, certainly, the anti-Christ comes as little under this name as the devil himself (II Corinthians 11).

Under these circumstances, we shall observe whether it is not necessary for us to first be converted so as to become Christians and whether we ought not to be fearful of the anti-Christ in the world and whether we do not have to be persecuted on account of the truth, along with all those who have *at any time* belonged to Christ: for never yet have great numbers walked on the narrow, dangerous path of life but only the fewest; great numbers however walk on the broad way to destruction and even if one offers them salvation in Christ they will still not have it.

But now it is the reversed condition from what it was in the time of the apostles. At that time the church as a whole was holy and the ones who were pretentions separated themselves from it. Now however, the church in general is an anti-Christendom and the true Christians, for that reason, must separate themselves from it so as not to become partakers of its sins and punishments.

If we could find the Spirit and Life of Christ in the world, we would be willing to remain in the state church, for we seek only Christ; but if we do not find the love of the brethren and the fellowship of saints, in spite of all the outward profession, it then is not the church of Christ and we dare have nothing to do with it.

October 4, 1840 (Sunday); Morning Meeting; I John 2:18 ff.

> "Little children, it is the last time: and as ye have heard that anti-christ shall come, even now are there many anti-christs; whereby we know that it is the last time.
>
> "They went out from us, but they were not of us; for if they had been of us, they would no doubt have continued with us: but they went out, that they might be made manifest that they were not all of us.
>
> "But ye have an unction from the Holy One, and ye know all things."

In the Old Testament, the devil fought against God so as to ruin His people Israel for Him and to frustrate His first household; in the New Testament, he instated a representative, the anti-Christ, and through him strives against Christ so as to make His kingdom contentious for Him amongst men, in that he has perverted the institution of salvation into an institution of destruction for most men.

For what is Christ and His kingdom? He is a King of Truth, of Righteousness and of Peace (John 18:36 ff.; Hebrews 7 and 1:8 ff.):

> "Jesus answered, My kingdom is not of this world: if my kingdom were of this world, then would my servants fight, that I should not be delivered to the Jews: but now is my kingdom not from hence.
>
> "Pilate therefore said unto him, Art thou a king then? Jesus answered, Thou sayest that I am a king. To this end was I born, and for this cause came I into the world, that I should bear witness unto the truth. Every one that is of the truth heareth my voice.
>
> "Pilate saith unto him, What is truth? And when he had said this, he went out again unto the Jews, and saith unto them, I find in him no fault at all."

---

> "But unto the Son he saith, Thy throne, O God, is for ever and ever: a sceptre of righteousness is the sceptre of thy kingdom.
>
> "Thou hast loved righteousness, and hated iniquity; therefore God, even thy God, hath anointed thee with the oil of gladness above thy fellows."

and thus is His kingdom also, and by this divine nature of His all His subjects are to be known, that they do the will of God and no longer the will of the devil, like the unconverted, who live in unrighteousness, lies, hypocrisy, malice, envy, strife, war, lust of the flesh, pride, etc., even though they bear the name of Christ. But the firm foundation of God still stands and has this seal, "Let every one that nameth the name of Christ depart from iniquity."

From this, it is clear that the nominal Christians are not subjects of Christ but anti-Christians, for they have not been freed from their old devilish nature so as to serve Christ in truth and love, in righteousness, in peace and the joy of the Holy Ghost (Romans 14). Whoever does not serve Christ surely serves the anti-Christ, for every person must serve a master: here, there are no absolute lords who would be their own lord and master to do as they pleased. The unconverted cannot do what they would like if they commit sin (Romans 7) and the converted are not permitted to do what they like but what God wills (Galatians 5), namely righteousness, not humanness which insists strictly upon its demands, but the divine which accomplishes the good unto all men and seeks peace with all as much as is possible; they prefer to suffer wrong than to do it or to firmly demand their rights; by all the injustice they do not open their mouths; to him who smites them on the one cheek they turn the other also and him who takes their coat they let have their cloak as well (Matthew 5; I Peter 2:23).

> "Who, when he was reviled, reviled not again; when
> he suffered, he threatened not; but committed himself to
> him that judgeth righteously:"

This is what the disciples and subjects of Christ are, but where does one find this mind in the nominal Christians? Each one feels that he needs not leave unrequited any wrong done to him. That is what anti-Christendom is, which adorns itself with the name of Christ, and is opposed to His kingdom.

Thus has the devil won again in the world under the New Testament as well, with the mask of the anti-Christ, who had to come after Christ and has come, according to the prophecy. This is the highest culmination of sin and is all the more a serious matter for us since there does not, after this time of the New Testament, follow another time as there was another time prophesied in the Old Testament, namely, the coming of Christ, Who should restore the lost.

October 4, 1840 (Sunday); Afternoon Meeting

The great conflict in the world is between Christ and the anti-Christ for the possession of mankind. Man is the slave or subject of either one of the two whom he serves (Romans 6:16; II Peter 2:19).

> "Know ye not, that to whom ye yield yourselves
> servants to obey, his servants ye are to whom ye obey;
> whether of sin unto death, or of obedience unto right-
> eousness?"

---

> "While they promise them liberty, they themselves
> are the servants of corruption: for of whom a man is
> overcome, of the same is he brought in bondage."

Whoever does not belong to Christ belongs to the anti-Christ even if he does not mean to. The matter determines itself, and Christ is deserving of it that everyone who wishes to belong to Him, resolutely declare himself to be on His side and fight against the deception of the anti-Christ, indeed not with weapons of flesh but with those of the Spirit, for if we, after knowing the truth and being converted to Christ, still take part in the anti-Christ, we then strengthen others in their error, as if they were Christians too, and thereby deny Christ in the deed for fear of the suffering that we have to undergo to openly oppose the great masses: for every converted person knows that he also was formerly turned away from the right and in Satan's power, as all are by nature without knowing it; therefore we ought to tell them so that they may be saved, whether they listen or not.

We dare not be frightened by the anti-Christ for God is with us; and if we look not upon the visible but upon the invisible, that we love not our life in the world for Christ's sake, Who is our Eternal Life, we overcome the world and shall inherit the future one (Matthew 5:5; Hebrews 2:5, 16), the new earth, in which righteousness dwells.

> "Blessed are the meek: for they shall inherit the earth."

_____

> "For unto the angels hath he not put in subjection the world to come, whereof we speak."

_____

> "For verily he took not on him the nature of angels; but he took on him the seed of Abraham."

And even if a hundred thousand oppose us, we shall not fear, for more still are with us. Nor dare we be ashamed of Christ before men for we are not worthy of Him. In the New Testament everything revolves around Christ as the Axis, even the battle of the anti-Christ. He is a Sign spoken against for the fall and rising of many, and he who resolutely gives testimony of the truth shall be contradicted and evilly entreated everywhere.

The true Christians, as opposed to the anti-Christians, must be called a sect, seducers and seduced ones. But even though we do belong to the party of Christ, we still do not constitute a human party or faction like the many of the world but belong to the great church of God; for when John says of the anti-Christs, "They went out from us," it means that they grew in the same field of the church of Christ, however not from the good seed of Him but from the seed of the devil.

According to their inner condition, they never rightly or actually belonged to the church of Christ because they never let their hearts really be converted or cleansed from sin (Matthew 13). They came into the church unrightfully and were afterwards revealed as false, for a rebellious spirit cannot remain concealed for long. They cannot deny their nature; they must make sects (I Corinthians 11); but it is not the fault of nor a charge against Christ and His church that such false members are in it (Acts 20:29 ff.) (below), and they either separate themselves as dissension makers from it or they are put away from amongst it so that they do not contaminate the rest (I Corinthians 5), for which men would now like to hold me responsible, but I know which Lord I serve and suffer for.

> "For I know this, that after my departing shall grievous wolves enter in among you, not sparing the flock.
> "Also of your own selves shall men arise, speaking perverse things, to draw away disciples after them."

October 6, 1840 (Tuesday); Evening Meeting; I John 2:18 ff.

> "Little children, it is the last time: and as ye have heard that anti-christ shall come, even now are there many anti-christs; whereby we know that it is the last time.
> "They went out from us, but they were not of us; for if they had been of us, they would no doubt have continued with us: but they went out, that they might be made manifest that they were not all of us.
> "But ye have an unction from the Holy One, and ye know all things."

The apostle gives the believers the sign for proving the times and for guarding themselves against seduction. He who does not take the signs of the times into consideration is mistaken about the anti-Christ, like the Jews were mistaken about Christ in His time, for by His sayings and works they should have recognized Him from the prophecies as the Promised King of Israel (Matthew 16:1 ff.):

> "The Pharisees also with the Sadducees came, and tempting desired him that he would shew them a sign from heaven.
> "He answered and said unto them, When it is evening, ye say, It will be fair weather: for the sky is red.
> "And in the morning, It will be foul weather to day: for the sky is red and lowring. O ye hypocrties, ye can discern the face of the sky; but can ye not discern the signs of the times?"

and thus also shall we be able to recognize the anti-Christ by his word and work, to prove the times we live in and not let ourselves be blinded by the false impression of the great masses of anti-Christians, when, for all that, the Unction (Christ's Spirit and Life) is not to be found in them but the spirit of the world, which would cover its wickedness with the name of Christ, and, right in this, bears the sign of the anti-Christ, and all false Christians become revealed as oppositionist-Christians as soon as Christ by His Spirit shows Himself as living in His members and saints.

## Chapter XXXV

### Righteous Fellowship

There is no failing of the enmity of the world against Christ but only of true Christians and witnesses, and although the false Christians are divided into many parties, yet they are all one against Christ, just as the Spirit of Christ also is One and works in all who have Him. The spirit of the world in the nominal Christians now is precisely the same one which was in the Jews and heathen before Christ. Yes, the false Christians live as if no Christ had ever come to redeem the prisoners of Satan; they could not live worse even if Christ had not come, for no one in and by himself is saved through Christ, but only him who is converted.

The same devil still rules in all the unconverted now, as in the Old Testament, and now the power of darkness and the deception of men is double because, with their sins, they still think they are Christians, from birth on. So they think there is nothing to fear and it is impossible that the devil should still reign over them, but just this false Christendom is anti-Christendom and the devil reigns under another name and illusion now. No attention is paid to the ungodly life of men, their reciprocal hatred, enmity, etc., whether they live continually in war and strife, as revealing what is in the spirit of the anti-Christians. However should any commotion arise on account of witnessing for the Gospel, the anti-Christians instantly clamor about injustice, disturbers of the public peace, disorder, inharmony, sectarianism, and the like. But false Christendom does not destroy Satan's power over men; it much more strengthens it to the utmost.

And, as in the beginning, the anti-Christians went out from the Christians, now, inversely, the Christians must go out from the anti-

Christians. And if false members show up among us, who, according to their mind and spirit, do not really belong to Christ, we are not to grieve when they go back again and are left behind (John 6); but it, to be sure, is a most regrettable thing if they also draw the hearts of the simple and guileless with them (Romans 16).

October 8, 1840 (Thursday); Evening Meeting; I John 2:19

> "They went out from us, but they were not of us; for if they had been of us, they would no doubt have continued with us: but they went out, that they might be made manifest that they were not all of us."

It serves to our instruction when John says, "They [the anti-Christs] went out from us, . . . that they might be made manifest that they were not all of us." Compare Romans 9:6 ff.

> "Not as though the word of God hath taken none effect. For they are not all Israel, which are of Israel:
> "Neither, because they are the seed of Abraham, are they all children: but, In Isaac shall thy seed be called.
> "That is, They which are the children of the flesh, these are not the children of God: but the children of the promise are counted for the seed."

In the true church of Christ, the false members will indeed be revealed, those who are unapproved by Christ, and consequently did not come into His church of the saints rightfully but brought their old, crafty heart along with them (like Simon the sorcerer, Acts 8).

The church of Christ, as the body of Christ, consists of the sanctified only, who, together, are one body and one Spirit, and the acceptance or entry thereinto is indeed by baptism, after one has heard and believed the Gospel of Christ (I Corinthians 12:12 ff.; Romans 10):

> "For as the body is one, and hath many members, and all the members of that one body, being many, are one body: so also is Christ.
> "For by one Spirit are we all baptized into one body, whether we be Jews or Gentiles, whether we be bond or free; and have been all made to drink into one Spirit."

but not by infant baptism, by which the world, it is true, means to gather all into one body (the state church), however not under the head of Christ, because they do not believe and have not been filled with Christ's Spirit for the fellowship of the saints. Therefore they have not come in upon the right way and are not the church of Christ, but an anti-Christendom, from which we, for just this reason, must separate ourselves, after the grace of God has redeemed us by a holy calling from the principality of darkness and has incorporated us into the body of His Son (the great church which is above).

Now, in this, we do just as the apostles did in their time: they preached the Gospel unto *all* men without exception and those who willingly accepted the Word and let themselves be baptized, they separated unto the church, and even in this way they could not be held responsible if, with them, false members were intermingled who were made manifest afterwards. But in the state church this is impossible because none have entered by faith and baptism; and when we go out from them we do not separate ourselves from the church of Christ on that account. We must indeed rather withdraw ourselves from the wrong church so as to unite with the right one, for when we hear that Paul (II Timothy 3:1 ff.) (below) describes the so-called Christians of the last days before the coming of Christ as being even worse than the heathen and Jews (Romans 1 and 3), with the additional word, "from such turn away," what then should we do?

> "This know also, that in the last days perilous times shall come.
> "For men shall be lovers of their own selves, covetous, boasters, proud, blasphemers, disobedient to parents, unthankful, unholy,
> "Without natural affection, trucebreakers, false accusers, incontinent, fierce, despisers of those that are good,
> "Traitors, heady, highminded, lovers of pleasures more than lovers of God;
> "Having a form of godliness, but denying the power thereof: from such turn away."

A church communion with them is a sin; the believers shall not be unequally yoked with unbelievers, and here we shall not let ourselves be deceived by the cry of the masses, "We are the Christian church," etc., for the church of Christ is not everywhere on earth and least of all is it the world, which lies in wickedness, where men much prefer to be lovers of pleasure than lovers of God and only affect an appearance of godliness and deny its power.

Yet we must be careful that we, in that we have gone out from the state church, do not *ourselves* form a carnal-minded sect, but, in truth, belong to the body of Christ as the reborn and the sanctified, and even if there are impure ones among us who do not belong to Christ, those then who are approved in Him shall hold together all the more closely in brotherly love and the fellowship of the Spirit, as *hard* as it ever is in our time to attain unto faith and to abide therein.

However, it is now to be noted seriously that John calls those who abide not in Christ, anti-Christs. But no one can abide in the fellowship of the Spirit of Christ who does not remain in the fellowship of His body, for Christ and His body are but one; consequently, whoever does not continue with us has really never belonged to us, even though he once confessed the faith and was baptized.

October 11, 1840 (Sunday); Morning Meeting; I John 2:20 ff.

> "But ye have an unction from the Holy One, and ye know all things.
> "I have not written unto you because ye know not the truth, but because ye know it, and that no lie is of the truth."

In the way of contrast with the anti-Christians, who have fallen away from the truth and gone out from the church, John says of the true Christians, "But ye have an unction from the Holy One, and ye know all things," can discriminate between the truth and the lie. By this unction the true believers are to be recognized, namely, by the Spirit of Christ, just as Christ Himself was to be recognized as the Son of God in no other way than by His Spirit, for in His outer form and being He was like another man (Philippians 2), indeed more lowly than all men (Isaiah 53, Matthew 8:20).

> "And Jesus saith unto him, The foxes have holes, and the birds of the air have nests; but the Son of man hath not where to lay his head."

Prejudice on every hand was against Him: He was from Nazareth (John 1:46 ff.):

> "And Nathanael said unto him, Can there any good thing come out of Nazareth? Philip saith unto him, Come and see.
> "Jesus saw Nathanael coming to him, and saith of him, Behold an Israelite indeed, in whom is no guile!

126

"Nathanael saith unto him, Whence knowest thou me? Jesus answered and said unto him, Before that Philip called thee, when thou wast under the fig tree, I saw thee.

"Nathanael answered and saith unto him, Rabbi, thou art the Son of God; thou art the King of Israel."

of Galilee (John 7:52):

"They answered and said unto him, Art thou also of Galilee? Search, and look: for out of Galilee ariseth no prophet."

had not studied and was rejected by those in authority. Only a few unprejudiced ones observed the Spirit by which He worked and spoke (John 3:2; 9:29 ff.).

"The same came to Jesus by night, and said unto him, Rabbi, we know that thou art a teacher come from God: for no man can do these miracles that thou doest, except God be with him."

———————

"We know that God spake unto Moses: as for this fellow, we know not from whence he is.

"The man answered and said unto them, Why herein is a marvellous thing, that ye know not from whence he is, and yet he hath opened mine eyes.

"Now we know that God heareth not sinners: but if any man be a worshipper of God, and doeth his will, him he heareth.

"Since the world began was it not heard that any man opened the eyes of one that was born blind.

"If this man were not of God, he could do nothing.

"They answered and said unto him, Thou wast altogether born in sins, and dost thou teach us? And they cast him out.

"Jesus heard that they had cast him out; and when he had found him, he said unto him, Dost thou believe on the Son of God?

"He answered and said, Who is he, Lord, that I might believe on him?

"And Jesus said unto him, Thou hast both seen him, and it is he that talketh with thee.

"And he said, Lord, I believe. And he worshipped him."

He Himself, as the Son of man, had been anointed with the Holy
Ghost without measure (Luke 4:18; John 3:34; Hebrews 1:8 ff.):

> "The Spirit of the Lord is upon me, because he hath
> anointed me to preach the gospel to the poor; he hath
> sent me to heal the brokenhearted, to preach deliverance
> to the captives, and recovering of sight to the blind, to set
> at liberty them that are bruised,"

> "For he whom God hath sent speaketh the words of
> God: for God giveth not the Spirit by measure unto him."

> "But unto the Son he saith, Thy throne, O God, is
> for ever and ever: a sceptre of righteousness is the sceptre
> of thy kingdom.
> "Thou hast loved righteousness, and hated iniquity;
> therefore God, even thy God, hath anointed thee with the
> oil of gladness above thy fellows."

and precisely the same Spirit is imparted to all members. For that
reason, we, in our judgment of anyone, must take note of the spirit
which dwells and is effectual in him, whether it is the spirit of the world
or the Spirit of God (I Corinthians 2). Mankind looks only upon the
physical structure and the human appearance and easily lets itself be
blinded and deceived by a false appearance, but God looks upon the
heart (I Samuel 16). By His physiognomy, Jesus was hardly recognized
as to Who He was (as Laventer thought). But the flesh, which is proud,
must be abased if the spirit shall live in God, "for that which is highly
esteemed among men is abomination in the sight of God (Luke 16:
15b)."

The spirit of the world is nothing else than the devil, which by nature
lives and reigns in all and must be driven out in advance, before the
Spirit of Truth from God, that is, Christ, can live and reign in us.
The two do not mix. Therefore a man of God is single-minded, pure,
unmixed (Matthew 10:16; Philippians 2:15).

> "Behold, I send you forth as sheep in the midst of
> wolves: be ye therefore wise as serpents, and harmless as
> doves."

> "That ye may be blameless and harmless, the sons of
> God, without rebuke, in the midst of a crooked and per-
> verse nation, among whom ye shine as lights in the
> world;"

A fountain does not send forth both sweet and bitter water (James 3:
10 ff.).

> "Out of the same mouth proceedeth blessing and
> cursing. My brethren, these things ought not so to be.
> "Doth a fountain send forth at the same place sweet
> water and bitter?
> "Can the fig tree, my brethren, bear olive berries?
> either a vine, figs? so can no fountain both yield salt
> water and fresh."

Now, whoever overflows with the world-spirit in word and deed,
his piety is merely pretence and hypocrisy, for there are no Pharisees
who do not have an appearance of godliness. Therefore we must be
careful for not everything that glitters is gold. Indeed the higher one
stands in the power and honor of the world, the more he is filled with
the world-spirit. It is difficult for one to become nothing and a fool in
this world and no one becomes a believer otherwise, so as to become
anointed with the Holy Ghost of Power and Love and accordingly be
sanctified and sealed therewith (II Corinthians 1:21 ff.):

> "Now he which stablisheth us with you in Christ,
> and hath anointed us, is God;
> "Who hath also sealed us, and given the earnest of
> the Spirit in our hearts."

and known of Christ as His brother (Hebrews 2:11 ff.):

> "For both he that sanctifieth and they who are sancti-
> fied are all of one: for which cause he is not ashamed to
> call them brethren,
> "Saying, I will declare thy name unto my brethren,
> in the midst of the church will I sing praise unto thee."

for Christ and His saints are of one Father.

# Chapter XXXVI

## The Holy Unction

October 11, 1840 (Sunday); Afternoon Meeting

Unction is a figurative term and (establishment) concept carried
over from the Old Testament, under which an external anointing with oil
was practised in instances in which an inner spiritual unction had al-

ready existed: such anointed ones were set apart for God, and thus are all anointed believers now set apart as a people of God and as a church of Christ, all without exception and without discrimination; for John signifies by "unction" not an especial gift of the Spirit, but the new creature and the divine nature in general.

One perhaps speaks also of anointed teachers and unctuous sermons which are indeed not distinguished by lofty words of human wisdom but by manifestation of the Power and the Spirit, so that they, like a two-edged sword, make a separation between the *soulful* and the *spiritual;* since those neither understand nor accept the Word of God, for to them that is foolishness which is of the Spirit of God, in Whose place human wisdom is without effect (I Corinthians 2; Hebrews 4:12; Matthew 7:29):

> "For the word of God is quick, and powerful, and sharper than any twoedged sword, piercing even to the dividing asunder of soul and spirit, and of the joints and marrow, and is a discerner of the thoughts and intents of the heart."

---

> "For he taught them as one having authority, and not as the scribes."

but is praised by the carnal-minded.

But the world does not only not know the Spirit of Christ, it cannot endure it beside its own spirit. They hate it without cause and persecute it. They slander the saints because they no longer run with them in the same riotous manner (I Peter 4): whom this does not befall, in him the unction of the saints is not to be found, but the world-spirit, even though he adorn himself like Jezebel.

Therefore, "Ye have an unction," means: Ye, all, are spiritual or in the Spirit and no longer of the flesh; that is, if the Spirit of God dwells in you, but if one has not the Spirit of Christ he is not His (Romans 8). However for this, the cleansed and the saints must accordingly separate themselves from the unclean ones (II Corinthians 6; Titus 1). By this, and in that they abide in the Word of Christ, they are enabled, as His true disciples, to know the truth and by the truth become free from sin (John 8). By this also, the anointed become independent of men and human opinions so as not to be deceived and misled by the many lying-spirits, of which the world is full. They can discern what the truth and the lie is, for the Spirit of Truth, which the world cannot receive, is self-governing in them. They are taught inwardly by

130

God Himself; otherwise they could not guard themselves from seduction. But for this, the heart must be cleansed of the lust and love of the world and of the flesh, so that the holy, pure Spirit of God may dwell in them and Christ may be transformed in them.

## CHAPTER XXXVII

### DISCERNMENT

October 13, 1840 (Tuesday); Evening Meeting; I John 2:21 ff.

"I have not written unto you because ye know not the truth, but because ye know it, and that no lie is of the truth.

"Who is a liar but he that denieth that Jesus is the Christ? He is anti-christ, that denieth the Father and the Son.

"Whosoever denieth the Son, the same hath not the Father: [but] he that acknowledgeth the Son hath the Father also."

The intention of John is to enable the believers to discern the truth and the lie, Christ and the anti-Christs, so as to be guarded from seduction, inasmuch as the lying-spirits are subtle—often hard to recognize. Even at that time, they forced their concealed roots into every kind of deviation from sound doctrine and the truth (for instance II Timothy 2; II John 7 ff.), and no lie (wrong doctrine) is from the Truth (the Spirit of Christ).

"For many deceivers are entered into the world, who confess not that Jesus Christ is come in the flesh. This is a deceiver and an anti-christ.

"Look to yourselves, that we lose not those things which we have wrought, but that we receive a full reward.

"Whosoever transgresseth, and abideth not in the doctrine of Christ, hath not God. He that abideth in the doctrine of Christ, he hath both the Father and the Son."

Now, the apostle designates the liar in this way, that he denies Jesus, that He is not the Christ, and such anti-Christs went forth from the *church*. This denial of Christ has reference to:

Either *His eternal sonship* (as for instance the Socinians say Christ was neither with the Father from all eternity nor descended from the

Father, but was merely the natural son of Joseph and Mary and by reason of His piety was exalted to sonship of God). Then He would be no greater than any other man who is exalted to adoption by God.

But Jesus is infinitely much more than all others who are saved: *He* is the *Way* to the *Father*. We must become participant of His divine nature. His obedience as the *Son of man* has become only the means thereto. But he who does not consider Him the natural Son of God but only a Son of man, cannot seek his redemption and blessedness in Him and therefore it is only a lying, sham confession of Christ, which is not in accord with the Word of God and by which men are not saved from sin. Or, the denial of Christ has reference to:

*His new position to us,* which He has entered upon since He has accomplished our reconciliation, as our *King* and *Lord,* to Whose commands and will we *unconditionally* owe implicit obedience if we call and confess Him as our Lord and Savior (I Corinthians 12; Philippians 2). But also in this sense, the false Christians have fallen away from Him and denied Him as their King, in that they have refused Him obedience (Luke 19) and serve another. But so as to confess Christ as the Lord and to serve Him, one must not only believe that He died for the reconciliation of our sins, but also firmly believe and have the confidence in Him that He rules for us and over us and all things at the right hand of God, that we must be in subjection to Him and that not even a hair will fall from our head without His will (Matthew 28:18).

> "And Jesus came and spake unto them, saying, All power is given unto me in heaven and in earth."

October 15, 1840 (Thursday); Evening Meeting; I John 2:22 ff.

Although the apostle, with respect to the believers and the faithful, was convinced that they themselves also knew the truth, yet he would not forbear giving them more specific instructions to discern the good and the evil, the true and the false Christians, or those who are within and those who are without. Actually there are no false Christians (it is a contradiction). A Christian is always something genuine, a reflection of the Son of God and a temple of the Holy Ghost, for there is no falsification or darkness in one; instead the light and life of God is his nature. His glory is no longer in the flesh as formerly (Philippians 3) but in Christ, in the Spirit and in the Truth.

All those who are not thus in Christ as a new creature and walk not according to this rule—as belonging to the Israel of God, to the Upper

Jerusalem, to the church of the Firstborn (Galatians 6; Hebrews 12), over whom is peace and mercy and to whom the future kingdom of Christ (the sabbath of the people of God) is promised—are still without, out of Christ and His church, even though they would presently be in the outer court (in the outer church) and for that reason would think they also belong to the church of Christ: for the outer court itself no longer belongs to the holy temple of God; it has been given over to the Gentiles (the nominal Christians) to trample underfoot until their time is fulfilled and the time of Israel comes. That is why John was not permitted to measure the outer court of the Gentiles with the temple but had to leave it out.

Now, if we have gone no farther than this outer court of the Gentiles, we, by all means, are then without, where the dogs, etc. are (Revelation 22) and the deception is all the more profound, since they, in that place, think they are within by reason of their infant baptism, etc. And because we all were in the outer court—were born and reared in it—we must go out of it by the call of God and enter in the inner court of the Israelites so as to be in Christ and be saved by Him. An ever so great a change must have occurred in us that we appear as a miracle of grace to ourselves (II Corinthians 5:17) (below), and he who has not experienced this, his glory is still according to the flesh and not spiritual and consequently he will not be acknowledged by Christ as a Christian.

> "Therefore if any man be in Christ, he is a new creature: old things are passed away; behold, all things are become new."

So we dare not recognize such false Christians as Christians but as anti-Christians and liars, who pervert the truth of God into lies; for the way of salvation, which has been opened to the Gentiles, from beginning to end, is attained by faith in Christ and His Gospel and he who cannot or does not wish to believe, remains to be an over-plus of Israel. To Israel, the kingdom and the promises really belong and when her time is fulfilled, it will no longer be attained by faith but instantly by the beholding (Revelation 1:7).

> "Behold, he cometh with clouds; and every eye shall see him, and they also which pierced him: and all kindreds of the earth shall wail because of him. Even so, Amen."

But as long as the believing children of God are in this world, they are still only in the court, although no longer in the outer court of the

Gentiles but in the one of the Israelites upon hope, that they will afterwards enter into the holy place as priests of God. But even though one invites the false Christians to come from the outer to the inner court by a true conversion, they decline, and consider themselves as being right and conversion an error and sectarianism.

October 18, 1840 (Sunday); Morning Meeting; I John 2:22 ff.

> "Who is a liar but he that denieth that Jesus is the Christ? He is anti-christ, that denieth the Father and the Son.
> "Whosoever denieth the Son, the same hath not the Father: [but] he that acknowledgeth the Son hath the Father also.
> "Let that therefore abide in you, which ye have heard from the beginning. If that which ye have heard from the beginning shall remain in you, ye also shall continue in the Son, and in the Father.
> "And this is the promise that he hath promised us, even eternal life."

"Who is a liar?" By nature all men are liars and accordingly children of the devil (Romans 3:4; John 8:44).

> "God forbid: yea, let God be true, but every man a liar; as it is written, That thou mightest be justified in thy sayings, and mightest overcome when thou art judged."

---

> "Ye are of your father the devil, and the lusts of your father ye will do. He was a murderer from the beginning, and abode not in the truth, because there is no truth in him. When he speaketh a lie, he speaketh of his own: for he is a liar, and the father of it."

Lying is the principal sin of man from his youth. The entire life of natural man is lies. All his thoughts and endeavors follow after that which is vain and sinful and not after the living and true God; all is high-mindedness and pride, lust of the world, etc. God however is the Father of His own children only, who, in their entire life and being, are true, like He is, not liars like the devil.

The lie (sin, death, the devil) came into man by faith in the lie and with that a great change took place in him so that he was ashamed, afraid, etc. (Genesis 3). With the word of the liar, his spirit also entered

134

man and in this way the truth of God in him was changed into the lie, the image of the devil engendered (darkness) and the image of God destroyed. Now, in the same way also, in Christ, the engendering of the divine image takes place. First, man must hear the word of truth and by faith in the Word of God, truth must again enter man and where the Word is accepted, there it is also sealed by the Spirit as a divine, eternal life.

Now, one might think it is an easy thing to believe God, but that is missing it by much. The lie has completely filled man. With all his might he offers resistance against God and His Word of Truth and makes Him a liar. God may say whatsoever He will, the liars will not believe it. Indeed it appears, as they say, that they believe all that is written, the entire Gospel of Christ, but it again is only a lie, a delusion and imagination. It is not faith of the heart but an ineffectual understanding of it. They very willingly ascribe the comfort and the promises of the Gospel to themselves without authority and right, so as to apply a plaster to—but not heal—their wound. They take that which does not belong to them because they are not prepared for it and that which is for them, they do not accept. They pass over the Word of the beginning, unto repentance, and wish to be comforted before they have mourned and have been afflicted by their misery and the death of sin in Adam (Matthew 5; II Corinthians 7).

But if one comforts the uncontrite they are then only strengthened and hardened in their wickedness. They must first have been led into the hell of their darkened hearts, in recognition of their lost condition by the preaching of John the Baptist and be broken and suffer in godly sorrow, before they can be transplanted with Christ as new creatures in heaven by faith and the knowledge of the truth and its representation in their hearts and lives. The spirit of lying must leave if the Spirit of Truth shall enter and for this they must first believe what God says, that they all by nature are sinners, liars, children of the devil, lost and damned. With that the foundation must be laid and the hard heart broken up by the plow; otherwise the divine seed of life does not enter into it.

It is true, one sees men mourn, weep and lament also, however not after God unto salvation but after the world unto death — like the heathen (I Thessalonians 4)—if they perhaps have suffered earthly loss; however over themselves, their sins and their own death, they do not sorrow. In fact, when anyone sorrows and weeps after a godly manner, they consider that mockery and foolishness and insanity, but it is very much worth while to mourn over ourselves if we have learned to know ourselves in our death, so that the stone may be rolled away from the grave and the dead awakened by the voice of Christ (John 5; Ephesians 5). Without knowledge of his damnation, man cannot believe in the Crucified Christ unto eternal life, but sinners are so proud and conceited that they do not accept God's judgment over them. They repel every word by which they think their honor has been touched; they are so vile that they slander one another and so high-minded that they cannot endure it.

## Chapter XXXVIII
### Denial of Christ

October 18, 1840 (Sunday); Afternoon Meeting

John asks who the liar is, and answers that he who denies Christ is the anti-Christ. Thus, to John, the liar and the anti-Christ are one, as it were, the arch liar, in comparison to whom all other liars are as nothing, for the other liars were born thus; they cannot help it that the lying-spirit has been transmitted to them from Adam. God accordingly has forgiven all these sins of the old nature to them and does not take them into account for He has laid them upon His Son as the Sin- and Curse-Offering for our reconciliation.

But the people who now hear that, think: "Under these circumstances, everything is right again, for what Adam had lost Christ has won anew. There is nothing to fear on account of our sins now. They have all been wiped out by one sacrifice. We believe in the Gospel," etc. With that the people peacefully and securely remain in their sins and lies and enmity against God, deceive themselves and accordingly deny Christ, Who, in the deed, has purchased them while they, by word, feign to confess Him.

Here the last deception is worse than the first. They do not realize that Christ, the Other Adam, has come and died so as to re-establish that which the first Adam ruined. Now, as many as remain in the death of the first Adam deny Christ, are liars and anti-Christians, and abide in death and condemnation eternally because they do not accept the only salvation that is offered to them in the Son of God (John 3), for which Adam is as little responsible that we remain unbelieving toward Christ as we are responsible that we are sinners in Adam. But Adam received such a Substitute to redeem us from Satan's power that it is as though we had never descended from Adam or had been born of him, and it is our own fault and choice if we have not been born again in Christ. Everyone who becomes a believer in Christ is also born again a child of God, is participant of the Holy Spirit and freed from sin (Galatians 3:22 ff.; John 7:37 ff.).

"But the scripture hath concluded all under sin, that the promise by faith of Jesus Christ might be given to them that believe.

"But before faith came, we were kept under the law, shut up unto the faith which should afterwards be revealed.

"Wherefore the law was our schoolmaster to bring us unto Christ, that we might be justified by faith.

"But after that faith is come, we are no longer under a schoolmaster.

"For ye are all the children of God by faith in Jesus Christ."

———————

"In the last day, that great day of the feast, Jesus stood and cried, saying, If any man thirst, let him come unto me, and drink.

"He that believeth on me, as the scripture hath said, out of his belly shall flow rivers of living water.

"(But this spake he of the Spirit, which they that believe on him should receive: for the Holy Ghost was not yet given; because that Jesus was not yet glorified.)"

Therefore He in whom these things have not taken place, bears the marks and seal of unbelief upon him, and unbelief is the principal sin (John 16), from which all other sins originate, as fruit on a tree. He is the liar and anti-Christ who denies the Father and the Son, for in the denial of the Son lies also the denial of the *Father*.

The harm of Adam has therefore not been made good by the death of Christ for those, nor has it been healed in them, who remain in sin and the lie, but there the harm has first become really incurable, for the lie is not a single word or deed, nor a thousand, but is instead a spirit, which must be driven out so that the Spirit of Truth and the Life of Christ may take its place, and Christ lights His candle only for the reason that it may give light in the darkness of this world, that men may learn to know God (Matthew 5; Philippians 2) by His children.

137

October 20, 1840 (Tuesday); Evening Meeting; I John 2:22 ff.

There is a two-fold denial of Christ and each is the sin against the Holy Ghost, which is not forgiven. Some deny Him right in the beginning if He is preached unto them, that He as the Son of God has come into the world to seek and to save the lost. These deny Him as *Jesus* (Reconciler and Redeemer); the others deny Him *afterwards,* insofar as He is the *Christ* and as Son of man, after having accomplished our reconciliation and redemption, was lifted up to the right of God as our Lord and King so as to rule over the new humanity.

The former deny that He has come in the flesh and died for the reconciliation of sin, and just this constitutes their lie, that they are Jesuits and nevertheless anti-Christians who deny Him in the deed, in that they boast of Him with their lips. The former do not believe unto redemption and the latter do not believe unto obedience, but neither have Christ: for there is only *one* true Christ, Who has come that He might destroy the works of the devil in all who believe on Him so that they might have eternal life, according to the promise of the Father.

But he who denies the Son does not have the Father either, for there is no other way to the Father for fallen mankind than by the Son, Who is one with the Father, yet not so, that there should be no difference between the Father and the Son, or the Father would not have sent the Son. However They are thus One, that he who sees the Son (knows Him through His Spirit) knows the Father also (John 14) and he who has not the Son, does likewise not have the Father; that is to say, he has no God (II John). And just because there is only *one* Christ, namely, He Who brings the dead to life, so also is there only *one* true Gospel, namely, that which is the power of God unto the salvation of the believer, which is effectual upon all and in all who hear it, decisivelv and forcefully from the first day on, be it unto life or unto death (II Corinthians 4:2 ff.):

"But have renounced the hidden things of dishonesty, not walking in craftiness, nor handling the word of God deceitfully; but by manifestation of the truth commending ourselves to every man's conscience in the sight of God.

"But if our gospel be hid, it is hid to them that are lost:

"In whom the god of this world hath blinded the minds of them which believe not, lest the light of the glorious gospel of Christ, who is the image of God, should shine unto them."

138

and the preaching which does not have this effectual working is not the Gospel of Christ (the Word of God), but a false, fabricated word of man, which indeed works unto death but not unto life.

Therefore, he who has once received a new divine life through the Word and has tasted therein the powers of the world to come, he most certainly has heard the only true Gospel and has learned to know the true Christ and the Father in Him and he dare not thereafter wait for another Christ or for another true Gospel; and as many as may come later and would preach another Gospel and another Christ to him, he shall consider seducers and refuse them outrightly. Here will apply what is written in Deuteronomy, chapters 13 and 18, and for this reason John says to the believers, "If that which ye have heard from the beginning shall remain in you, ye also shall continue in the Son, and in the Father (I John 2:24b)."

October 22, 1840 (Thursday); Evening Meeting; I John 2:22 ff.

In order that we fully understand what an anti-Christian is, we must include the citation of chapter 4:1 ff.:

> "Beloved, believe not every spirit, but try the spirits whether they are of God: because many false prophets are gone out into the world.
> "Hereby know ye the Spirit of God: Every spirit that confesseth that Jesus Christ is come in the flesh is of God:
> "And every spirit that confesseth not that Jesus Christ is come in the flesh is not of God: and this is that spirit of anti-christ, whereof ye have heard that it should come; and even now already is it in the world.
> "Ye are of God, little children, and have overcome them: because greater is he that is in you, than he that is in the world.
> "They are of the world; therefore speak they of the world, and the world heareth them.
> "We are of God: he that knoweth God heareth us; he that is not of God heareth not us. Hereby know we the spirit of truth, and the spirit of error."

where John calls especial attention to the other side of the denial, so that we think not, only that man is a liar who does not confess that Jesus Christ has come in the flesh (as the Son of God), but *he also* is an erring spirit and seducer who does not confess that Jesus of Nazareth is the *Christ*, King, Lord and Commander and Possessor of all things, but especially the Head and Firstborn of His brethren, raised up, as the Son of man, to the right of God, that He reigns over us by the commandments and laws which He has given us in order that we may be saved, so that we obey Him unconditionally, are subject to Him and follow Him and serve no other master beside Him.

## CHAPTER XXXIX

### A WILLING PEOPLE

But Christ would have a willing people, not a forced one, and therefore He gives all believers of His own Spirit and writes His laws into their heart as the eternal life from the Father, according to His promise and the way of the New Testament (Hebrews 8), so that we no longer follow any other law and will except His, whether it pleases our flesh and the world or not, for all who shall become children of God and be heirs of the kingdom must also be brethren of Christ and His servants, must follow after Him in the form of a servant as He, according to His hidden counsel, wishes to lead them.

We cannot keep the commandments of Christ if we obey the commandments of the anti-Christ, for the latter are the opposite of the former. We must obey the laws of the king whose subjects we are. Now, if we wish to be subjects of Christ, we shall then not observe the commandments of the anti-Christ (we can for instance not observe the order of Christ in baptism if we baptize infants, etc.). But the commandments of Christ pertain mostly to the *inner* life so that *eternal life* may be in us, that we keep them and thus have fellowship with the Father and Son and enter into the same relationship with the Father as the Son Himself has entered into: for if we do not, in this world, enter into the relation of sonship to God by quickening knowledge and love, we shall then not be able to draw near unto Him in the future world.

According to the revelation of the New Testament, we stand in no other relation to God than through the Son, so that in the denial of the Son there is already comprised the denial of the Father, and the first-fruits of the Spirit, which the believers receive now already, are of the same divine nature as the future glory. The children of God must *here* accustom themselves to association with the Father and to being minded like Him, as Jesus Christ also was, but by that we glean no honor of men, only scorn and reproach, if we walk as Jesus walked. Thus all those are anti-Christians and liars who keep not the commandments of Christ, who deny Jesus as the Christ, for, of and to the people of the state church, one cannot say what John says: "Let that therefore abide in you, which ye have heard from the beginning," etc., for one can keep only that which one has received. But the nominal Christians have not the Word of Truth in them; instead they have the lie, the spirit of error, and as long as that abides in them, Christ cannot take up a dwelling-place in them.

October 25, 1840 (Sunday); Morning Meeting; I John 2:23 ff.

"Whosoever denieth the Son, the same hath not the Father: [but] he that acknowledgeth the Son hath the Father also.

"Let that therefore abide in you, which ye have heard from the beginning. If that which ye have heard from the beginning shall remain in you, ye also shall continue in the Son, and in the Father.

"And this is the promise that he hath promised us, even eternal life.

"These things have I written unto you concerning them that seduce you."

Those deny the Son of God as Jesus, who reject Him in the Word of Truth right from the beginning and never at all receive Him so as to be saved and become blessed; but, as Christ, only those who have once known, believed and received Him can deny Him. John here warns the believers against this latter sin of apostasy from the perceived truth, for over each one who has come to the knowledge of the truth and has been converted and has become a believer in Christ, the devil most certainly comes with all manner of temptation and seduction and apostasy from Christ, and he then who is not *firmly established,* falls away again. That person, namely, who does not let his heart be purified through faith and who in his faith is still fundamentally earthly-, worldly- and carnally-minded, will not be able to withstand the attacks of the tempter because he has the enemy within himself, without which the outer enemy can accomplish nothing.

But who are those who have no firm foundation of the truth in them? They are those who do not do the Word of God, do not live and walk according to the commandments of Christ (Matthew 7). It is for this reason that God permits all believers to be tempted, that it shall be made known whether their faith is a power of God unto salvation or a shallow, unquickening knowledge. That is why the true believers and children of God count temptation and suffering as real joy, so that they *through patience* become accomplished and are made perfect unto salvation (James 1). Fire must prove their foundation.

But those whose faith is founded upon the Rock, Christ, and upon His Word and His Spirit of Truth and Life, shall nevermore yield nor waver in the storms of temptation or in every wind of doctrine (Psalm 16; Ephesians 4). "For other foundation can no man lay than that is laid, which is Jesus Christ (I Corinthians 3:11)," and he who has received this foundation from the Word has heard the true Word and Gospel, beside which there is no other. And whatsoever teacher brings not this Word of Truth—Which creates life and immediately sets a humble heart on fire and takes root—is a seducer and an anti-Christian (II John), whom one shall not receive, for he cannot build up but only destroy the temple of God; and even though a thousand teachers, educators and learned men should come afterwards, they can still only come to and build further upon the foundation which is laid if they speak through the Spirit of God.

But he who violates and does not remain by the teaching of Christ (by the word from the beginning), but accepts an other foundation, that man has no God and becomes a vagabond of the Gospel, which is much worse than when one comes to ruin under the law (like the prodigal son, Luke 15), for a restoration is possible for the latter but not for the former (Hebrews 6 and 10). But he who continues in the doctrine of Christ has both the Father and the Son, and however difficult it now is until one sinner is converted, it is yet a still more difficult matter for one who has been converted to be preserved until the end.

October 25, 1840 (Sunday); Afternoon Meeting

Why is it that John (like all the other apostles) so very strongly insists that those who were once converted and saved and have become believers, should remain in and by the word which they have heard from the beginning? Because this word is the seed of God, without which they cannot continue in the Son and in the Father or be saved in eternity, upon which all depends, that we lose not our present life in the Spirit and thus our soul's salvation, in the time of grace.

The word which we have heard from the beginning is indeed a small seed grain, but sealed by the Spirit it becomes a tree in whose branches the birds of the heavens build their nests. It must enlighten, fill and permeate man wholly that no part of the old darkness remains over. The believer must now already be filled by (and become full of)

God and His eternal life; the kingdom of God must now already become manifest in him, for which purpose Christ appeared in the flesh and sends His Spirit. But because God has become inapproachable, unknown and hidden to carnal man on account of the darkness into which man has fallen by faith in the lie, there is no other reascension unto God possible except by faith in the word or in the truth, and he who cannot believe is not capable of fellowship with God, either now or eternally.

But as the first man, by faith in the lie, fell away from God and became darkened, so must we now, by faith in the truth, fall away from the devil so as to become enlightened. Then God establishes His Kingdom in us in righteousness, peace and joy. This inner kingdom of God is indeed still invisible and hidden at the present time, as the fruit of the first appearance in the flesh, but at the second appearance of Christ in glory it will be revealed. And he who has not now received the inner kingdom of God cannot enter in the future kingdom of glory (Luke 17). Therefore all is established upon faith and our eternal salvation depends upon the use we make of the time of grace. But as faith in the word from the beginning works unto salvation, conversion and rebirth, so must it afterwards work unto obedience, in love, unto the end, so that in the foundation of the right faith there is nothing else than love, which keeps the commandments of God or continues in Christ and *then* in the Father also. We believe only in the proportion that we love.

## CHAPTER XL

### LOVE, THE TREE OF FAITH

Love is the tree which has grown from the original mustard seed of faith and bears fruit. Now, if John makes the abiding in the word which they had heard from the beginning, the condition of salvation for the believers of his time, it then applies to us also; that is, we must have heard and accepted just *that* word which, from the beginning onward, was preached by Christ and the apostles, else we cannot be saved now nor be blessed in eternity, for no other word than the Word of God has a regenerative power. Therefore we must return to the teaching of the apostles and not let ourselves be held captive by the error of the delusive teaching of man, which is now general in the world (Romans 10). Had the people heard and believed the original Gospel, they would also be converted, new creatures in Christ, and only there where man hears the right Word of God is it a question of who shall be saved by faith and who lost by unbelief, and even with the believers the possibility of eternal salvation is decided only by their abiding in Christ and their remaining stedfast in the Word of Truth until the end.

October 27, 1840 (Tuesday); Evening Meeting; I John 2:24 ff.

"Let that therefore abide in you, which ye have heard from the beginning. If that which ye have heard from the beginning shall remain in you, ye also shall continue in the Son, and in the Father.

"And this is the promise that he hath promised us, even eternal life.

"These things have I written unto you concerning them that seduce you."

The intention of the apostle in his entire writing is to guard the true believers from seducers. But so as to know what seducing is, we must note John's continuity and order of thought. We then find that the anti-Christ's spirit of lying and error, from the beginning onward, went forth for the purpose of perverting the way of Christ and foisting another way of salvation upon deceived men which does not lead to the goal of salvation but to damnation, while men always think they are still upon the right way to blessedness.

But the only way to salvation is Christ Himself and so as to be saved by Him, we must be in Him and abide in Him and walk as He walked, in righteousness. That is the eternal life which He proclaimed to us and promised to give to all in whom the word that was preached to us from the beginning by Christ and the apostles, abides. If this word is not in us, we are not in Christ; if it does not remain in us, we do not continue in the Son and in the Father and we cannot be saved eternally.

For if one is called a brother (Christian) and is at the same time still a fornicator, etc., he cannot inherit the kingdom of God for he has not eternal life in him. Or can it be said that the nominal Christians continue in the Son and in the Father and have eternal life in them, when they live entirely in the flesh and in all kinds of sins and seek and love only that which is in and of the world and not of the Father—indeed forbidden by Him? They walk in a way that is altogether contrary to the one of Christ and are cheated out of their salvation. According to their church liturgy, they are pronounced blessed from birth to the grave, but according to the Word of God they are condemned as sinners for the word and way of God has become no other during these

144

1800 years; and if they, upon their wrong way, would refer to their great numbers, it does not change God's judgment (Matthew 7:13 ff.):

> "Enter ye in at the strait gate: for wide is the gate, and broad is the way, that leadeth to destruction, and many there be which go in thereat:
> "Because strait is the gate, and narrow is the way, which leadeth unto life, and few there be that find it."

that they should not be wrong or lost because there are many of them and only a few of the children of God (who find and walk upon the way to life).

The deception lies in this, if one applies what John said to the believers of his time, without distinction to the unbelievers of our time, they then think: "Who are the seducers from whom we ought to guard ourselves but the new believers, anabaptists, who go out from us and make sects?" —and they do not know that they themselves are in error and have been deceived. Men are now entirely different from what the believers of the early times were, but Christ as the Way, the Truth and the Life, has remained unchanged for all who shall be saved. And when we now witness that men on their wrong, evil way will be condemned according to the Word of God, we are considered by the world as being hard-hearted and desirous to condemn others, but we must do this for the sake of the love of God, for the salvation of men, according to James 4:17: "Therefore to him that knoweth to do good, and doeth it not, to him it is sin."

## Chapter XLI

### Spiritual Weapons of Light

October 29, 1840 (Thursday); Evening Meeting; I John 2:25 ff.

"And this is the promise that he hath promised us, even eternal life." The fulfillment of this promise is carried out in the believers in two terms: According to the beginning, Eternal Life, that is, Christ, is given to us in this time through the firstfruits of the Spirit, for although it is an everlasting life, still for *us* it has a *beginning* because we, by nature and our descent from Adam, are in death; but its completion is retained for the future world. Yet it is promised only to those who have here received the *beginning* (in advance) and who then pre-

145

serve the same unto the end, since only those can be saved who endure unto the end; that is, do not fall away again from the living God after they have once found and tasted Him, for it is possible for only those to lose eternal life again who have once received it in Christ; namely, if they love, instead of hate and deny, their sensual and earthly life in the world (flesh and blood).

For we, insofar as we are still visible in the body, stand in danger of apostasy and the denial of Christ, and just from this side the devil and the world set against us, that we should look back to the earthly (which by conversion lies behind us), like Lot's wife, and John, on this account, has made the denial of the visible a condition for all followers of Christ in order that they might attain the eternal and not again deny Him before men by love of the *earthly,* in which the *only possibility* of apostasy for a believer lies, just as the *love of the world* is the reason why most men are never at all converted and saved but remain in the power of Satan and live without God and without hope in the world.

Now, when the living God ceases to suffice a believer so that his life is lived in the Spirit, he then falls into the flesh and death again, but he who endures in faith and in the hope of glory can nevermore die for he has eternal life in him. The death of the body is no longer a death but a departure from every necessity and danger and an entry into everlasting rest and security. The believer therefore does not fear the death of the body but only apostasy from the living God, Who, for him, is a high and mighty Fortress and a Deliverer (Psalm 18), in Whom he can glory in the hope of glory.

Therefore, it cannot fail: either we have not yet received Christ the Eternal Life at all, or we really have it within us, and then we must be aware of it also and feel that Christ lives in us. But His divine, eternal life is revealed in all righteousness, truth, longsuffering, faith, hope, love, gentleness, humility, purity, etc., and these again are our spiritual weapons of light for the battle against our spiritual enemies (Ephesians 6). For only then are we strong to overcome, when we have put on Christ in His holy, divine, eternal life (Romans 13), and to these overcomers is the crown of righteousness and life then promised in the revelation of the glory of the children of God, which is still hidden now and will first be fulfilled in the Millenium of Christ, in the first resurrection (Revelation 20). So we shall take heed that we abide in Christ and live and walk in the Spirit, so that no one may rob us of our crown and *for it* we must let our rejection as offscourings in this world be acceptable to us.

November 1, 1840 (Sunday); Morning Meeting; I John 2:26 ff.

"These things have I written unto you concerning them that seduce you."

(Namely verse 18 ff.)

"Little children, it is the last time: and as ye have heard that anti-christ shall come, even now are there many anti-christs; whereby we know that it is the last time.

"They went out from us, but they were not of us; for if they had been of us, they would no doubt have continued with us: but they went out, that they might be made manifest that they were not all of us."

Seduction is the opposite of guidance. A true spiritual guide first leads the souls into the Word of Truth, Christ, and then further on therein unto the end, unto eternal blessedness. Christ is the Way of Life from the beginning to end and faithful souls obey their guides, and another, whose voice they do not know, they will not follow but will flee from him as from seducers (John 10). An upright guide gathers his sheep to the (only) real Shepherd, Christ, and under His staff they all become one, like-minded, for all have in them the same law of the Spirit and one aim; they are united in the highest of interests, the kingdom of God and eternal blessedness; therefore the vile, human, earthly interests are not able to separate them.

By nature all go astray; each one turns to his own way and seeks his own (Isaiah 53). But in Christ, that is, in the converted, this old law of sin and death—the principles of the devil, selfishness, self-love, obstinacy, willfulness—has been destroyed and in its place the new law of the Spirit of Life—of Love, the Holy Life of Christ and His Divine Mind—has been implanted (I Corinthians 2). The old law of sin—selfishness, egotism—is inseparable from the old heart, as it is deeply buried therein, and there all outward laws and preaching are in vain and lost. Only there where the old law is broken and dashed to pieces does the law of the flesh cease to be in power.

But the devil can tie the old threads into the weft again through stubbornness and the selfishness of man, if this poisonous root has not been utterly destroyed and the converted one does not watch over himself, and then the last state is worse than the first. Where each one seeks his own, looks to his own way, there the devil and the way of the error of seduction are to be found. And if a child of God becomes aware of something of this kind, he battles against it and will not suffer it within him and here no enemy can accomplish anything.

With the converted it is the reverse of the unconverted. The former have the law of God within them, the Spirit of Christ as their eternal life, and Christ can never deny Himself; where He is and lives He is the same yesterday and today (II Timothy 2; Hebrews 13), but if we are minded otherwise and do not walk as He walked, we deny Him. As long as the law of sin is within all preaching is in vain; men still remain selfish; no real conversion has taken place but the inner knave has merely been whited over and comes to the fore at every opportunity. There one finds nothing but strife and war (James 4) and each one is in the other's way with his carnal ambitions.

However he who remains stedfast and firm in the Word and Spirit of Christ must as well have a divine persistence and perseverance for the good, like the old man has a devilish persistence for the evil. But the world considers a firm believer who abides in Christ, a stubborn, stiff-necked person whose headstrongness should be broken by the rod. Here Christ is in real power, where the devil employs all his means in vain to cause one to waver in the confession of the truth. The living Christ, Whom the world hates, is here, and whoever will be saved in another way has been deceived by the devil, has long ago been led astray and would not first be deceived now.

## Chapter XLII

## Guidance Into All Truth

November 1, 1840 (Sunday); Afternoon Meeting; I John 2:27 ff.

"But the anointing which ye have received of him abideth in you, and ye need not that any man teach you: but as the same anointing teacheth you of all things, and is truth, and is no lie, and even as it hath taught you, ye shall abide in him.

"And now, little children, abide in him; that, when he shall appear, we may have confidence, and not be ashamed before him at his coming.

"If ye know that he is righteous, ye know that every one that doeth righteousness is born of him."

"But the anointing which ye have received of him abideth in you." *(And you who have received of him the anointing, which abideth in*

148

*you.*) The addressing of them as "you," which otherwise is omitted, is not superfluous as it stresses the rejoinder: *I have written unto you, and you already know it otherwise also.* Here one might think the writing of it were useless, but it is still necessary for the strengthening of the truth, for the testimony of two persons is true (John 8:13, 17 ff.).

> "The Pharisees therefore said unto him, Thou bearest record of thyself; thy record is not true."

---

> "It is also written in your law, that the testimony of two men is true.
> "I am one that bear witness of myself, and the Father that sent me beareth witness of me."

Even though Jesus bore record of Himself, yet it was no presumption but the truth for He knew whence He had come as the Son of God, but if another person would speak in that way about himself he would be a liar. But men like to betake themselves to human authority and thereby become devoted to a party and are deceived, and Paul, already in the early life of the Corinthian church, had to repress this evil.

> "Who then is Paul, and who is Apollos, but ministers by whom ye believed, . . . ?"

Let no one boast of men; they are too inconsiderable, as servants. We have not yet attained to lordship; there is only one Lord over all, in heaven. We dare not take any man except Christ Himself—and only Christ—as our Pattern; otherwise one would even be worse than the other and each one would comfort himself with someone who is worse.

However, when an apostle witnesses by Christ's Spirit of Truth and those who teach and those who hear it, find exactly the same testimony of the Spirit in them, these then know that they are in the truth and have the Spirit of Christ. It is true, we no longer have any apostles in person among us, but in their place we have their written word of Christ, and if we now come before this testimony and examine ourselves according to it, the inner testimony (Christ in us) is then either in harmony with it, or if we have not the Spirit and Life of Christ in us, we do not understand the written word, and in that case men read it like an almanac and fiction or not at all.

We have no other choice here: either we must find Christ through His Spirit incarnately (essentially) in us, that He teach us all things and guide us into all truth, to not only know but also do the will of God (II Corinthians 13), or we are unqualified and reject Christ as

149

the Truth and the Life. He must be so near to us that we need not run hither and yon in uncertainty and perplexity (Romans 10) or we are never secure from deception and temptation if we have to depend upon other men.

It is indeed good that we still have the written word or we could no longer find Christ at all. Yet, even with the written word, we nowadays must needs be called heretics and seducers if we cling faithfully to the truth. And, in this world, men can indeed set the written and the preached Word of God aside so that they need not endure His eyes which search the very bottom of their hearts, but how confounded and ashamed will they be in their nakedness when the Lord Himself appears again, Whose eyes are like flames of fire and before Whom they must stand and receive their sentence, for (II Timothy 2:19):

> " . . . the foundation of God standeth sure, having this seal, The Lord knoweth them that are his. And, Let every one that nameth the name of Christ depart from iniquity."

However, if we are free from all unrighteousness, nothing else than righteousness remains and if we know that He is righteous, we then know that everyone who does righteousness is born of Him. In the New Testament, the heart and mind of man is the ark of the covenant, where the living law is laid down and preserved.

November 3, 1840 (Tuesday); Evening Meeting; I John 2:26 ff.

> "These things have I written unto you concerning them that seduce you.
> "But the anointing which ye have received of him abideth in you, and ye need not that any man teach you: but as the same anointing teacheth you of all things, and is truth, and is no lie, and even as it hath taught you, ye shall abide in him."

In reference to the besetting lying-spirits, the seducers and false brethren and disguised servants of Satan (II Corinthians 11; Galatians 2), the apostle wished it to be made known to his young brethren that they were self-reliant and independent so that they, by means of the unction, might be in a position to prove all teachers and teachings and discern the truth and the lie, so as not to be deceived and led astray. He who can judge all teachers stands above them in this respect and consequently is independent of the judgment of others in reference to the truth, and it must be so with all the anointed or they would be at the mercy of every seducer and lying-spirit (Romans 16).

Yet the believers, by reason of this spiritual self-reliance, are still not *in the same degree* as independent from the teaching of the truth itself as it is revealed by the older, experienced servants of Christ through the Holy Ghost. Only the fathers in Christ are independent in this respect also, but all the younger ones shall be desirous of the sincere milk of the truth (I Peter 2) and continue stedfastly in the instruction and advice of the leaders (Acts 2), so that they, through the same, may increase in the true wisdom and knowledge of God. It is the same in this respect as with children: as long as the child is in the womb of the mother, its life is wholly bound with that of the mother and is dependent (absolutely) upon her, but when it is born, it, at that state, has received a separate life, yet it is not so independent that it could sustain itself, but must even then receive its nourishment from the mother that it might live.

As necessary as self-reliance may ever be in reference to the erring spirits, to slash them to pieces with the Sword of the Spirit (the Word of God), just as destructive also is the high-minded conceit, self-knowledge and self-sufficiency of so many beginners and novices who have been puffed up by the devil against the truth and imagine that they need learn nothing more. They are the first to become seducers of others. Paul warns us against this old and self-conceited way (Romans 12; I Corinthians 8, etc.).

" ... if any man think that he knoweth any thing, he knoweth nothing yet as he ought to know."

Such independence is neither right nor good for eccentricity, the lying-spirit, is behind it and such inexperienced ones imperceptibly depart from the truth. "A little leaven leaveneth the whole lump." For, as we are indebted and obligated to accept the whole truth as the counsel of God unto our salvation, so must we also avoid every lie if we are to be saved. It is not for us to be concerned about adding to or taking away from the truth at discretion.

The self-reliance and independence of which John speaks is therefore not absolute or unconditional, but conditional and relative, and we must guard ourselves just as much from our own mind as from the strange lying-spirits so as not to be deceived, for we can never finish learning the truth and wisdom of God, and we must keep our heart pure from sin in order that the Holy Ghost may dwell and abide in us, guide us into all truth and keep us from seduction.

November 5, 1840 (Thursday); Evening Meeting; I John 2:27 ff.

The anointing which the believers receive from Christ is known by this, that it instructs them in all things according to the truth, leads them in all truth and also reminds the anointed to walk in the truth and to do the will of God in all things so as to please Him. So we shall consider nothing that we say and do, accept or reject in the name of the Lord as insignificant, so as not to grieve the Holy Spirit wherewith the Father has sealed and anointed us unto the day of redemption.

By the unction, we are, in advance, designated, declared and destined of God as children and heirs of His Kingdom, as kings and priests in eternity, and accordingly the unction has its design upon the invisible— the veritable and the eternal and the future—so that our mind must be directed thereunto and not upon the timely and visible, for the latter is not our own and we cannot take it with us to the future world because it is perishable and vain. But the invisible, the veritable and eternal, is our real property, for which we shall strive so as to become rich in God (Luke 16).

So he who considers the earthly as his property, like all the un- anointed, is a thief, for he appropriates unto himself that which is not his but is only entrusted to him. He who is so unfaithful with that which is not his own, how would God entrust the veritable to him? That is why the children of God do not yet, in this world, receive the actuality itself but only the seal and the pledge therefor, so that they, on earth, learn to be heavenly minded and to live a godly life.

So he cannot be blessed in the future world who has either not re- ceived the unction (because he did not believe from the beginning) or has not preserved that which he received (did not further believe until the end), for how could he redeem his property if he cannot proffer the pledge therefor or how could he enter into the kingdom of God if he has no passport? The called, the anointed and sealed have it within them, like David who had indeed in advance been anointed King of Is- rael, but did not attain unto rulership as long as Saul lived and was per- secuted and fugitive, uncertain of his life, on account of the jealousy of Saul. Likewise the prince of this world knows very well who the anointed and sealed are who shall inherit the future kingdom of God, and he perescutes them for this reason and would like even to deprive them of their livelihood because they no longer serve and obey him;

and whoever is offended by that and doubts God's faithfulness, falls away again and does not attain unto the kingdom of God.

But persevering godliness has the promise for this and the future life. These are assured of their blessedness and glory in their adoption and heirship of God because they have the pledge and seal thereof within them; but those who, without this, imagine that they will be saved too, according to the wrong way of the world and seduction, are deceived. Indeed the unanointed and unsealed also like to boast that they are children of God and God is their Father, like the Jews (John 8), and also want to be saved, and therefore hate and revile the anointed and sealed, who boast with an entirely different certainness and confidence of their future blessedness and their sonship of God.

And just as the Jews noticed that it was something entirely different when Jesus called Himself the *Son of God* and God His *own Father* (John 5) than when they said God was their Father, thus the nominal Christians also notice the difference between their own false, carnal boasting and the real spiritual boasting of the true Christians, from which they draw the right conclusion; namely, that this "high-minded" sect imagines that it *alone* shall be saved and all others are damned. This conclusion hurts them; such pride is unbearable and yet it *is* so, that no one can be saved who does not have the unction for a holy, godly life and walk and the striving after the veritable, which is above and not on earth. And although the believers and anointed have not yet received the kingdom, still Christ, their Firstborn Brother, has already taken possession of it for them if they abide in Him (Hebrews 2).

## Chapter XLIII

## "Abide In Him"

November 8, 1840 (Sunday); Morning Meeting; I John 2:27 ff.

"But the anointing which ye have received of him abideth in you, and ye need not that any man teach you: but as the same anointing teacheth you of all things, and is truth, and is no lie, and even as it hath taught you, ye shall abide in him.

"And now, little children, abide in him; that, when he shall appear, we may have confidence, and not be ashamed before him at his coming."

153

In those who have received the Holy Ghost, He abides constantly as a Teacher in their home and heart and the longer we are in His school, the more we learn of God. If we follow His guidance and are still, we then *at all times* hear His voice, "This is the way; walk thereon and, besides, turn neither to the right nor to the left." An outward teacher cannot always be with us and his voice dies away, but this Inward Teacher is ever attent upon His office, and the children of God are known by this, that the Spirit of God—that is, God Himself—dwells and speaks in them.

For this, Christ went to the Father, so as to give all the believers of His Spirit, that He may be and abide in them as a constant Inspirer of the will of God (Paraclete); by this, the Spirit of Truth in the children of God has taken the place of the lying-spirit, which by nature possesses mankind; and as the latter, like an inward and indwelling law of sin, incites them to all that is evil, thus the Holy Ghost urges the children of God onward to all that is good, if God has become an Inner Law, and without that we are not children of God (Romans 8).

God is indeed near unto all men and they cannot flee from before Him (Psalm 139), but they are far from Him; they sin before His countenance; they know not the way of peace; there is no fear of God before their eyes (Romans 3). On the other hand, the children of God at all times have God before their eyes and in their hearts and He never forsakes them. His seed abides in them and if they abide in Him, it is impossible that they could be removed or separated from Him; "Like will to like," the children and the Father. But if they abide not in Him as in their Fortress, they may then be very easily captured and overcome again. The children of God are sure of their matter and of their way for they know whither they go, but all other men only imagine that they will be saved, for they have not the pledge of the Spirit because they will not surrender themselves to God so that the devil would have to depart from them and his works in them would be destroyed.

Every unconverted person is a stronghold of the devil (II Corinthians 10), and God sends His ambassadors to this stronghold to invite them to a voluntary surrender, "Be ye reconciled to God," —and as many as yield to Him for weal and woe obtain grace and the gift of the Holy Ghost and become strongholds of God, but those who resist God's invitation in the time of grace must afterwards fall on the day of the wrath and righteous judgment of God, like the cities of Canaan. Thus there is a war in this world between God and the prince of the world: God seeks to conquer the strongholds of the devil and the devil would like to regain the strongholds of God. But he who surrenders himself to God and receives the forgiveness of his former sins, him the devil must not only free, but the anointed can also resist him in faith and overcome him by patience, for in the new man the Holy Ghost is the Commander, just as the devil is in the old one.

November 8, 1840 (Sunday); Afternoon Meeting

On the one hand, the anointing itself teaches the children of God to abide in the Son and in the Father, verse 27:

> "But the anointing which ye have received of him
> abideth in you, and ye need not that any man teach you:
> but as the same anointing teacheth you of all things, and
> is truth, and is no lie, and even as it hath taught you, ye
> shall abide in him."

and, on the other, the apostle exhorts them to just the same thing, verse 28:

> "And now, little children, abide in him; that, when
> he shall appear, we may have confidence, and not be
> ashamed before him at his coming."

The anointing is *Christ in us,* and this Spirit of Christ awakens a constant longing, yearning and sighing in us for Him, Who is at the right hand of God, and for our redemption and eternal union with Him.

We shall not think that the unction is only the gift to speak the Word; this is something purely additional to and not even necessarily connected with it, but the unction is necessary in all believers for the holy life of Christ, as the glory of the hope of glory (Colossians 1:27; Romans 5).

> "To whom God would make known what is the riches
> of the glory of this mystery among the Gentiles; which
> is Christ in you, the hope of glory:"

But our abiding in Him is the ground of the hope and toward this the unction aims and has a tendency, that we abide in Christ; namely, walk upon the way which leads to eternal life and not depart from it again, not contemptuously sell our right of the firstborn again for the perishable food of this world like ungodly Esau, and even if we could gain or lose the whole world, we would still have need of Christ as our Eternal Portion and with Him indeed *all things* are ours. After all, we do not come into temptation to gain or to lose the whole world but only a bit or a small part of the same, and should we be so foolish as to sacrifice Christ for that!

But even though Christ is in us by His Spirit, there is still a great difference between the Christ dwelling in us and the Christ sitting at the right of God. No anointed one can say, "I am Christ." Even with the anointing, man is always still a man and his mind is distinctive from the unction; for it is just this mind of man which must be controlled, renewed and sanctified according to the mind of Christ, against the day of redemption and, in this, man can also withstand the Holy Spirit, that he does not abide in Christ and accordingly does not attain unto the goal of the heavenly calling. To be sure, those whose names are written in the Book of Life cannot be torn out of the hand of Christ and of the Father's for they abide in Him. But we do not know them by name and it is just as possible that a beginning believer may fall away as that he will remain faithful and constant unto the end. It depends upon one's using well that which was entrusted to him, the pledge of the Spirit.

November 10, 1840 (Tuesday); Evening Meeting; I John 2:28 ff.

"And now, little children, abide in him; that, when he shall appear, we may have confidence, and not be ashamed before him at his coming.

"If ye know that he is righteous, ye know that every one that doeth righteousness is born of him."

"And now, little children, abide in him;" That is the conclusion drawn from the foregoing, in contrast to the anti-Christians, liars and seducers, who fell away from Christ and consequently, like their father, the devil, did not endure and remain in the truth, while others do not even accept Christ as the Way, the Truth and the Life. Thus it must be revealed by Christ and His Gospel who of Adam's children can be saved and who, on the other hand, will be lost and condemned; that is, who of them become devils and who children of God, which is still undecided where Christ has not yet been preached. For indeed by nature all men are sinners and the devil reigns in them by his lying-spirit, but they are not yet devils on that account, not until they decide for themselves to be them, by rejection of the truth and the salvation in Christ. For those who do not accept Christ at all and those who do not abide in Him (do not endure in the truth), both come to the same end of condemnation because there is no salvation and no way to God except by

Christ; but in Christ the believers are reborn as children of God and created anew unto good works.

And just as the lying-spirit in the children of the devil is the root of all the sin and unrighteousness they commit, also, inversely, is the Spirit of Truth in the children of God the root of all the righteousness and truth they do. That is why one and the same person cannot commit sin and do righteousness, for he who still commits sin is not reborn (not of God but of the devil), and Christ in us cannot sin and where the Spirit of Truth is, there the spirit of lying is no longer to be found. He who says, "Indeed the new man in me does not sin, but the old one," is not yet a new man at all (is not in Christ), for who else is being born again and created anew if not the man himself? A new man therefore is no longer an old one; otherwise he is not new, and just this is the lying-spirit of seduction which teaches that one can *at the same time* be a sinner and a child of God (old and new).

They have denied Christ, for it cannot be said that the unconverted, carnal, nominal Christians are in Christ; consequently they abode not in Christ as the church of the believers and saints abode in Him from the beginning, from which they originated, and this apostasy of the so-called Christians from the Christ the Truth, is just what the Spirit of Prophecy warns us against (II Peter 2; Epistle of Jude), by alluding to the examples of the fallen angels who kept not their first estate and habitation. How then shall those judge a true Christian and his spiritual riches who themselves are not in Christ and have never experienced His power of life? Or how can we let them tell us what a Christian and a child of God is since they themselves have not been born of God?

It can, of course, not be said that the nominal Christians ever were in Christ (for the apostasy took place in earlier times and is perpetuated traditionally), but even though one offers the truth and salvation in Christ to them, they will not accept it, which proves certainly that they love the lie and hate the truth. For unto them who believe in Him, Jesus says (John 8):

> " If ye continue in my word, then are ye my disciples indeed;
> "And ye shall know the truth, and the truth shall make you free."

But if the righteous in this world must undergo such judgment that they can scarcely be saved, where then shall the ungodly and sinners, who do not believe the Gospel, appear (I Peter 4)? We shall therefore not let it grieve us when we are judged by the world for the time is coming when the world shall be judged by us.

November 12, 1840 (Thursday); Evening Meeting; I John 2:28 ff.

The abiding in Christ pertains to the future revelation of the children of God, so that the pardoned and sealed may be saved in eternity, because anyone who is not in Christ or does not continue in Him is excluded from the kingdom of God. Now, if we know that Jesus Christ is the Only Way thereto and if we have once known and experienced Him, it is then a necessity and duty of ours to continue in Him and not let ourselves be led astray anew.

But to be in Christ and to continue in Him does not just mean to claim His passion and death for the reconciliation of our sins and for justification before God and to *thus* confess Him as the Only Way to God, for, with that, many still remain in sin, in the disposition of the flesh, in enmity to God and in death and do not, through Christ, come to God and His fellowship, His friendship and sonship. If those who boast of Christ were, as well, in Him, they, on the average, would all be new creatures and then one could easily recognize and count the false ones among them. But John now gives us the only infallible sign of those who are and abide in Christ: "If ye know that he is righteous, ye know that every one that doeth righteousness is born of him," —of His seed, participant of the divine nature, which is pure righteousness and holiness without any admixture of unrighteousness and sin.

If we know God, we must simply be astounded that we shall attain unto the incomprehensibly high rank of becoming and of being called children of God, and indeed not falsely and without cause but in truth, by an essential conformity to and like-mindedness of the Father and the Son, in that His Spirit is and abides in us. And this does not first occur with the death of the body, but during the time of our life we must die unto sin and become alive for God and His righteousness; for even Christ, what He died unto, that He died for sin *only,* so as to remove the partition-wall between us and God and to make an approach to God and His fellowship possible for us. But the main thing is that we receive the life of Christ in order that we may be able to glory in Him in the hope of glory, that, at His coming, He will not find it necessary to send us away in shame and disgrace, for many shall say unto Him on that day:

"Lord, Lord, have we not prophesied in thy name? and in thy name have cast out devils? and in thy name done many wonderful works?"

and He will nevertheless say unto them:

"I never knew you: depart from me, ye that work iniquity."

Therefore, we must be concerned about that which Jesus looks upon at the judgment, so that we may not deceive ourselves with an imputed righteousness of faith without having an actual righteousness of life, without which nothing has merit before Him because, without that, we are not children of God, have accordingly never truly believed in Christ. For as Christ, as the Son, even became a Servant and was obedient unto death, so also must we, as children of God, rejoice to become servants of righteousness, in that we do His will.

But how great and wonderful is the transformation which we must have undergone! For as Adam after the fall begot children who were of his likeness—that is, sinners—so God, by the resurrection of Christ, begets children who are of His likeness—namely, saints and the righteous. And as the seed of sin develops in man from his youth, until little children are adult servants of sin, so also must the seed of God develop in the reborn, that they gradually become accomplished servants of righteousness, doing nothing but righteousness and sinning no more (Romans 6 and 8).

## Chapter XLIV

### The Prudence of the Righteous

November 15, 1840 (Sunday); Morning Meeting; I John 2:28 ff.

"And now, little children, abide in him; that, when he shall appear, we may have confidence, and not be ashamed before him at his coming.
"If ye know that he is righteous, ye know that every one that doeth righteousness is born of him."

Christ is our Lord; therefore we owe Him submissiveness and obedience. He has purchased us with His own precious blood from our vain walk (I Peter 1), not with gold, and even if He had purchased us with money (like the slaves in America who are forced to obedience),

He would still have the most perfect right of possession to us. But Christ as well is a good Lord, as Polycarp said, "It is now eighty-six years that I serve Him and He has done only good to me and no evil; why then should I curse Him?" It is true that we have to suffer many evil things in following Him, not from Christ however, but from the devil and the world for Christ's sake, so that we may learn what kind of master the devil is: for if he persecutes those who no longer serve him by sinning, what then will first befall those who have served him all their life long?

We must all give account to Christ of the use we have made of His Grace and Gift. Now, if we are carnally minded and desire good days according to the flesh, we bargain with Satan and the world that they let us alone, and thus bury the pound of Christ. Those are they who will say to Him on that day, "I knew thee that thou art an hard man. There thou hast that is thine. —Under these conditions I do not wish to serve thee," etc. But if we are spiritually minded and live in the Spirit, we consider the suffering of this time nothing but joy and the reproach of the cross an honor, for the sake of the glory which follows thereupon (Romans 8; II Corinthians 4; James 1).

Yes, if we possess the prudence of the righteous, with a glance at the recompense of the reward we shall wish nothing but much tribulation for ourselves and, like Moses, much rather choose to share affliction with the people of God than to have the timely pleasures of sin, although Moses made the sacrifice of a kingdom on this point, which is not the case with us, for he counted his real relationship to Israel for more joy than the feigned one of pharoah's daughter. Now, if the glory and honor to belong to the people of God and to be the Lord Jesus Christ's own is the greatest and most precious thing to us—although He and His people are very lowly and despised in this world—we may then also look forward to the recompense of the reward at His coming. However, He really owes us nothing; everything that we are and have is indeed His Grace and Gift: but He will crown His own work, and even a cup of cold water offered in His name will not be left unrewarded. He is not unrighteous to forget the work of faith and the labor of love and the patience of hope; He is a Rewarder of them that seek Him (Hebrews 11). Yet we shall know this also, that the crown of life is not offered to us for nothing at all, but is given to the fighters and overcomers only, and for that we must be in earnest.

It is not an easy matter, but with much affliction do we enter into the kingdom of God, and those who now seek good days with the rich man and have them in the court of the state church and will not refuse to be called children of pharoah's daughter, can, for just this reason, not be or be called children of God, and shall suffer torture and agony for it in the future world, while the poor, despised Lazarus, who had his evil days here, will be comforted. Therefore we shall say with Peter (John 6), "Lord, to whom shall we go?" etc. To be and to abide in Christ shall not be just a necessity and duty for us but our delight and joy when we consider what our redemption has cost, and we shall not hold Him accountable for the evil we must suffer for righteousness' sake.

November 15, 1840 (Sunday); Afternoon Meeting

Now, because we know that we must give account to the Lord on that day of our use or nonuse or misuse of His Grace and Gift, we must travel the sojournings of our pilgrimage with fear and keep a daily account of our income and expenditures as householders of God, so that we are ready and come not to shame when He comes.

Not all, however, have received the Grace and Gift of God, but that does not excuse them for not having them. It, much more, is their own fault because God offers them to all by the Gospel of His Son and He gives them to all who ask Him for them and turns no one away empty with hard words, as perchance men do. But since only few have the Gift of God, it is evident that men do not ask, because they do not feel poor and wretched and yet, by nature (in Adam), all are poor and therefore all mouths shall be stopped as guilty before God, and this knowledge is the first step toward the kingdom of God (Matthew 5:3; Romans 3).

> "Blessed are the poor in spirit: for their's is the kingdom of heaven."

God calls but they do not answer: therefore His wrath comes upon the world—because it does not accept the salvation in Christ and scorns His love (John 3); for, since we read in the Gospel how kindly Jesus offers and recommends the Gift of God to the Samaritan woman, we shall think this concerns us just as much as it concerned her and should ask Him for His Heavenly Gift and not give up until we have received it, for eternal life lies therein. And if the Lord allows us to implore Him for a longer time, it is because He knows very well with whom He is dealing and we shall just ask all the more urgently (Matthew 15).

The greatest sinner is not excluded, as we see in the case of Paul, if he but answers the Lord Who is calling and knocking, by asking, "What shall I do?" But instead of accepting Him as the Eternal Life (the Gift of God), men let Him stand outside or hang on the cross, continue in sin and would be saved by the Crucified One only, when His friends have long ago taken Him down from the cross and the Father has received Him up into glory so that, by His Holy Spirit, He might give us eternal life and seal us and we need not be uncertain about our salvation but know how we stand with the Lord and Judge of all the world, need not be fearful but much more joyful at His coming and wait thereupon like servants who would be ready at any moment that He comes, with burning lamps and girded loins, ever mindful that the Lord is coming to give each one His reward.

However, because we now furthermore know that the day of Christ is not only coming for the entirely secure world like a thief in the night, but also that such who have already received the Heavenly Gift, the Holy Ghost, and have tasted of the powers of the world to come, can fall away again (Hebrews 6), we shall all the more diligently abide in Him, be ever at home with Him in the Spirit and make our calling and election sure, so as not to be rejected with the foolish virgins. The Lord may then come whenever He will, we are ever prepared.

For, as the world, taken as a whole, is not one day secure with respect to the Advent of Christ, so also does the individual one not know either when the end of his earthly life is reached. Therefore, as children of God, we must ever be pure and holy; for those are cheated out of their eternal blessedness, like downright fools and irrational people, who think that their salvation is a matter of course after death, without the necessity of their having endeavored to obtain it in this world. How will those stand in the judgment who have not had Christ as their eternal life because they have scorned His love!

## Chapter XLV

### The Spirit of Christ in Us

November 17, 1840 (Tuesday); Evening Meeting; I John 2:28 ff.

The mystery of faith and godliness consists herein: that we learn to walk before the invisible God and Lord and to cling to Him as if we beheld Him, as Christ *for just this reason* was removed from the sight of our mortal eyes and left His Word behind Him—in His place—as a touchstone for us so that by it, it may become known who may be saved and who will be damned at His coming, for whoever does not accept His Word has made Him a liar and is without excuse (John 15); but he who accepts His Word in faith accepts God Himself and will be sealed with His Spirit of Promise unto the Day of Redemption.

His Word and His Spirit are the two pledges wherewith God has assured our eternal salvation, which do not waver because God cannot lie. The Spirit of Christ is the affirmation upon oath of the Word (Hebrews 6) and by both of these, the living, true God is as near to us as He can be at present, namely, *in us,* and what the Unction teaches us is the Truth also—not a lie—and we shall abide in it.

Christ cannot impart or reveal Himself to the world because it is unqualified for faith and, therefore, for all good works of righteousness, in which the divine nature in the children of God subsists, by which they know and possess the Father and the Son, and as Old Irsael *in certain instances* could inquire of God by the breastplates of the high priest (Urim and Thummim), so can we now much more perfectly *in all instances* experience God's counsel and will, light and right, by His Word and Spirit dwelling in us, that we need not go far nor ascend into heaven (Romans 10). Christ in us is the Oracle Indeed (Urim and Thummim), by which His glory reflects in us and through which we are changed into the same image (II Corinthians 3); but for this we must abide in Him and at all times behold Him in the Spirit, stand before Him, pray and ask Him. Then He always answers as our High Priest with the Father, with unveiled face.

This mystery of the nearness and revelation of God is hidden from the world. The unbelievers consider this nonsense and fanaticism. They are too untoward with their carnal mind to become advanced to the fellowship of the invisible God, and His Word, by which He could enter in them, they do not accept. Thus they are without God in the world and when He appears they will be confounded, but the children of God have great confidence and a good assurance for the Day of Christ for they already know Him in advance.

November 19, 1840 (Thursday); Evening Meeting; I John 2:28 ff.

The only true, infallible sign of those who are born of God and abide in Christ is that they do righteousness, as He is righteous, far from all unrighteousness. This is the standard, inviolable rule of the children of God and, by it, they have no thought of praise or honor, advantage or gain in this world or before men, but in all that they do they speculate upon the good pleasure of God and upon their eternal recompense from Him for what they do in righteousness, for the children of God are still concealed, veiled and covered with outward disgrace, dishonor, affliction and persecution in this world, unknown for what they are and do in righteousness; however they wait for their recognition from the Lord on *that* day.

Their way through the world appears to be full of suffering, but yet it is blissful, full of peace and grace, blessing and joy, for God, Whom they fear and honor in their hearts, is with them. He is their constant Witness. They are revealed before Him and wish to keep nothing from Him; they shun sin and avoid unrighteousness for His sake, and say with Joseph, "How then can I do this great wickedness, and sin against God?" Therefore they never come to harm or to shame with their breastplate of righteousness, girdle of truth, shield of faith, sword of the Spirit, etc., and even though they should be cast into prison on account of holding fast to righteousness, like Joseph, they nevertheless would not consent to sin, but in patience would wait upon their justification from God and for the revelation of the children of God.

Yes, even in this world, the godly one has his promise, as David says: "I have been young, and now am old; yet have I not seen the righteous forsaken, nor his seed begging bread (Psalm 37:25)"; and Solomon: "Better is a little with righteousness than great revenues without right (Proverbs 16:8)," —upon which the curse of God rests, that they, for the greatest part, come to shame in this world already as a proverb has it, *"Unrecht Gut gedeiht nicht"* ("Ill-got, ill-spent") and again, *"Ehrlich waehrt am laengsten"* (Honesty is the best policy"); and Christ says (Mark 10:29 ff.):

> "Verily I say unto you, There is no man that hath left house, or brethren, or sisters, or father, or mother, or wife, or children, or lands, for my sake, and the gospel's,
> "But he shall receive an hundredfold now in this time, houses, and brethren, and sisters, and mothers, and children, and lands, with persecutions; and in the world to come eternal life."

Therefore, with respect to Christ, the Gospel and faith, it is not merely a matter of a fanciful, imputed righteousness, as one fixes pillows and bolsters for people upon which they may comfortably sleep and dream of blessedness while they remain in sin and unrighteousness; but in the following of Christ, a positive, active, real righteousness of one's life and walk, according to the law of the Spirit, is required in order that He may once, in the resurrection of the just, recognize and acknowledge us according to the rule given in I Peter 2:1 ff.:

> "Wherefore laying aside all malice, and all guile, and hypocrisies, and envies, and all evil speakings,
> "As newborn babes, desire the sincere milk of the word, that ye may grow thereby:
> "If so be ye have tasted that the Lord is gracious.
> "To whom coming, as unto a living stone, disallowed indeed of men, but chosen of God, and precious,
> "Ye also, as lively stones, are built up a spiritual house, an holy priesthood, to offer up spiritual sacrifices, acceptable to God by Jesus Christ."

To this end, it is necessary that we meditate day and night upon the law of God (Psalm 1) and study His good and acceptable will (Romans 12:2) (below), not as learned, carnal men but so as to live according to it, without deviation, and to think continually of whatever things are honest, just, true, pure and lovely (Philippians 4:8):

> "And be not conformed to this world: but be ye transformed by the renewing of your mind, that ye may prove what is that good, and acceptable, and perfect, will of God."

---

> "Finally, brethren, whatsoever things are true, whatsoever things are honest, whatsoever things are just, whatsoever things are pure, whatsoever things are lovely, whatsoever things are of good report; if there be any virtue, and if there be any praise, think on these things."

and then, when the heat of affliction comes over us for righteousness' sake, we shall still be unafraid and shall not faint for we are planted by the brooks of the Water of Life.

November 22, 1840 (Sunday); Morning Meeting; I John 2:28 ff.

> "And now, little children, abide in him; that, when he shall appear, we may have confidence, and not be ashamed before him at his coming.
> "If ye know that he is righteous, ye know that every one that doeth righteousness is born of him."

The apostle directs the believers to the revelation of Christ and their own revelation with Him as the goal of faith and hope, so that they continually strive thereafter and may have joyousness and confidence at His appearance and not come to shame. Therefore it is now our task to walk by faith and to be true therein, as if we saw Him, for as long as Christ, the Head of the body, is invisible and undisclosed, for so long a time is the church His body. Yet He is with us in the Spirit and *in the Spirit* we shall abide with Him and cling inseparably to Him by love and keep ourselves pure, holy and undefiled for Him: for our relationship with Christ in this world is like that of a betrothed virgin to her far-distant fiance. Our betrothal to Christ took place in baptism and He thereupon gave us the pledge and the seal of the Spirit until the Day of the Marriage of the Lamb with His holy, elect bride-congregation, and so as to test our faithfulness, He leaves us for a time alone in the alienage of faith.

But now, what would a bridegroom do whose betrothed has trifled in love and whored with another during His absence? Would she not be a faithless adulteress? He who thus denies Him in the brideship of faith, him will He also deny when He comes in glory. The church of Christ goes on to perfection upon the same way He *Himself* has gone upon before us—through suffering to glory (Luke 24; Romans 8). Now whoever does not wish to share His suffering, can afterwards not share His glory either. But love, as the bond of perfection, constrains us to the fellowship of His sufferings, as it constrained Him to offer Himself up to acquire and sanctify us.

It is true, we ourselves cannot love Him without His Spirit, nor preserve ourselves; therefore He Himself in us is the One Who loves and Who brings about an unspeakable desire, sighing and longing in us for the eternal union with Him. The Spirit and the bride say, "Come, Lord Jesus!" This love however is not one-sided—only in us—but is a mutual yearning in Him and in us (compare verse 8):

> "Again, a new commandment I write unto you, which thing is true in him and in you: because the darkness is past, and the true light now shineth."

for He must wait for the time of the Father's for fulfilment, as we must wait. He longs for this union as His bride longs for it, and by this imuplse and the sighing of His Spirit in us, we shall know whether we belong to His betrothed church or not.

Besides, our heart can not and dare not be divided—our love to Christ may not be lukewarm; it must be fervent as His love to us is, as a lukewarm love is a divided heart and such are unbearable to Him:

166

He will spew them out of His mouth. He most certainly has not deserved it that we divide our heart between Him and another. That is what Old Israel did, which should also have been a peculiar, chosen people of God, whom He betrothed to Himself in Egypt and in the wilderness and they had promised obedience and faithfulness but did not keep it. Therefore, on account of their apostasy, unfaithfulness, courting, whoring and adultery, the Lord punished them by His prophets and their example should be a matter of reflection for us (I Corinthians 10).

## Chapter XLVI

### Love, The Gift of God

November 22, 1840 (Sunday); Afternoon Meeting

"If ye know that he is righteous [without sin], . . . "

We might think, who doesn't know that? Or who doubts that Christ is righteous, perfect, pure, and holy like the Father? But if we now know this, we ought to observe what kind of conclusion and inference John draws from it with reference to *us,* if we want to say: "We are now children of God and brothers and sisters of Christ, the Son of God," —"ye know that every one that doeth righteousness is born of him [descends from God like the Son]." Consequently he who does not do righteousness but commits sin is not of God, no child but a bastard, if he wishes to be called a Christian and nevertheless denies the blood of Christ (the doing of righteousness).

This verse forms the pivotal point of the whole epistle and the basis and foundation of the third chapter. We shall therefore not pass over it lightly. John therewith puts an end to every seduction—all false, erroneous anti-Christian ways and teachings and ideas about salvation, God's sonship and righteousness in Christ—as if one could be righteous and unrighteous at the same time, a child of God and a sinner, holy and ungodly; namely, in Christ justified by faith and a child of God, but in himself and in his daily life a sinner, as, for instance, Luther expounded the righteousness of Christ as if He, by His death on the cross, were a footman of sin and it would therefore be necessary that a sinner only say, "I believe in Christ, I ascribe and impute to myself His merit, so that I may no longer be punishable on account of sin."

John most determinately declares himself as being opposed to such distortion of the Gospel, that no one may think the sonship in God took place by adoption only and not by the divine nature and birth in God, like the Son was of the Father, for an adopted child is not a natural one. But God has no unnatural but only natural children, who descend from Him like the Son, and just for this reason Christ must dwell and live in us by His Spirit, so that we become children of God (John 1:12 ff.).

> "But as many as received him, to them gave he power to become the sons of God, even to them that believe on his name:
> "Which were born, not of blood, nor of the will of the flesh, nor of the will of man, but of God."

For Christ died just once for our sins, that we become cleansed of them by faith, but He lives eternally so that He might give us His eternal life if we believe. The real believers therefore are not to be known by this, that they have lied themselves into the righteousness of Christ and sonship of God, for with the lie no one can stand before God but only with the truth, which is in Christ, and subsists herein, that we do righteousness, just as He is righteous and not a sinner.

If we are thus in Christ and He is in us, we do not then have a falsified, an imaginary, but a true righteousness of life in Christ, since we no longer live unto *ourselves* but the Son of God lives in us, for as the Son is, so also are all the rest of the children: they stand in one row, and although we are first adopted by the justification of faith as ungodly ones and sinners, yet we directly afterwards by baptism, as reborn and recreated men of God, become natural children of God, begotten of His seed. There is then no longer Jew or Gentile, but all in all, Christ,

November 24, 1840 (Tuesday); Evening Meeting: I John 2:28 ff.

Now, if we expect the second coming of Christ just as certainly as we believe in His first appearance in the flesh, how must we then be prepared so as to appear with confidnce and stand before Him without coming to shame? The answer is in verse 29:

> "If ye know that he is righteous, ye know that every one that doeth righteousness is born of him."

We must have *in* us and bring *with* us the fruit of the first appearance of Christ, that we have died unto sin, live unto righteousness, love Him as our Bridegroom and keep His Word; then we can lack nothing. This is especially necessary in these last evil times, when Christ finds so little faith because, with unrighteousness getting the upper hand, the love of many waxes cold (Matthew 24; Luke 18), that few will be able to endure in faith, hope and love unto the end and therefore only few shall be saved, because they are not prepared as wise virgins, who have not only a burning lamp of knowledge of the truth and of faith but besides an oil vessel also—the unction and the bride-love—so as to always be assured of a new supply from above for their lamp, that if the Bridegroom tarries longer than we think and it would appear that God has forgotten us, our devotedness, faith and love would still not diminish. For if one had all faith and knowledge and had not love, it would still not help him to enter in the kingdom of Christ and of God, in which no impure or unrighteousness one has a share (I Corinthians 6 and 13).

Pure love alone constrains us to no longer live for ourselves but for the Lord (II Corinthians 5) and consequently do righteousness for love's sake. Therefore we shall pray without ceasing and not become weary, for the higher unrighteousness rises, the nearer the redemption of the children of God is. That is the faith which righteousness brings about and which is powerful in love; for true love is strong like death and overcomes all things, that many waters of tribulation cannot quench it, and if one should give all his possessions in exchange for love, it would still be as nothing. That is why Paul says that if anyone loves not the Lord Jesus Christ, he is henceforth accursed (I Corinthians 16), and Christ looks upon nothing as upon love, which at first is so tender and fervent that it can endure all manner of suffering for His sake and can sacrifice the visible (Hebrews 10:32 ff.; Revelation 2:4):

> "But call to remembrance the former days, in which, after ye were illuminated, ye endured a great fight of afflictions;
> "Partly, whilst ye were made a gazingstock both by reproaches and afflictions; and partly, whilst ye became companions of them that were so used.
> "For ye had compassion of me in my bonds, and took joyfully the spoiling of your goods, knowing in yourselves that ye have in heaven a better and an enduring subtance."

---

> "Nevertheless I have somewhat against thee, because thou hast left thy first love."

and it shall afterwards not diminish, but increase and ever become more ardent, the more we learn to know Christ and approach His coming in glory.

Love does not come from us ourselves but is given to us by God the Father, and is shed abroad in our hearts by the Holy Ghost as the pledge and the sealing of the hope of glory (Romans 5): "Behold, what manner of love the Father hath bestowed upon us,"—that is the reason why we may be called the children of God!

## Chapter XLVII

### The Purpose of Redemption

November 26, 1840 (Thursday); Evening Meeting; I John 2:29—3:1

> "If ye know that he is righteous, ye know that every one that doeth righteousness is born of him.
> "Behold, what manner of love the Father hath bestowed upon us, that we should be called the sons of God: therefore the world knoweth us not, because it knew him not."

Just as we, by a new birth, have entered into a new relation with God (to the Father as children, to the Son as brothers and sisters and do righteousness, as He is righteous), thus we enter into a new relation with the world also. It is as if all the bonds of the former relationship had been dissolved, as soon as our new relationship to God is consummated by our conversion from darkness to light; it is as if the evil spirits which went out from us had entered others to avenge themselves. Our best friends and nearest relatives—our own folks at home—become the worst enemies. Before the coming of Christ, it cannot be otherwise in a home and heart. Division and the sword enter with Him.

Then it is said: "As long as these fools, fanatics, sectarians, new believers and anabaptists were not here, things were peaceable and went well." Here one, all at once, loses one's self respect, honor and good name in the world—as soon as one becomes minded like Christ and confesses Him before men without being ashamed of Him. For this reason, few distinguished persons of the world accept and follow Christ, preferring the honor of men to the honor of God.

One can therefore easily recognize the children of God by their new mind and life from and of God, which is strange to the world, for the children of God also were once in the wrong and darkened like all the rest, and after their conversion and redemption they are not ashamed to admit it and to testify of the great change which, by the power and grace of God, has taken place in them, to the glory of God, although they gain no honor on earth by this but rather become dishonorable without cause, but they receive another, new name in heaven for it and honor from God.

We cannot be citizens and feel at home in both places. Besides, as the unconverted are aliens in heaven and enemies of God, so have the converted indeed become strange and unknown on earth, but, on the other hand, are at home in heaven and the friends of God, and whenever they must depart from this world, they come to no strange place but to one with which they have long been acquainted, where their heart has long since been. And as we have lost the time of our former life in the death of sin, we must now purchase the remaining time to win our salvation (I Peter 4).

The children of God therefore do not fear death like the children of the world, who have no God and no hope with their counterfeit worship and blind zeal for their ancestral religion, on account of which they hate the children of God, persecute and slander them as apostates, for they do not know that Christ did not come into the world to set up an outer, formal religion but to reveal His divine life in us. For how can anyone serve God with anger and a carnal zeal?

Still the unconverted imagine that they are zealous for God when they persecute and kill His children (John 16), and if that does not happen to us, we are not true Christians or children of God, for the world knows neither the Father, nor the Son, nor His children who have His Holy Spirit, and we ought to remember the word of the Lord Jesus: "The disciple is not above his master, nor the servant above his lord." "If they have called the master of the house Beelzebub, how much more shall they call them of his household?"

The true Christian who has become a light by the indwelling of Christ cannot remain hidden, but just this light reproves the darkness and its works. Yet we shall not hate those in return who hate us for Christ's sake but love them and pray for them, for they know not what they do, and who knows whether we, by our witnessing of Christ, may not be able to help some to life? Save them from the error of their way?

— END OF VOLUME I —

171